success @ e-business

profitable internet business & commerce

success @ e-business

---

profitable internet business & commerce

Peter Morath
American Management Systems

THE McGRAW-HILL COMPANIES

London · Burr Ridge IL · New York · St Louis · San Francisco · Auckland
Bogotá · Caracas · Lisbon · Madrid · Mexico · Milan
Montreal · New Delhi · Panama · Paris · San Juan · São Paulo
Singapore · Sydney · Tokyo · Toronto

Published by
McGraw-Hill Publishing Company
SHOPPENHANGERS ROAD, MAIDENHEAD, BERKSHIRE, SL6
2QL, ENGLAND
Telephone +44 (0) 1628 502500
Fax: +44 (0) 1628 770224   Web site: http://www.mcgraw-hill.co.uk

---

British Library Cataloguing in Publication Data

A catalogue record for this book is available from the British Library

ISBN 007 709625 8

Library of Congress Cataloguing-in-Publication Data

The LOC data for this book has been applied for and may be obtained from the
Library of Congress, Washington, D.C.

Further information on this and other McGraw-Hill titles is to be found at
http://www.mcgraw-hill.co.uk
Author's Website address: http://www.mcgraw-hill.co.uk/books/morath

Publisher: David Hatter
Produced by: Steven Gardiner Ltd
Cover by: Yvonne Booth
Printed in the United Kingdom by Bell & Bain Ltd., Glasgow

5 4 3 BB 4 3 2 1

For my daughter Larissa, wishing her a life with many opportunities to exploit – and may she be supported by a wide set of convenient services

CONTENTS

FIGURES

TABLES

It's not the strongest of the species who survive, nor the most intelligent, but the ones most responsive to change

Charles Darwin

FOREWORD

We are at the dawn of an Internet era. It's a time of excitement and confusion, opportunities and risks. No one is certain of what's happening now, what's coming next. Is this a technological breakthrough as important as the development of electricity, the telephone network or the railroad? Or is it comparable to the invention of the transistor and the integrated circuit? Clearly the Internet is at the crossroads of different new technologies but it is mainly an innovative process opening the way to a multiplication of new services. In the industrial sector, we usually start with the product and then move to the most suitable production process. In the service sector, it's often the new process, in this case the new network, that will lead to new services and products.

How far will this Internet wave go? In which direction? No one really knows, but out of this "primordial technological swamp" new companies, new business relationships, new corporate structures are emerging. We know that it will affect our lives. All managers and organizations are concerned. Startups are sprouting up all over and they capture our imagination. The more we develop services and professional organizations, the more we become a learning economy and the more we have to develop according to a learning mode. Better things, better ideas, better solutions will appear in the future but we have to go along with the learning curve. The innovation process is neither sequential or orderly, nor is it a matter of random trial and error. We have to learn while going with the flow.

If you don't understand what is going on at stage one, you will find stage two more difficult to embrace. If you miss mark one, it could be more difficult to target mark two. You should not wait too long to get started. Two steps forward, one step backward is acceptable as long as you get started. You have to learn to manoeuvre during the journey, but you cannot control the flow.

Thus I encourage you to read this book and take in as much as possible. It will give you hands-on guidance and show where technology meets value. It will give you an overview of the actual technology and guide you to meet value by focusing on the "three C"s: Customers, Competition and your own Capabilities.

It will give you examples of emerging best practices and embrace the whole value chain, from business to business applications, to e-commerce. The supply chain is the backbone of service opportunities: enlarging the customer base and boosting world trade, providing economies of scope, adjusting supply and demand, enhancing efficiency, effectiveness and flexibility of different players in the chain. This book will help you to understand present limitations, and where a new technology may lift a constraint and introduce a different route. So don't hesitate to plunge into the book and go with the flow. I wish you good luck and even more importantly consistent luck in your *e*Venture adventure.

James Teboul

INTRODUCTION

This book provides a practical guide for launching businesses on the Internet. You should read it and use the practitioner's advice, practical examples and checklists to prepare your launch, if you are:

- a start-up entrepreneur or an owner of a small or medium enterprise,
- a Project Manager in a big company in charge of going online,
- a Senior Manager or Strategic Planner who needs to oversee the new business evolution,
- an Information Technology manager who needs to make your team and environment ready for the changes in your business.

Lots of analysis is available for big corporations and many articles on specific aspects of electronic commerce and business have been written for the interested entrepreneurs and consumers. Only rarely though is there a synthesis of the various pieces of the puzzle. This book provides the "how-to" guidance: it is written for practitioners and for everybody interested in the business potential of the new technical device.

In contrast to many other books, this is a truly international book. It's written by a German working for a US-based consulting company, with a foreword by a French professor at a leading international university, published in the UK and it looks at many international case studies. The book reflects the different stages of maturity of electronic business in the various countries. This global perspective provides the different answers for the different situations and it allows the reader to leverage the lessons learned.

The book guides you through the launch of an "electronic" business. It explains the strategic issues to be considered before starting the project. The descriptions include the necessary observations and analysis to perform and indicate tools that can be used in coming up with a business plan. Then, the globally emerging best practices and the underlying technologies that make the new type of business possible are described and used as the baseline for identifying the key project tracks. Finally, activities to implement the electronic business are described.

As a summary, a checklist for self-assessment is provided for each of the strategic and implementation considerations.

If you are a private reader or a student, you will also benefit from this book. You will probably be most interested in a look behind the curtains at how electronic business is approached by the providers – and what improved interaction between them and their products and service providers can be expected. One aspect of this is the emerging of "communities" of which the consumers will find themselves becoming members. Another aspect is the increasing power of these consumers who can now, by reverse auctions[1], even define the price of their providers' products and services.

Structure of the book

The book is structured in three parts. First, the strategic considerations for launching an eVenture are elaborated. Second, the emerging best practices are described and the technical background to the ongoing changes in business due to Internet and similar electronically supported interactions are discussed. Third, the implementation of such a project is described, based on the lessons learned by the pioneers of eBusiness so far. This implementation focuses on the organizational and information technology aspects.

Each part includes checklists to use in setting up and validating your own project approach. Key Success Factors are highlighted.

Part I addresses strategy considerations:

* A new paradigm in business
* Know your customer
* Know yourself
* Know your competitor
* Innovative.

Part II describes the leverage of emerging best practices for eVentures together with the stages of maturity of electronic business, lessons learned by larger enterprises, the roadmap to a customer-focused organization, the best practice information technology (IT) architecture, and the Internet technology background.

Based on the project roadmaps described in Part II, Part III then describes the implementation tracks:

* Organizational evolution

---

[1] See Section 1.1.4 for an explanation of the reverse auction approach.

- Processes for a learning organization
- Information technology implementation, including a market survey of currently available software components
- Solid financials with a business plan and risk mitigation
- Getting ready with project plans for a variety of business scenarios.

In each chapter, a checklist is provided to help the practitioner organize an eVenture project and to help the consumer understand the way electronic enterprises will present themselves to their customers.

Those checklists reflect and integrate best practices from supporting disciplines, for example Change Management, Business Process Redesign (BPR) and IT Project Methodologies.

The checklists are also available on the web and can be downloaded to be used as work sheets for your analysis. On the web there are also additional examples and readers are invited to share their observations with other entrepreneurs starting their electronic business. Please see the website at www.mcgraw-hill.co.uk/books/morath and www.success-at-e-business.com.

Acknowledgements

I'm enthusiastic about the potential for new and convenient ways of interaction between the customers and their suppliers. I'm glad that so many pioneers show with their day-to-day presence on the electronic markets, that they share my enthusiasm for creating offerings and markets for easy and customer-friendly ways of doing business.

My special appreciation is for my editor, David Hatter, who believed in this book from the beginning. He encouraged me to invest the necessary time to get started and to continue with the research and analysis necessary to refine the materials. Thanks to Catherine Griffith from ic*parc (www.icparc.ic.ac.uk), who reviewed successive drafts intensively despite her very busy schedule; I was able to make many substantial improvements following her comments, and the recommendations for the readers have been expressed much more crisply.

I want to thank my family who had to suffer from my long working nights, and many colleagues and friends who not only tolerated my different mental focus during the book writing phase, but also contributed many valuable suggestions.

And last but not least, I'm grateful that my employer, American Management Systems, gave me the opportunity to use a broad fund of case studies and research materials plus a sabbatical to condense those materials into the book you now hold in your hands.

PART I
Reasons for starting an *e*Venture

1

A new paradigm in business

The time is NOW to start exploiting the new technical possibilities by selling your offerings on the web to consumers and business customers via PC, mobile phones or TV.

1.1 HOPE – OR HYPE?

Consumers in many countries are getting ready to buy electronically and, as Jupiter Communication puts it, "the Internet market is beginning to explode". Consumers have instant access to goods, services and knowledge and they can buy and communicate globally. European radio stations had a little competition on how long you can survive with just the things you can buy on the Internet – the teams easily made several days, but stopped the exercise after a hundred hours, because the participants voted to get a real shower. So the markets and the public opinion are getting ready.

Now is a good time for you to start a new venture and to gain shares in the growing markets pretty successfully. You can hope to get rich with your new business ideas. On the other hand, there's much hype – look at the stock market, where it was enough for a long time to be a "dot com" company or to mention the Internet somewhere in your mission statement in order to have a stock price raising to levels nobody every dreamed of. Now, there's more sense of reality. Some frustration is even around, because despite growing market activities it takes much longer to get rich than anticipated. And the stock prices are back to a level where there's some connection with financial performance of the companies. Reality tells, that it's not sufficient just to have a website – you need to organize your business approach and processes thoroughly in order to be successful in your exploitation of the virtual markets.

My goal for this book is to equip you with the necessary methodology for being the *e*Business pioneer in your market. Following this pro-active and customer focused methodology, you will be able to outperform your traditional competitors that continue their old behaviour. Also, if you have your ongoing business and want to add *e*Commerce, i.e. an electronic channel for your marketing and sales or do your procurement electronically, this book will lead the way.

"Electronic commerce" in my definition is a rather narrow initiative, e.g. opening an electronic channel for one particular aspect of the overall business, such as sales via the Internet, electronic procurement or electronic payment. Adjustments to the existing business model of the company will in this case only be necessary in the specific area where *e*Commerce will be launched.

"Electronic business" in contrast is either the launch of a completely new company or business unit or the redefinition of the overall business approach of an existing company. This will usually be done by launching new types of services and products reflecting the possibilities provided by interactive selling, interactive production and supply chain management, interactive ("just in time") delivery. In both cases, strong leadership needs to guide the implementation in the organization, the dealing with the customers, partners and suppliers.

In the book, I indicate if specific recommendations are only relevant for either *e*Commerce or *e*Business. Additionally, I use a term for describing activities to launch either *e*Commerce or *e*Business: "*e*Venture". This word was chosen for its connotation with the new frontiers we are about to explore and the risks and opportunities related to such explorations. It also indicates the necessary energy and action to be taken.

1.1.1   Opportunities and challenges

The good news for startups is, that the Internet provides a marketing and sales channel much cheaper to implement than a brick and mortar business. On the other hand, this new market is more demanding than the traditional physical outlet market, it's faster and more competitive because the customers have all the information at their fingertips. Descriptions of the offering, reviews of the products by various individuals and organizations, the service quality and the prices can easily be compared. So you need to be very clear about the capabilities you can offer to your customers.

At the same time, many traditional companies are facing new competitors from within their country or from other parts of the globe; they initiate electronic distribution, too, in order to defend their market share. To be successful, they need to adopt the approaches from the Internet community – in particular they need to forget their traditional way of customer treatment scattered over a variety of responsibility areas. Instead, they need to focus on the relationship with each particular customer and realign all their business processes around him. As difficult as this realignment is, they need to speed up – there's no longer the room for a nine to five attitude, now the customers expect twenty-four hour service availability at 365 days per year.

1.1.2   Current situation for Internet business

Electronic commerce and electronic business has made lots of progress with more than a hundred million people worldwide having access to Internet communication. But the capabilities for interactive selling can only be anticipated and we are still at the beginning of explosive growth. Electronic business-to-business transactions are estimated to grow to more than 1,000 billion € (Euro)[2] in the next three years globally, while consumer transactions are still a small fraction of that, they have the bigger potential in the long run.

The initial wave on the web was focused on providing information and company presentations and some pioneers have started to do business online. These pioneer businesses have found their market acceptance and can serve now as role models. The initial activities were focused on presentations on desktop personal computers and have primarily taken place in the US. We observe an initial structure of customers, namely the better educated part of the population with higher income.

Now we see more and more companies using the Internet as a facilitation for transactions with their customers and as a support for the business processes between themselves, their customers and their suppliers. The second wave in the evolution of Internet has started. In this second wave, the business models of the pioneers are adopted in other business areas and web presence becomes a must for each company in the USA. The recent merger of AOL and Time Warner shows that the fight for complete control of the interactions with the consumer has started – Internet shopping is no longer a playfield for computer-addicts, but will be interweaved with entertainment and will become a mass media event.

Significant market penetration begins in countries outside the USA. In comparison to the initial customer target, two large additional market segments can be approached now. Mass market consumers not using PCs can get their web access via TV sets connected to the telephone network and business people as well as young spenders can surf the web on their mobile phones[3]. "We are just waking up to the reality that phone calls as well as Internet access will be wireless; that's the new battleground" says Atlanta telecoms analyst Jeff Kagan.

The benefits of the Internet are broadly perceived and accepted. For consumers, convenient shopping is possible by a few mouse clicks. Businesses can cut back their time to market for the initial launch and for additional products and they can react quicker to market changes than in "brick and mortar"

---

[2] Source: Forrester Research. Throughout this book, I use € (Euro) as the standard currency. For the readers not familiar with the new European currency: 1 € is approximately equivalent to 1 $ US (the exchange rate on Feb. 22nd 2000 was 1 $ US = 1,0063 €).

[3] Mobile phone vendors like Nokia and Ericsson estimate that in year 2000 15 per cent of the mobile phones in Europe will be capable of providing Internet browsing capabilities. UMTS Forum estimates, that the worldwide number of mobile phones will grow to 950 million by 2005, and 2.7 billion in 2010 with more than half in Asia/Pacific.

businesses. Those time savings are due to the automated support of the "production", the no longer necessary creation of a physical sales outlet and the adoption of best practice approaches.

Speed and growth are the two most important factors in an eWorld. Supporting them requires ongoing investments and dedication of you and your team – and you may be incentivised by getting rich through an Initial Public Offering (IPO) of your company at a stock exchange once you've grown large enough. There's another option, though, namely to be one of the niche providers using the low cost marketing and sales capabilities of the web. In this case, you can earn your living with less stress than the people shooting for an IPO – provided you keep your costs tight.

With the examples explained below and the discussed approaches distilled from various projects, you will understand how the online technologies allow a quantum leap of interaction between providers of services and products on one hand and consumers on the other hand. This leap will be in quantity with an expectation of thousand million people being online in a few years as well as a leap in quality with other ways of selling, servicing and product packaging. This new quality will be for the providers and for the consumers – it will be a great new experience for entrepreneurs to exploit new ways of selling and for consumers to enjoy the new ways of shopping and additional services.

Several aspects of the paradigm shift can already be observed in the United States, and some of the US offerings are accepted by the consumers around the globe where a pioneer has teached how to approach the opportunities.

One of those aspects is a re-distribution of market share and market power. In the book market for instance, two per cent of the overall transactions are channelled through online retailers such as amazon.com. While two per cent are only a small fraction of the whole, it has to be noted that those two per cent are handled by very few online book sellers while the other 98 per cent are handled by millions of book stores. So, the online sellers have a much larger buying power, can achieve better economies of scale and sometimes offer their goods cheaper (or with a better margin) than the competition. This will lead to even growing market share and les expenses for supplies – you can expect a "virtuous circle of success" as Aran Nathanson from the marketing research agency Janus Enterprise International calls it.

The example of the book pioneer Amazon (www.amazon.com) is now copied by several other providers and Amazon themselves re-uses their approaches developed in book selling for music selling and auctions. Bank of Montreal (www.bmo.com) who cut back the traditional approval times for loans from several weeks in the physical branches to two minues on the web, has now created a spin-off company doing consumer loan decisioning as a service for other banks or even retailers. Similar evolutions can be observed in the car market – interestingly, though, there are already a handful of competitors that all try to adopt the book market experience for the car market.

Even amazon.com, though, is only starting to be profitable. This is no surprise – actually it's rather a surprise that they are already making money. Before you can benefit from the economies of scale you need to implement the appropriate environment. The investment need during growth periods is significant –

traditionalists would say, that you shouldn't exceed a growth rate of 30 to 50 per cent annually[4]. Your banker would have been very concerned about how you can absorb all the growth and the continuation of investments. But this figure is from the pre-Internet days. During the initial boom of the *e*Businesses, venture capitalists and stock markets have been very generous with Internet companies, but now as the financial markets begin to settle, you shouldn't expect someone to throw money at you, you have to avoid the trap of growth. This trap would be to always expand your environment and let the investment for the expansion always eat up next year's profits, before you really have earned something – so we may even get back to the experience of the above mentioned traditionalists where you can grow AND earn money. This is supported by observations in the USA, that the Internet becomes a normal way of shopping with more than 70 per cent of the Internet users already having made purchases online and prices more or less the same as in physical outlets or in traditional mail-order. Large companies move now into *e*Commerce and *e*Business, too. They have the funds to cross-subsidize the launch of an Internet spin-off plus they have many customer and supplier relationships to build upon. Don't wait too long with your launch – many others are ready for stepping ahead.

Three more big changes will start to influence all of us:

Web access will soon be possible for additional types of consumers. Connections between the TV set at home and the Internet start now to be rolled out on a large scale. This opens the door to the broad mass market and allows even more types of converging entertainment and information, the so-called "infotainment". And Internet capabilities on the mobile telephones allow to approach the highly mobile upper class more easily than by desktop PCs.

National borders diminish in their importance. Electronic commerce and electronic business can be done, no matter if provider and consumer are in the same region or country or in different countries. Within Europe, this development is even accelerated by the Euro currency, so the same transparency is given for the provided services, for the payment and thus the costs and benefits can be easily compared.

Also, entry barriers into markets built up by large enterprises dissolve as well: there's no longer a dependency on large production facilities – the fabrication of many goods can be outsourced, purchased from another

---

[4] Guess you are having a sound margin of 50 per cent per sold item. If you could invest all this contribution into your growth, you could grow at exactly those 50 per cent without needing fresh capital – but also without making a profit. Unfortunately, several factors are missing in that equation. Tax is one of them: your investments need to be amortized over several years, so even if you don't have liquid funds left after your re-investments, you will have taxable profits and thus need to pay the appropriate taxes. Probably not all your sales are at that 50 per cent margin, because surely you have some promotions or special sales, even some write-offs may occur. You have capital costs for the investment and for the time you have your resellable items on stock when you have already paid your supplier but not received the money from your customers yet. So that's why usually 30 per cent is more realistic than 50 per cent.

company at the other end of the globe and delivered just in time to the consumer. The more "commoditized", i.e. standardized a product is, the quicker the change is coming. Electronic handling of banking and insurance products have already a significant market share. Electronic book sales, travel reservations and "mail" orders have started to grow quickly. And the gold digger country is open for your pioneer activities.

The snapshot of current positionings can provide an idea of the additional turmoil in business to come. Small companies that were not known by the broad public a few years ago, have a continuous growth while the market share of the established, monolithic enterprises is shrinking:

- Amazon's bookselling success story is copied by other book retailers and by music retailers.
- The whole banking industry is shifting from physical outlets to online transactions, e.g. with investment brokers like E*Trade or Charles Schwab, the real time round the globe investment brokers, together with other online traders having gained 25 per cent market share.
- In the travel industry, eBay and TISS, the award winning discount airline ticketing service, have added a new dimension to "grey market" tickets.
- Dell computers have quickly gained a big market share and have a stock price outperforming the other PC providers.

So, the Davids, i.e. startup companies or small and flexible units within big enterprises, gain leeway and get significant business size while traditional players have to fight for their standing. Those giants that are capable of exploiting the strengths of the web (as Microsoft or AOL/Time Warner), will also be successful by boosting their market penetration via online sales.

The clue for success is to be best in something: either your unique offering if you decide for the "boutique" approach or the perfection of your processes if you go for the economies of scale.

And the speed of innovation is now measured in days or weeks and no longer in years or even decades. As the speaker of BOL Klaus Eierhoff put it: "In the Internet world, three months are equivalent to three years in traditional business".

1.1.3   The options for your launch

The time is now to balance the expectation in the continuing boom of online business with some traditional considerations. In the book we'll use two distinct business models to clarify the range of strategic options you have.

- The first model is a small start-up with low cost: a little "boutique" business, usually mail-order or auction type offerings, with selected products, and with a very targeted group of customers. In this approach you should use the electronic interaction capabilities of the web to outsource everything that's not your core business, but make money based on the uniqueness of your offering.

- The second business model is the full service provider, often the Internet spin-off of or add-on to a large existing company: grab a big market with an extensive offering and strive to be profitable due to your economies of scale. You will then start with an existing costumer base and can quickly expand your market reach by delivering all or some of your services via the web. Much of the implementation will be handled in house.

No matter which of the business models best reflects your situation, I recommend for the project you're considering to factor in time and effort for explorative tasks, as we are still in the pioneer times to transform the technical possibilities into profit generation. Start your *e*Venture with a concise subset of test offerings for a test target market. Think of your project in iterations, allow for trial runs and pilot applications – and prepare yourself for errors and failures. Observe the results and learn from those errors and failures. With such first-hand experience, you have a competitive advantage compared to companies starting later than you and you can cover market positions while the others may still be sleeping. Be ready also to expand quickly from your initial test products and test markets to a fuller coverage and to support the boom you have created.

1.1.4 Examples of *e*Ventures

In this place, let me frame the discussion of various aspects of *e*Ventures and indicate the different business strategies for small start-ups versus larger companies. Regarding the definition of *e*Commerce and *e*Business, please refer to the beginning of this chapter.

Table 1-1: Examples of *e*Ventures

	Electronic Commerce	Electronic Business
Retail/ consumer market	Book Marketing: McGraw-Hill/ electric-press	Book business: Amazon.Com, Adobe
	PC sales: IBM	PC ordering and manufacturing: Dell, FreePC
	Finance: Home banking for standard transactions (transfers, account statement)	Financial Self service for complex transactions: automatic loan approvals via Internet, Investment brokerage. e.g. Bank of Montreal, Charles Schwab
Business-to-business	Online bookings of air transportation usable by travel agencies and other large professional users: START and Amadeus	Sale of cheap tickets and last minute offerings to private travellers: TISS, EBay

Table 1-1 (continued)

	Electronic Commerce	Electronic Business
New Markets	Selling and distributing Enterprise Resource Planning (ERP) Software via the web: SAP/mysap	Online Auctions: eBay, Priceline
		Outsourced loan decisions: Competix
	Selling information items via the web: Hoppenstedt,	Automotive industry: eProcurement
	Renting software: Intuit	Interactive search: the-seeker

Let me now give you some background information on the mentioned examples.

The book business examples

Amazon launched their business with a re-invention of the bookselling business:

- Virtually all books available in each country can be purchased.
- For some books excerpts from the actual text can be browsed.
- Free shipment of books and often interesting discounts are offered.
- By a sophisticated collaboration via electronic media with their suppliers, Amazon has drastically cut back their inventories thus achieving better margins, and at the same time they can deliver the books faster than physical booksellers could do with ordered books. So Amazon is really *e*Business.
- The readers can join a community[5] where they can publish their book reviews and make them available to other customers.
- And beyond that, Amazon is also selling music with a very similar approach.

With this new approach, Amazon has 16 million items on sale and generated more than € 600 million revenues in 1998. This forces the existing marketeers to react. For example, McGraw-Hill offers an electronic Reading Room, where many professional books can be read – not only an excerpt but all pages. This electronic marketing has important advantages.

- The cost of the marketing information is smaller than any broad mailing activity.
- People browsing the electronic reading room will buy more probably than the average recipient of the broadcast mailing.

The disadvantages are less critical. The current reach of the marketing restricted to PC users only will change soon, e.g. with the roll-out of Internet-

---

[5] The new marketing concept of communities is the ideal way to strengthen the relationships with the customers. This concept will be explained in the next chapter. The basic observation that has led to the concept of communities is the fact, that customers have a higher loyalty and buy more frequently when having an additional engagement with the company. Communities can be created on any topics, e.g. profession, health, family, sports, entertainment.

TV. The Internet marketing being an additional cost to traditional marketing leads to balancing cost and expected outcome by focusing on specific books where interactive searches can be assumed – as for this book. The idea is to make readers curious and motivate them to purchase the books eventually – because it's more natural for a prospective buyer to browse through the book, as in a bookshop, than only to refer to a brief excerpt plus some reviews. With the selected format, by the way, printing and downloading of specific pages is possible, but it would be very cumbersome for the whole book. Still, McGraw-Hill uses this technology only as a careful expansion of their traditional sales channels. So it's "just" *eCommerce*.

Other participants in the book value chain have reacted as well. Books can be printed on demand (e.g. www.bod.de). Adobe (www.adobe.com) has announced a new version of their publishing software which will allow reading the downloaded files only after the reader has paid some fees. The publisher can use the Acrobat Merchant software, and the consumer Acrobat web-buy reader. The web-buy function built into the new reader software will accepts digital coins from the reader and pass them onto the publisher. Until that payment has been executed, the file content can't be seen by the consumer. So, either long texts like books, or small texts like an online help, can be made chargeable. Barnes & Noble as well as Simon & Schuster have started their marketing activities, also for short articles from magazines and newspapers, with the new Adobe approach. Adobe works with the company Intertrust Technologies Corp. (www.intertrust.com) on extending that to music and video formats, so you will be able in the future to download individual songs from the web for some fee. This is a big step forward for the consumer online business, because all the interaction between provider and consumer regarding his payment details won't be necessary any more.

Conclusion:

- The book market is in turmoil due to the changes introduced by an Internet start-up.

The PC examples

Dell (www.dell.com) has started the "tailor-fabrication" of PCs, i.e. the PCs are configured exactly to the order of a particular customer. The customers configure their PCs in self service on the Internet – they can select from more than 10,000 different configurations! Like in Amazon's case, Dell is also working together with his suppliers and the producers of the PCs via electronic SCM (supply chain management). Dell is actually the company with the highest online revenues: they made more than € 600 million in 1998.

FreePC (www.freepc.com) has created another new business approach, namely giving away the PCs for free as long as the customer commits to viewing the advertisements from FreePC's advertising partners that are downloaded from the Internet. For those advertisements, Free PC gets their revenues from their marketing partners – so FreePC is both a marketing agency and a PC distributor.

FreePC had some initial success, but now there's a challenge from another Internet corner. The idea to make money by selling advertisements has been adopted by the providers of free Internet services (free ISPs[6]) and they are much faster in penetrating the market by making consumers subscribe to their services than FreePC's hardware distribution. The prices for banner ads are under pressure as well, because the responsiveness to such ads is little. Only when an ad is dedicated to very specific customer segments, or in particular if it can be proved, e.g. by click stream analysis, that the ad was actually seen be the customer, higher prices can be maintained. For such sophisticated approaches, rather ISPs have the appropriate data available than FreePC.

The existing marketeers reacted like in the book business example. IBM (www.ibm.com), for example, now uses the Internet as one of many sales channels without largely changing the overall PC sales approach.

Conclusion:

- The PC sellers have managed to keep the market amongst themselves, but those players that invented the new business approach gained a large market share.

The banking examples

In the finance industry, home banking was invented in the 1970s to do simple transactions. It was infrequently used by the customers, though, and it was just another cost for the banks. Only when the banks rethought their whole approach and thus transformed into an *e*Business it became successful. With an aggressive new business model of online discount brokerage services, Charles Schwab (www.schwab.com) together with other companies that copied his business model has grabbed more than a quarter of the traditional US investment finance business. Bank of Montreal (www.bmo.com) now presents itself as the friendly partner of the customer, the customers are engaged by a service oriented approach – and they get online confirmations for complex transactions like approving a loan within minutes. Such transactions took weeks before and many clerical staff were needed to check, sign and shuffle application forms around. Today, these modern approaches are even offered as a service for other financial institutions who want to outsource that piece of business.

Conclusion:

- The financial institutions with a good idea how to leverage the potential of the Internet have gained a large share of their respective markets.

---

[6] The first ISPs paying the consumers money for surfing have even shown up: www.gotoworld.com pays 40 cents per hour of using their Internet browser plus additionally up to 75 cents per hour for referrals.

The travel offerings

In the START and AMADEUS projects dedicated to airlines and travel agencies, reservation systems have been integrated on a global scale quite a while ago using EDI (Electronic Data Interchange) standards:

- General terms with the various airlines have been agreed.
- Each travel agent can make reservations in the pool of the participating partners.
- The reservation is processed electronically between the travel agent and the suppliers.

Now the potential of existing reservation systems, together with the ubiquity of the Internet, is exploited by bringing such reservations systems to the home of the consumers in the same way as a professional travel agent can see them. It redirects the travel agent's commission to the providers of the Internet reservation systems such as TISS (www.tiss.com) and eBay (www.ebay.com). While the START and AMADEUS projects were still geared towards professional users (dedicated computer terminals being necessary and being pretty expensive, and a training for data entry on the complicated screens being necessary), TISS, eBay and Priceline (www.priceline.com) make the distinction between "business" and "consumer" disappear. In fact, they even make the business model of some of the professional users, the travel agencies, obsolete. Moreover, they have inverted the pricing for tickets. Airlines and IATA are no longer in control of the ticket price, and the travellers make a bid how much they are willing to pay for a specific distance. So, if the consumer is flexible regarding his travel time and he wants, say, to travel from Amsterdam to Boston, he can bid € 300 through eBay, and the airline first accepting the bid and coming up with a reasonable travel schedule, will get the deal. So the airlines have to deal with the consequences like price erosion in the mass market and distinctive service levels for the business tariffs.

No matter if price reductions are enforced by customers making a bid for a specific transportation or by the airlines pro-actively pushing "last minute" prices down in order to get their planes filled – the consequences are the same. The prices erode. So the airlines need to carefully examine where it's still profitable to continue their services and have to adjust their flight patterns according to the up-to-date demand.

Conclusion:

- A few start-up online distributors are challenging the existing marketeers, i.e. the airlines and travel agencies, by establishing a more transparent travel market where the prices are adjusted permanently according to the respective balance of supplies and demand.

Summary for discussed cases

With the offerings discussed so far, we've covered more than half of the current product (or, mail-order) business on the web, i.e. books, music and PCs and more than three quarters of the service business. The market has accepted these offerings and they have some characteristics in common:

- The successful companies have a clear **customer** orientation.
- They focus on their **core competencies** and outsource all other activities necessary to provide the offerings to third parties; those third parties are treated as **partners** and are neatly integrated via electronic communication into the overall network of value generation.
- The use of online customer interaction as well as electronic integration with the partners and suppliers helps them to gain a **unique position against their competitors** and thus allows a quick gain of market share.
- They **continue to improve** and extend their offering.

In the next chapters we'll discuss each of those aspects in detail. But before we do that, let's look at some more business ideas.

New markets

Whole new markets are being created by the *e*Venture pioneers. These business ideas as of yet went only through a short life cycle, so the business success stories haven't been fully publicized. Some of their characteristics may be interesting for you, anyway.

Online auction

The traditional (physical) auction model has been refined and extended by companies like eBay (www.ebay.com). Now, participating in an online auction is not only a means to fulfil a need, but it's rather a game to play for the participants how cheap they can get something attractive. Additional entertainment is provided to keep the consumers buying and selling – and to keep the commission and advertising revenues flowing. The benefit for the provider from eBay-like auctions is that you have zero inventories, so you just need to handle the interactions between the sellers and the buyers for which you get your sales commission. The next refinement is the reverse auction model of Priceline (www.priceline.com). Reverse auction means that the customer quotes a price for an item (no matter if it's a car or a hotel room, for example) and the providers can accept – who acts first will get the deal. There, the provider eventually has the same benefits, but it requires more preparation. You need to create a shopping community with a big buying power and you need agreements with the suppliers in your region or for a specific market (e.g. hotels, car-rentals) for flexible price schemes in order to allow your customers the quotation of prices. This preparation, on the other hand, will be an entry barrier for upcoming competitors.

Another refinement of the auction model is to provide little robots that surf the web automatically, compare the prices at various auction sites and are authorized by the consumer to buy or sell on their behalf. Prototypes exist already like the auction rover from Research Triangle Park (www.ncsu.edu).

ASP (Application Service Provider)

ASPs, for example SAP (www.sap.com, www.mysap.com in cooperation with Qwest and Hewlett-Packard) have complemented their traditional licence business to sell software licences for components of their ERP software by a usage based business model, where the customer can use SAP's accounting and controlling services via the Internet. Rather than investing significant amounts into the software (and the underlying necessary hardware), those customers can pay on an as needed basis while the ASP provides the hardware, software and operates and maintains them. With this approach, the large target markets of SMEs and individual professionals can be made interested in the offering in addition to SAP's traditional customers, namely larger enterprises. Additionally, the mySAP concept allows the participating companies to collaboratively work together as partners in the electronic mySAP.com Marketplace business directory with already more than 1,000 companies registered. So, SAP has created the community of electronic buyers and sellers by enabling them to do *e*Business; it's still labelled as *e*Commerce "only", because these ASP services are just a slight extension to SAP's traditional business behaviour.

Another example for an ASP is Competix (www.competix.com), a joint venture of the Bank of Montreal with the provider of the automatic decisioning tools, American Management Systems. They provide the online service to come up with consumer loan decisions. This capability can't be afforded by smaller banks or retailers in a sophisticated enough way to survive in today's market – so even the traditional core of banking, namely risk management, can be externally contracted now.

The ASP market will become hot very quickly. Many large companies intend to rent their software via the web. Microsoft prepares a version of Office-2000 to be rented and distributed via the Internet, Sun (www.sun.com) plans to distribute Staroffice the same way and Verio Inc. (www.verio.com), a US hosting provider, is about to make Microsoft Office accessible via the web, either, as a complementation to Microsoft's own plans.

ASPs are possible on a smaller scale as well. One example: in our quickly changing world, people are losing sight of friends (and even sometimes of relatives). In the US the company www.the-seeker.com helps to find the friends again. They have a steeply growing number of users with more than a million hits per month. Other search engines, e.g. for dedicated product searches and price comparisons helping the customer to reduce the time for surfing the web by identifying his needs and submitting an automatic service agent like www.respond.com, should also gain a quick market acceptance.

For ASPs there's a good way to enter into the market by providing the services initially for free. You can allow a new user to make some ten inquiries in your database without charge like Hoppenstedt (www.hoppenstedt.de) is doing with their database of company profiles, or give your software for 30 trial days for free like McAfee does with his virus checker, or have the first month of a rental agreement for free as Intuit does with his Turbo Tax Filing software.

Local service offering

Local offerings can further expand the community idea. For example, you can extend the relationship between the customers and the physical retailers in the neighbourhood. That's a suggestion for Internet starters with little investment possibilities. You can start in your home town, in particular in big cities or the "sleeping villages" around the big cities where the young professionals with little time live. Allow the young professionals to select a recipe for evening cooking during their lunch break and have everything ready for pick up when they pass the grocery store on their commute home. Or start in a region with elderly people and bring the groceries to the door of your customers. This offering can resemble as much as you like to the "good old days" when the milkman brought milk, rolls and the newspaper. Preparation is necessary to get the agreements with the grocery stores in the neighbourhood, investments are necessary only for a little Internet shop with regular updates of the catalogue and a little car for deliveries. Example: www.my-world.de.

Other possibilities include helping your fellow Internet start-ups. My book and the related website is an example, and www.checkmarkinc.com is another one. They test professionally the Internet presence and offerings of new Internet entrants and identify areas for improvement in the presentation and order handling.

New types of ideas for local services are possible by mobile phones and the WAP technology. As the physical location of the mobile phone is approximately known to the telecom provider (due to the cell, i.e. the antenna, that currently keeps the connection), specific proposals can be made to the travelling person. Hotel and restaurant recommendations, navigation aids, connecting train schedules can become a combination of information and marketing with possibly revenues from both the consumer and the hotels or restaurants. The consumer will pay for the connection time when he's looking for information, the partnering hotel will pay commission for the reservation.

For the big money: car selling

Let your customers configure their cars like Dell's customers configure their computers. This might be the next big wave after the success of book selling! Forrester Research estimates by 2003 five million cars being sold via Internet. Preparation is necessary to get the agreements with the car manufacturers, and banks. Investments are necessary for the electronic sales and purchase channel infrastructure. Examples: CarPoint (www.carpoint.com), Autobytel (www.autobytel.com) providing car sales, leasing, financing and insurance, Autoweb (www.autoweb.com), AutoTrader (www.autotrader.com), www.Cars.com, www.CarsDirect.com.

1.2   WHAT'S THE IMPACT ON YOU – READY FOR SUCCESS OR DOOMED TO FAILURE?

Electronic business is not (only) about technology, but primarily about processes and organization. With the increasing competition and the rising power of the customers, you should seek to centre your organization around the customer. You have to embrace the demands and needs of your customers and align them with your core capabilities.

Figure 1-1 illustrates the types of activities that require an alignment with your customers' needs.

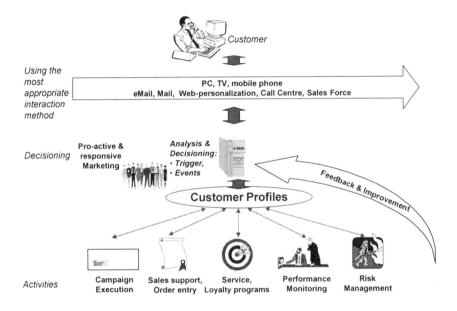

Figure 1-1: Customer centred approach: consistent sales messages across all channels and products

At the top of the chart we see the customer with his Internet access. Your customer may have one or several of the possible Internet peripherals; currently most probably a PC, soon often also TV and mobile handsets. While the different formats of the output displays can be adjusted automatically by the ISP, the customer will use his different equipment for different needs, e.g. his TV set for watching a Video-on-Demand, his mobile phone for doing a quick day-to-day transaction (e.g. for some movie tickets or bank transactions) and his PC for downloading music. The standard interactions between your customers and you can be handled automatically, but for additional functions, e.g. sales and customer support, you need to use a wider set of channels and methods, e.g. your sales force staff, your call centre, or even traditional means, such as mail or eMail. In fact, eMail should become one of your favourite marketing tools. It costs little, can be dedicated to very targeted customers and raises their awareness more than other broadcast marketing means. Next to eMail, you can use web-personalization, i.e. specific marketing messages displayed for the particular customer. That sounds great, but how do you get all those automated and integrated features? Well, you have to be clear about your activities and the related processes such as marketing campaigns, sales, service performance, and monitoring performance and risk. Those processes won't be sufficient, though, for continuously successful interactions with your customers. In order to present the "right" approach or message to the appropriate customer, automatic decision support is necessary as soon as your number of customers grows larger. This automatic decisioning consists of two steps. First you need to assign your customers to certain profiles in which the buying behaviours are expressed. Secondly, you can define specific approaches and activities that can be automatically started for the customers with the particular profiles.

The key evaluations based on the mentioned profiles have to include the performance of your various products and services and have to give indications of trends of demand in order to trigger the appropriate actions. In parallel, you have to monitor the performance of your market segments and products in order to slow down in unfavourable market segments and to increase the sales in favourable segments. Should risks arise, e.g. payment defaults of particular customers, you have to adjust your interaction with such customers, e.g. stop credit lines and offer pre-paid services instead.

The basic idea of the described approach is like motherhood and apple-pie, but the only types of shops where such "customer profiles" are constantly available are the very small businesses where the sales people know their customers, i.e. the "profiles" are stored in the brains of the sales people or on little cheat sheets they use. Most of the larger corporations see the customers only as an anonymous entity. Only a few leading examples exist; these are very large corporations that have set the new standards. In the US, this orientation towards the customers has started more than ten years ago when companies like Citibank or AT&T have implemented data mining activities in order to come up with customer segmentation and profiling. In Europe, recently similar activities have been started by the large corporations, e.g. Otto Versand in Germany (www.otto.de), a large mail-order company. They use data warehouses where all customer transactions and interactions are stored, they analyse them with data mining tools and organize their messages to the customers based on the insights generated from this analysis.

With your eVenture, you may fall into the trap of not knowing your customers, too. To avoid this trap, you need to have the informal activities like discussions with some key customers and formal processes like satisfaction surveys and buying behaviour analysis to achieve a good understanding of your customers. We'll talk more about those activities and the related processes in Chapter 2 and in the implementation part of the book, i.e. Part III.

1.2.1   What are the new benefits of an "electronic" launch?

With the increasing number of competitors and the acceleration of innovation cycles, the electronic interactions with customers and partners based on your basic assets are most important. Those basic assets are knowledge, creativity, and energy. Create permanently intriguing propositions to your customers based on your key competencies – and make them quickly available with high quality. Organizational efficiency by Internet enabled electronic integration of partners like your suppliers, your delivery and logistics companies or advertising allies will exploit big gains compared to companies without such integration. This electronic interaction between suppliers and their business customers will intensify no matter if a small or large enterprise or even a traditional business is concerned. Research agencies expect that the investment of enterprises for implementation of the appropriate electronic interaction tools will be initially even higher than the online sales to consumers. We will discuss the methods for the supply chain management in the implementation part of the book.

The electronic interaction with customers and partners has financial and non-financial benefits. You can use the lists below to identify the areas of improvement.

Benefits with direct financial impact

Reduced marketing costs: With the analysis of the customer buying behaviour you will be able to cut back the shotgun marketing approaches, and instead you can run one-to-one marketing campaigns based on the customer's actual buying preferences. So you can stop wasting tons of stamps for your marketing letters.

Additional sales: you can address new customer groups or you can step out to new countries and increase your sales accordingly.

Reduced cost per sold item: Compared to a physical shop, your cost structure is lower. Therefore you can offer your products cheaper than a physical store – or you can realize a better margin.

Reduced cost for field force and technical support: If you can concentrate your service staff in some central places, adjust your business processes to reduce the travelling times of your support staff and automate the replies to some frequently asked, general questions of your customers, you can reduce lots of wasted time and can better focus on value generation.

Reduced cost for supplies: With the productivity increases due to electronic procurement, the supply chain costs can be reduced. Experience from different projects in large enterprises as well as research, e.g. by A. T. Kearny, shows a cost reduction of 80 to 90 per cent after a streamlining of the paper shuffling "request – check – authorize – obtain offers – compare offers – order" procedures. Traditionally, the cost for procurement was often higher than the value of the purchased items. With electronic procurement, standard items can be purchased directly by the persons requesting it, thus allowing the procurement people a more careful evaluation of the larger investments.

Reduced working capital charges: Higher speed of delivery leads to a reduction of inventories and thus a reduction of financing costs plus lesser risk of having old items on stock. At least five to ten per cent of supplies costs can be saved and the accelerated delivery improves the customer satisfaction (and the company's liquidity) tremendously. For example, Ford could cut back their average delivery times from 50 days to only 15 days by operational efficiency gains during the last ten years. Even sales is supported, because customers urgently wanting a car come now rather to Ford than to a supplier who needs longer for delivery. While process efficiency and inventory reduction was the initial target of the activities at Ford, now they are doing the next step: a "business online" joint venture between Ford and Oracle, the company Autoexchange, will allow the customers to configure their cars online like Dell has shown in the approach with PCs. So, we are back at the beginning of this benefits list, i.e. the new approach generates now additional sales indicating that usually over time more than one of the benefits can be achieved by an *e*Business activitiy.

Benefits with indirect financial impact

Reduced time to market: New products can be launched more quickly, because the alignment of your operational processes necessary to support your changed business approach will allow you to understand the feedback of your customers more quickly, to configure the products flexibly and to adjust the pricing according to the market needs.

Growth of market presence and of market share: The ubiquity of Internet allows you to present your company everywhere. And you can open a virtual shop more easily and more quickly than a new physical shop. Thus you approach additional prospects at only little cost.

Process optimization and quality increase: Well, that's a side effect of your *e*Venture and you have to take care that it really materializes. But if you do so, additional benefits can be realized again and again – and excellent companies will strive for that continuous improvement over time. The optimization can be in the areas:

- **Automation of paperwork and documentation:** You can automate your paper work: orders, invoices, delivery notices, tax declarations can be generated as part of the overall process.
- **Improved forecast for delivery dates:** With electronic supply and delivery chain management and electronic procurement, you can let your customers know with high precision when they can expect your delivery. Realistic dates help your business customers to align their organizational processes, so you will achieve a higher customer loyalty.

And they help your private customers to select a gift for the upcoming birthday which they'll actually receive before the birthday.

- **Error reduction:** With a data entry done by the customer, sources of error will be eliminated. Cisco has observed a 25 per cent decrease in error rates for systems ordered directly by the customers.
- **Market transparency:** Product innovations can use the better tracking of buying behaviour and interaction information such as complaints, as those do exist then in a format that can be automatically evaluated.

To really be successful on the web and not to disappear somewhere as "background noise", you need to make your prospective customers aware of your presence and to offer a high perceived value to your customers. This can be achieved by thoroughly approaching the *e*Venture like a real project – with the appropriate funding, staffing and reasonable project milestone reviews.

The experience from many current *e*Ventures shows, that you best should adopt a stepwise approach.

1. Establish an initial web presence, i.e. your home page, and create the awareness in the market by using links, search engine entries and traditional marketing approaches. A great marketing idea was used by free4u (www.free4u.net), a free ISP service. Months before they launched their services, they offered value points to their subscribers which eventually can be transferred into shares of the company once they go public – but this offer was only for the first 10,000 subscribers. And the consumers could get additional points by referrals to friends and by sweepstakes for the highest daily score of referrals. Quickly they've won over 100,000 customers. In this initial step, you should present your marketing information on a static website and organize your customer contacts via *e*Mail and traditional marketing media while you organize in parallel the actual launch of your company together with your partners.

2. In the second step, you should allow interactions like ordering based on some selected offerings and for the first segment of your customers. With this step you can test if your expectations regarding the market acceptance have been realistic. If not, you can prepare to scale your organization up (or down), to what you need in place for the ongoing operations in the next phase.

3. In the third step, you should implement the processes with the service levels (e.g. timeliness of delivery) for the number of customers you expect now. All types of transactions as outlined in the figure above need to be implemented and integrated end-to-end between you and all your customer segments as well as with your suppliers.

4. Continue with an improvement of your services. Each of those steps will be discussed in further detail in the Implementation part of this book, in particular steps two and three regarding their organizational, process and IT aspects.

1.2.2   Where are the threats for your existing business?

In many industries, entry barriers have been existing in the past. A key reason has been the cost of implementing the processes in the back offices including all production-related machineries. While some of those barriers persist in the "heavy" industries, the service industry has virtually no "hard" entry barriers. This means that many offerings can be treated as a commodity – and that many good ideas will just be copied by the competitors.

The way to cope with those challenges is to put much emphasis on the quality of service and on the know-how behind the offerings. Quality and know-how can be copied, though, as well. Therefore, the time to market for each new idea becomes more and more crucial. In earlier days, innovation cycles were measured in years or decades while in the emerging service industries, new ideas need to be implemented within a few weeks in order to gain competitive advantages.

Additionally, customer loyalty needs to be nurtured without jeopardizing the profitability. Not every customer wants to get always the latest and greatest development, often the convenience of using something he's used to or his friends and colleagues are using as well is more important than having the last frills or the best price. At certain times, customers go through an explicit analysis for a provider, but then they stay loyal to him as long as no dissatisfaction or change in circumstances happens. The "art" of successful marketing is to inform the prospective customers with the "right" messages at the "right" time. We'll discuss the details of this "art" in the next chapter. Additionally, to marketing activities, provide added values to your customers where your cost of "production" is pretty low compared to the benefits the customer perceives – like customer conferences for traditional businesses, the readers' reviews of Amazon.com's book offerings or the value points from free4u in the virtual world.

1.3   IMPORTANT TRENDS

Let me share some figures with you. I've distilled the most important messages from the observations in statistical materials as checked in Q4/1999. As the detailed numbers are quickly overtaken by events I don't highlight them in the figures as long as the meaning of the analysis isn't changed[7].

Most important is the expected market growth in the next three years: from approximately € 120 billion[8] in 1999 to more than € 1,000 billion in 2002. This

---

[7]   Actually, many of the figures are now again 30 per cent higher than at the time when I started writing the book in spring of 1999. In some of the charts I've also put figures of different research agencies together despite the fact, that they don't necessarily have the same methods of measurements – as long as the overall trend can be seen. If you are interested in the detailed figures, please check with the various research agencies – their websites are indicated in Chapter 14.

[8]   Source of the estimate: Forrester Research, 1998.

is expected to be primarily driven by business-to-business transactions, in particular in the electronic procurement area while business-to-consumer is only less than ten per cent of those figures. However, the consumer market is growing at a faster pace and, in my view, will be much larger in the long run. The research figures were also prepared before TV and mobile phones could be used as "terminals" for Internet access, so the market reach of the Internet in the consumers area can quickly jump by a big factor.

The business-to-business market will be primarily focused on supply chain improvements and electronic procurement. In this area, primarily large corporations will push their suppliers to replace their order, delivery and invoicing paperwork by electronic media. Each of those projects will have a size of several million Euros thus leading to the huge overall numbers. Given the size of those projects, they will be primarily handled by large system integrators and consulting companies. Best practices are already emerging and I use some examples in the book such as from the car manufacturers and their suppliers to show the impact of the new approaches to small and medium companies.

The electronic business-to-consumer market on the other hand will focus on complementing or even replacing traditional physical point-of-sales activities, as we discussed for the book, travel and banking industry. New business approaches with services outperforming the physical stores are being invented. This is the field for start-up companies. Let's have a look at the current markets.

1.3.1   Current markets

Figure 1-2 shows that the segments on the right side of the pie charts, i.e. books, music, computers and to some extend fashion, are already pretty well covered with offerings, and the market demand is already channelled to some key providers. In fact, the examples of Yahoo or Dell indicate how to get the acceptance of customers: be very service minded, offer a high value to the customer and make it easy for him to get exactly what he wants.

Inform the customers very broadly, invite criticism and allow your customers to share their experience! If you want to be successful in those areas, you have to have a very specific niche of offerings – or you should be large enough to challenge the now established *e*Venture pioneers, like multi-million funded BOL (www.bol.com) is trying to gain market share against Amazon.

In the other areas, the markets are less developed. This means you will have more flexibility to define your part of the cake, e.g. what type of sports equipment you intend to offer, but on the other hand you need to invest more creativity, energy and experimental time to find out the right fit of your product with the marketing and sales approaches.

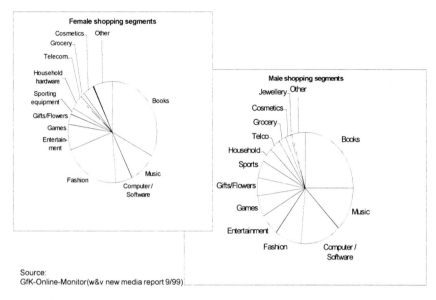

Figure 1-2: The current *e*Business market with consumers – product sales

Let's also have a look at the electronic services market as shown in Figure 1-3. Similar to the product market, we see some well-developed areas, namely online banking and travel. Most of the banks have now launched their electronic banking channel for the traditional types of transactions, and new types of deals are now implemented that are enabled by electronic transactions such as day trading or discount brokerage. Thus, a new combination of traditional players and new *e*Businesses has established itself. Still the business of the newcomers is growing at the cost of traditional banks that don't provide electronic channels, but that's no field for start-ups because you won't be able to step into the market of the established players easily with all their rules and regulations. The examples in this book will indicate how you can "blend" your offering.

In travel, the two big newcomers eBay and TISS issue already a good part of the "last minute" tickets with the combined approach of cheap offers from the airlines or the new auction approach based on the bidding request from the consumer for a certain ticket. Their market is also growing, but together with the traditional travel agencies and the direct sales of the airlines it will be difficult if you want to break into that business yourself. If you actually intend to, you have to find a very good market niche with an outstanding offering profile: e.g. focus on a region that's not so well covered yet or some specific offers beyond the current proposition of the existing players.

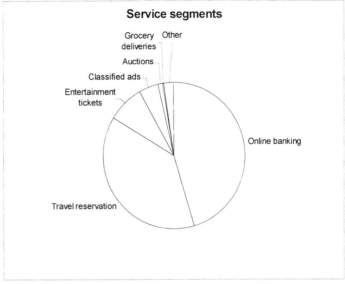

Source: GfK-Online-Monitor (w&v new media report 9/99)

Figure 1-3: Market breakdown for online services

So much for the existing markets. Let's now check the potential markets of the future in the next section.

1.3.2   Potential markets

Which additional markets can be expected? Currently the relatively established book market is expanded by extensions to the value propositions, e.g. electronic books to be downloaded from the web, printing on demand of personalized books, providing pieces of books like dictionary entries. At the same time, the approaches from online booksellers are adopted by US music retailers (e.g. CDnow – www.cdnow.com) and toy retailers.

Where can we expect the consumers to accept the new electronic offerings? As first indicator we can use the current and expected number of Internet surfers and the active buyers within those groups; another indicator is the PC availability. Those figures vary largely country by country.

The expected growth is enormous, so the timing is great for starting your eVenture! Below, some selected Western countries are shown. Actually, the European numbers reflect the latecomers in the Internet world – the Scandinavian countries show similar progress to the USA.

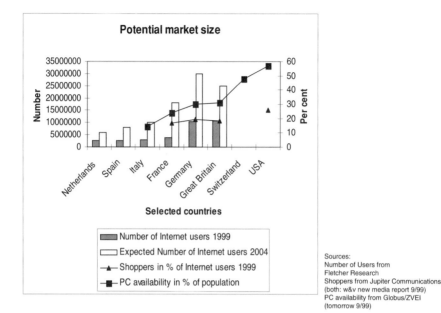

Sources:
Number of Users from
Fletcher Research
Shoppers from Jupiter Communications
(both: w&v new media report 9/99)
PC availability from Globus/ZVEI
(tomorrow 9/99)

Figure 1-4: Potential market size – Western countries

Let's also look at the expected trends for selected Asian countries below.

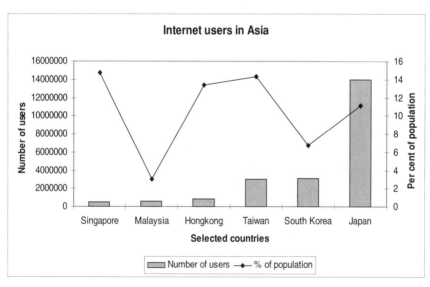

Source: Computer Zeitung 36/1999

Figure 1-5: Internet users in Asia

We see that for most of the countries (with the exception of Japan), the absolute number of users is much smaller than in the Western countries, and that on average also the penetration within the population is less progressed. However, the use of mobile phones in Asia is even further advanced than in Western countries. Thus, I expect and recommend focusing the activities for Asian customers on the very offerings that can be well described on the small screen of a mobile phone (using the WML standard). This also means preparing concise interactions with the customers that can be quickly brought to a closure of the sales deals. As a marketing tool, SMS can be used there in lieu of eMail.

For the PC based Internet, even between the various western countries important differences regarding the readiness of the markets exist. Those differences are due to customers' likes and dislikes, the progress of the infrastructure (in particular cabling), the PC penetration in the population and the formal environment (in particular legal and payment).

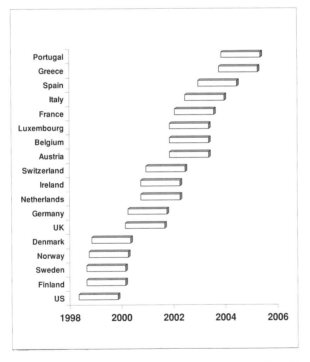

Source:
Forrester Research 99

Figure 1-6: Expected timing of market acceptance for _e_Business

The markets in the US and in Scandinavia are ready today – and in fact we see several strong new players emerging. The other countries will follow. So, start your offering in a country when it's ready; if you have your infrastructures idle while the critical mass in the market still builds up, you would only waste money. With the upcoming roll-out of TV-based Internet, some of the indicated dates may be pulled forward – a final hurdle still to overcome is that the consumer needs to get his set-top box to connect his TV with the telephone. Who will be the first to offer those set-top boxes for free when the customer commits to watch Internet through the provider's portal?

So, let me repeat the forecast mentioned initially: the Internet business is expected to grow by almost a factor ten in only three years – grab your piece of the cake now!

1.4   SCOPE OF AN eVENTURE

This book will help you understand:

- **How to use the Internet** to communicate electronically with your customer for your marketing and sales activities and how to keep your customer engaged in his relation with your company.
- **What type of organization and systems to use** to integrate flexibly your suppliers and to sustain the ongoing changes in order to maintain your competitive positioning.
- **What to do to get started** with your eVenture.

In the Figure 1-7 below I illustrate the scope of an eVenture.

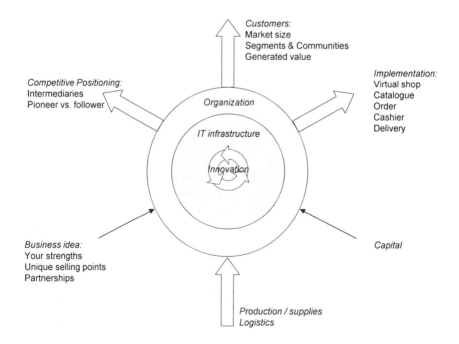

Figure 1-7: Aspects of getting started

This figure shows the necessary "input" into your *e*Venture project at the bottom and the "output" at the top. The thin arrows indicate what you need to contribute for a success, the thick arrows indicate where the Internet will support you. The centrepiece is the organization you have to build with its IT infrastructure and the readiness for ongoing innovations.

Those aspects are covered in the subsequent chapters. I recommend that you actively work through the book and use the checklists to document your considerations. In many areas, the insights from this book will trigger additional "homework" to be done by you like calculating your business case or doing additional research; in other cases you may already know the answer. Below please find my assumption, which type of homework is to be expected for each of the areas.

What you should have in mind when you are reading the book is your business idea – that's your contribution to a successful exercise in reading the book; and it will be the pillar of your success. Throughout this book several examples and some case studies will be discussed which you can use to identify additional facets for your business idea and which are the "strawmans" for the design of the implementation.

We'll start our joint work with the strategy considerations. In Chapter 3 we begin with the source of your revenues, namely the customers. The interactions with them are handled throughout the book. We'll discuss how to interact with prospects and customers, what to consider for servicing them and how to keep them engaged with your company. The actual production of your offerings is something you have to handle yourself, but the interaction and communication will be treated in the book from its organization and technical implications.

Secondly, in Chapter 4, we will examine your business idea and your strengths and map them in the best possible way to the Internet capabilities. Your ideas and the capabilities of your organization will create the selling arguments unique to your company. You need to nurture those strengths in order to stay ahead of anybody intending to copy your idea! In order to nurture your strengths and to get off the ground quickly, you should initially outsource all activities that are not your core competencies by interacting with some key partners. But also be aware of the dependencies you confront yourself with, when you outsource activities that are a core component to your offering. We'll discuss some risk mitigation strategies for that, but in the long run insourcing will become the best approach.

Thirdly, you need to position your company against your competitive environment and you have to create the awareness for your offerings in the market. That will be discussed in Chapter 5.

The discussion of innovation and knowledge management will conclude the strategic considerations in the book.

In Part II, the globally emerging best practices will be reflected. There, we will learn what organizational models and what IT architectures currently are the latest evolution for successful *e*Businesses. This discussion shows the organization of the companies enabling them to focus on the customer and explains how partnerships are approached. Additionally, we have production considerations and the necessary supplies and logistics. In order to organize them, i.e. if you want to produce some physical goods, you need to engage with the engineers to physically produce those products, you need to partner with your suppliers to provide the basic materials for your production. Or in the case of you intending to resell, you also need to organize your supplies and you need to package them appropriately. Finally, if you want to sell services, you need to provide them. This means to find the service people, the consultants and the technicians that will create the service. In the book, I assume that you know-how to perform this production. What we will address in the book are the communication aspects between the various players, such as the order management within your supply chain or the information to your customers about the progress of your production and delivery. This discussion will cover the organizational aspects as well as the information technology implementation of such interactions and communication.

Also in Part II, the technology background of Internet and the various peripheral devices is explained.

Finally, in Part III, we will discuss how to leverage the best practices for your company. For that discussion, four concrete business models are used and the creation of the virtual shop is explained: how the organization should look like and which IT components to install. Moreover, the actual marketing and sales is covered. In your virtual shop channel, the sales process has some different dynamics than in a physical setting. Your customer can't do a window shopping, nor can he touch and feel your different offerings. Instead, you need to provide a similar environment where the customer gets as much of a physical and personal impression of your offerings as possible. This is achieved by presentations, catalogues and references of other users. The closure of the deal is different as well: you'll have a remote order that requires also a tangible confirmation. And regarding the payment cash is no option – so you have to be sure, that your counterpart is giving you real money in exchange for your offering. Cheating is easier on the web, because people could use fake identities or credit card numbers intercepted from other web users. But fortunately, you can outsource the solution of this problem to payment service providers in similar ways as you could do it in a physical shop.

With all this information, a business plan and a project plan will be developed. The business plan will be necessary to convince your investor about the business concept – and to get the capital to actually execute the project. Only with your idea in mind, the investor probably won't be ready to listen to you. Therefore, you should carefully work through the book and use the checklists provided at the end of each chapter as your documentation of the business approach. With this documentation, you can show that you've done your homework and will be more easily able to convince him to invest his money in your activities. But even if you have the money yourself, your confidence in your plans will grow so you will be better off for the launch. To facilitate using the checklists, you also find them on my website: www.success-at-e-business.com. You should download the templates and use them as your working sheets.

Let me make one point before we dive into the details of your strategy: Your web business won't be successful by itself! Increase the awareness by different marketing activities. Use a combination of approaches: some are Internet based and others are traditional. As far as they are Internet based, we'll address them in the book, in particular regarding the establishment of communities and regarding technical tools like search engines and links. The concept of communities is highlighted in many places of the book. Even if you only want to browse quickly through the book, please check all the occurrences by reading the appropriate paragraphs as indicated by the index.

In order to create the appropriate awareness for your offerings, you should also use traditional marketing media. Use the same questions for deciding upon each specific marketing activity, e.g. newspaper advertising, TV spots, or direct mailing: what's the market reach of the media and which responsiveness can they generate?

1.5   DISCUSSION POINTS

At the end of this chapter, let's revisit our perception of the new opportunities and challenges. On my website www.success-at-e-business.com you'll find the answers to those questions and additional materials relevant for your launch.

- What are the benefits of doing business via the web?
- What type of challenges are those competitors in your industry facing that stick to the traditional approaches?
- Which web enabled possibilities to get in touch with additional customers do exist?
- What's the name of the concept to create customer engagement and loyalty?
- What are the two most important factors for success in your *e*Venture?
- When do you expect the readiness of the market in your target country?

Recommendations:

- Select one of the business models allowing quick benefits on the web – either a new business idea or the online extension of your current "traditional" business activities.

- Organize your activities for the launch of your electronic business like a real project with the steps Awareness and initial web presence, Initial offering and ordering, Full offering with ordering and delivery – and push for a quick delivery of the project results.

2

Strategic considerations

Create a unique offering for your customers using the electronic interaction possibilities of the web in cooperation with your suppliers and partners.

The strategic considerations for launching an *e*Venture initially are pretty similar to the assessment you need to make for launching any type of business or making any type of investment. In addition to those standard considerations, you need to factor in, how the Internet capabilities with their increasing speed of changes force you to be also very explicit about what NOT to do. As the Internet allows you a flexible configuration of your interaction with customers and suppliers and offers to more easily outsource many areas of operations, you should prepare a start of your business focussing on your core competencies. Reduce to the max! This means to start small, outsource all areas that aren't critical for your success – and be ready to re-configure and grow quickly.

In the subsequent sections of this part of the book, I'll guide you through the areas to cover for starting your *e*Venture. For those of you who are further interested in specific topis, I provide references like further reading recommendations to cover the respective disciplines.

2.1   ACTION ITEMS FOR THE QUICK READER: DEVELOPING A CONCISE STRATEGY

With the action items below, I want to show you possible abbreviations in organizing your strategic considerations. If you believe you have already covered certain aspects, just refer to the checklists at the end of the particular chapter to find out if you still should fill some gaps. If everything's fine, you can just proceed with the next chapter.

The overall goal of the strategic considerations is to prepare the necessary materials for the Business Plan describing quantitatively and qualitatively what you want to offer, in which markets, with which revenues at which costs – and the timing of your revenues and costs. The topics for each chapter are mentioned below.

I want to point out at this place that I recommend to the entrepreneur to get a good overall orientation by going through the checklists provided in this book. While the checklists are generic for *e*Ventures, I cannot advise you to start an *e*Venture by trying everything at once and spending money in a shotgun approach. The checklists should rather be used to identify:

- the best positioning and appropriate marketing approaches to create the awareness in the virtual marketplace for your offering;
- relevant Internet capabilities helping you to win new customers and improve existing customer relationships based on electronic interactions;
- key areas where you can create new markets based on your core capabilities and electronic interactions with your partners;
- the bottom line impact from continuous stream-lining of your front and back office activities, e.g. cost savings from optimizing the supply chain.

Ideally in just one or two key areas you should then start a very focused initiative, where again the checklists can be used to make sure that the activities of the initiative cover all relevant aspects. In the checklists (starting in this chapter), I've left room for your notes, priority considerations or questions in order to support our target for a practical use of the book. The action items below show how the following chapters fit together.

Table 2-2: Action items for defining the Strategy

Item/Target	Comments	Where you find details	Your self-assessment/ Questions
Establish a concise vision	Should fit on one page and be understood by staff and customers Should address the areas: Customers & Segments, Products & Services, Sales Approach	Refer to Balanced Scorecard example (Chapter 7) and Leadership discussion (Chapter 9)	
Develop a business model and plan	That's the overall purpose of the Part I	See examples in Chapter 12	
Understand your Customer	…in each important segment – better than your competitor	Chapter 3	

Table 2-2 (continued)

Item/Target	Comments	Where you find details	Your self-assessment/ Questions
Understand Yourself	…with your Products & Services, your Human Capital dynamics, and your partners	Chapter 4	
Understand your Competitor	…and revisit your plans and targets regularly vis-à-vis your competitor's moves	Chapter 5	
Innovate	You need to stay ahead of the market dynamics	Chapter 6,	
Understand the Emerging Best Practices	Based on electronic interactions with customers and partners	Part II	
Plan the Implemen- tation of your *e*Venture	Based on the Best Practice organizational and IT roadmap	Part III	

For a softcopy of this checklist see my website

2.2   FIRST TOP–DOWN PLAN

Your strategic planning should be organized in iterations. As a first result, you should get a high level plan. Below please find a template indicating possible scenarios. In this template, you can check off your first idea for a strategic plan. This initial plan should be refined by working through the subsequent chapters.

The checklists and templates can be downloaded from my website to give you a convenient way to document your considerations and to adjust them during the various iterations and refinements.

Table 2-3: Template for your strategic plan

Area	Possible targets	Your first idea	Considerations
Customers *Details in Chapter 3*	Business customers	☐ No ☐ Yes, namely: _____ _____	

Table 2-3 (continued)

Area	Possible targets	Your first idea	Considerations
	Consumers, e.g.	☐ No	Check the penetration of PCs, mobile phones, TV set-tops in each target segment
	• Juveniles	☐ Yes, namely: _____	
	• Students	☐ Yes, namely: _____	
	• Young Professionals	☐ Yes, namely: _____	
	• Families	☐ Yes, namely: _____	
	• Retirees	☐ Yes, namely: _____	
	• Rich	☐ Yes, namely: _____	
	• Bargain hunters	☐ Yes, namely: _____	
	Communities you can create	Topics: _____ Interaction: (e.g. room, expert group forum) _____	
Core Compe-tencices *Details in Chapter 4*	For example in the areas		
	• Marketing	☐ Yes, namely: _____	
	• Sales	☐ Yes, namely: _____	
	• Production	☐ Yes, namely: _____	
	• Logistics	☐ Yes, namely: _____	
	• Finance	☐ Yes, namely: _____	
	• Information technology	☐ Yes, namely: _____ _____	
	• Other	☐ Yes, namely: _____	
	Partners you intend to interact with electronically	e.g. marketing _____ suppliers delivery: _____	
	Positioning, as		
	• Quality leader	☐ Yes, namely: _____	
	• Price fighter	☐ Yes, namely: _____	
Compe-tition *Details in Chapter 5*			Their strengths and weaknesses; consider age, standing and reputation
	• Local	☐ Yes, namely: _____	
	• Global	☐ Yes, namely: _____	
	• Awareness creation	☐ Links with: _____ ☐ Index words for Search Engines: _____	
Innovation *Details in Chapter 6*	Anticipated approach for improvement of offerings, e.g.		
	• Own R&D	☐ Yes, namely: _____	
	• Partnerships	☐ Yes, namely: _____	
	• Knowledge Management	☐ Yes, namely: _____	

For a softcopy of this template see my website

Throughout the remainder of this part of the book, we will add details to your initial business plan. When you have completed the work with this book, you should revise your initial plan and use it as the masterplan for your discussions with your investors and banks.

Recommendations:

- Start NOW documenting your business model and business plan.

- Use the templates from my website as checklists for your documentation.

3

Know your customer

Analyse the market in order to prepare electronical interactions with your customers. Engage with your customers:

- *by eMail, SMS and personalized websites*
- *very regularly with high value contributors*
- *with specific marketing messages and special offerings triggered by an analysis of the customer behaviour*
- *in a combination of information, entertainment and business*
- *to have active relationships within the customer communities*
- *and to generate profitable business.*

Quantify your planned interactions and contribution and monitor your success.

In earlier days we said, the "customer is king". Some companies have even appreciated to serve the dignified king well, but today it's less a question of dignity, but a question of blunt might. George Bell of Excite concludes "The faster the delivery speeds become and the more efficient the Web becomes, the more power the consumer is going to have". To be ready for that battle of power, first and foremost you must know your customer. You have to internalize the answers to the following questions:

- How big is the target market?
- Who are your individual customers?
- What's the benefit you provide to your customers?

We'll discuss the approach to those questions in this chapter plus some more important aspects you need to cover – the latter aspects you don't necessarily need to memorize in each detail; it will be enough to do your homework and to revisit that homework in the light of the two overruling questions from time to time.

As far as the market size is concerned, some general observations and statistics have been discussed in the first chapter – for your exact target market, you should perform a focused research. If you intend to launch a local business, the chambers of commerce usually have sound statistical materials, if you are targeting a larger market, you can find statistics on the web. In Chapter 14, I indicate the websites of several research agencies providing much of the statistical materials for free.

In addition to the statistical research you should perform a market research for your specific target market including individual assessments of the prospects' interests and buying preferences. As a first assumption in the consumer market, you can start with the idea that your customer is in his early thirties, more male than female (female buyers represent 30 per cent to 45 per cent of the buyers), has a higher education and a high income[9]. Please also refer to the statistics provided in the beginning of this book.

Figure 3-8 below indicates the two major marketing models you can use for the consumer market, namely the buying preference model and the customer life stage model.

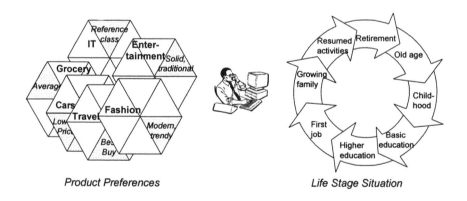

Product Preferences   Life Stage Situation

Figure 3-8: Models for consumer marketing

---

[9] Source: GfK-Online-Monitor (w&v new media report 9/99)

Product preferences: For different needs, your customer may show different buying preferences. He or she may wear the latest trendy and pretty expensive fashion, but rationalizes on expenses for his or her car and travel. Or a computer addict may have the latest electronics at home, but be a sloppy buyer in all other areas.

Life stages: At different life stages, your customers have obviously different needs and thus different buying behaviours. The most interesting point for sales decisions are, whenever the customer gets into his next life stage situation. At this point in time, he's actively looking for the best provider to support his new needs – and often he stays loyal to this selection throughout that new stage. Beyond the buying preferences, also the payment risk is different at the different stages.

To find these preferences out, there are two ways. One is just to talk to your customers; in a small market you can do that yourself, in larger markets you'll need to engage a market research company. The second approach is to monitor the behaviour of your customers with more or less sophisticated statistical tools starting with a count of sales in a small environment and ending with complex data mining activities crunching millions of data records to find out the patterns of the customer behaviour in very large markets.

3.1   OBSERVATION AND ANALYSIS

3.1.1   Market

How many customers are out there?

As a newcomer in the market, you should seek for good indicators for the overall market size. For consumers, the basic figure is the number of households or individuals that need your product or service annually. Such figures can be obtained by research, e.g. through statistical organizations. For business customers, the target market can be quantified by obtaining the appropriate business directories from research agencies, like Moody's (www.moodys.com), Dun & Bradstreet (www.dnb.com) or Hoppenstedt (www.hoppenstedt.com).

As an established corporation, you certainly have your sales figures available – but better use the opportunity during the launch of an *e*Business project to revisit the overall market size and to rethink, if there are areas of the market, which you have disregarded before.

Then, the number and positioning of the currently existing competitors should be examined. By that, you will get a first approximation of the overall market size and your possible market share.

Based on this anticipated sales figure, you should extrapolate the market dynamics: prepare a best-case and a worst-case scenario. The best-case scenario should include a growing demand for the new offering you provide. Imagine the growth of Internet usage where every forecast is scaled up after a few weeks – so prepare yourself mentally for an overwhelming success. But prepare yourself also for a flop: what if you are not alone with your great idea and someone else will come to the market a few weeks before you are ready? And what if the consumers don't like your offering as much as you thought?

Within this market, you will probably find segments, e.g. younger or older consumers, the genders, different regions. More often than not, the offering should be adjusted for the segments – in particular when there are several competitors out there you need to distinguish from.

The key risks for both the best and the worst scenario need to be analysed and mitigated. If you plan for the small numbers of the worst-case scenario and suddenly the customers dump their orders on you, you will get a reputation of a bad service enterprise. So agree on contingencies with your suppliers and configure your front and back office in a way to quickly scale up. We'll talk more about that issue in the implementation part of this book, but to give you a look ahead: your organizational structure, your processes and the targets of your staff should allow change readily and your infrastructure and IT systems should allow the easy addition of more performant components. If you plan for the best case scenario and the customers stay away, you'll have a big financial risk unless you have agreed with your suppliers to get out of delivery contracts without a big damage to yourself. A smart approach for your environment and logistics is to outsource many of those aspects in order to save the huge upfront investments instead of building everything yourself in the beginning. Once your growth starts to accelerate, you then can insource the activities again to achieve a better cost per transaction.

Recommendation:

- Start with documented assumptions of the market, compare them regularly to the actual development and prepare yourself for deviations in both directions: a much faster and a much slower progress is possible!

3.1.2   Customer value

How much does each customer contribute to you?

The contribution per customer is basically the net of the revenues generated by the transactions with him minus the cost associated with it. Nowadays, the controlling mechanisms are relatively well established for the back office activities, i.e. the costs of the products and services. But it would be too easy to do just a calculation of the margin per sold product or delivered service. Additionally the point-of-sales costs and other front office activities, e.g. the marketing cost and the cost of acquiring a new customer have to be considered as well. While *e*Business is still at an exploratory state, start with the A-Customers only. Once you have learned your lessons, you can expand to the B-segment.

Planning and controlling of those figures is well supported by ERP (Enterprise Resource Planning) software to analyse your financial results. You may not need to implement one of the huge ERP systems yourself, but you can either run it as an outsourced solution or buy one of the smaller packages that can run on a PC. Your accountant also should be able to provide you with the most important evaluations. On top of the retrospective number crunching, you may think of a sophisticated modelling of your revenue and cost structures, the customer buying behaviour and life cycle phases. But that's way too much for the beginning: For an initial business plan, some spreadsheet calculations (I would say not more than two or three pages) should be sufficient. This initial business plan has to be cross-checked against accounting and controlling data (your own if available, or industry benchmarks and standards, or documented assumptions). Then an A, B, C analysis of your customer segments has to be done: where do you expect the highest revenue, the highest retention, the least cost, the least risk for launch?

Also the monitoring, i.e. controlling of your customer performance will be supported either by an ERP system (for large enterprises) or by a spreadsheet. Unfortunately, the external as well as the internal accountants are rather used to orient themselves in accounting structures which don't support our discussed customer value model. Therefore, when you set up the reporting, insist on getting a break down by customer segments and include back-office and front-office costs into your reporting. Also, you should integrate your plans into the reporting to get an early warning, when your actuals deviate from your plans.

In some customer segments, it may be important to consider the evolution of the Customer Value throughout the lifetime of the relationship with them. You may have customers in your portfolio who just cover your cost for quite a while, but who become very profitable later.

But don't confuse yourself by mere hope – you should document your assumptions regarding the customer life cycle behaviour and cross-check them either based on your own records or using industry benchmarks. And you should avoid subsidizing your customers too much: it's easy to give free services to the Juniors, but will they grow into a very profitable customer once they are an adult? Such long-term offerings are an area primarily interesting for large corporations that can afford the subsidies – like the telecom carriers providing mobile phones almost for free to gain market share or Internet providers offering one year of free service. If you want to implement such a life cycle model, you have to have very strong customer retention programmes as well. Otherwise you'll end up with customers who do cherry-picking: they'll use up your subsidies and then exploit those of your competitor.

Recommendation:

- Focus on your most profitable customers!

3.2   CUSTOMER ORIENTATION AND INTERACTION

3.2.1   Segmentation

Who are your customers?

Maybe you're now enthusiastic about the money you dream of. But please push that dream away for a moment: why should anybody give you their money? The best sale is one where both parties believe, that they've got more value than they had to pay for. I don't want to talk about perception or sleazy salesman tricks – but I do want to drive your attention to the real needs of your customers or to the needs you can manage to create.

Put yourselves in the shoes of your customers: where do their desires, dreams, and needs match with your offerings?

Do you address business people's needs? Then you need to have a solid and functional presentation, be cost effective and show a solid track record how other businesses have benefited from using your offering. Can you convince reference customers to implement links to your offering from their Internet pages? Can you establish an active customer group? Can you gain leverage by multiple entries into search engines?

Do you address private people? Then anticipate what situation they're in when they surf on your Internet site. If you have some data about your existing customers, great. If you need to imagine, what type of people they are, good as well. To conceive the customer potential best, try to fully understand their situation:

- What's the typical age and gender of your customer?
- What's the social situation (parents, brothers and sisters, spouse, children)?
- How and where do they live and what's their profession?
- How do they spend their leisure time and what's their cultural and religious background?
- What's painful for them and what do they like?

You can match your customers to the three types of customers that research is indicating – and to their buying preferences. Initially, the segments should be pursued which can be most easily approached by *e*Ventures:

Table 3-4: Customer types to be approached by *e*Ventures

Segment	Attributes	Size
Quality shopping	Income > € 2000 Convenience driven, high quality expectations Forward looking Trust in product brands Age cluster < 40	35–40% of retail market **Focus for *e*Business offerings!**

Table 3-4 (continued)

Segment	Attributes	Size
Smart shopping	Income < € 2000 Cost / benefit awareness Sceptical regarding future Age cluster < 40	25–30% of retail market **Interesting for *e*Business**
Low budget purchasing	Income < € 2000 Much time for price comparisons, discount oriented Backward oriented High awareness of retail brands Age > 40	1/3 of retail market

Source: Market Horizons Smart Shopper Study, Grey Strategic Planning, 1995

What motivation do you expect from your customers? What private or company situation? Support the dreams of your target groups, e.g. help them find a nice travel location, a well-suited apartment for living, another job, a friend. And interweave this support of the desires of your customers with your offering. The more empathy you can create with the prospect, the more you can expect to close the deal. Just be nice to your customers – they've deserved it, because they give you their money.

Entrepreneurs and companies who took the effort to go through such an analysis and who invited their customers to share their needs with the provider, found results that were surprisingly easy to implement:

A car manufacturer executed a market survey and realized, that his customers wouldn't be only willing to buy new cars through the Internet (in some cases even together with a financing arrangement), but also used cars, spare parts and extra equipment. He had all pieces available to create a strong Internet offering serving many aspects of his customers' needs.

A bank analysed their credit card transactions and realized, that the credit card customers with the strongest usage and the best payment morale are football fans. They extended their leverage by engaging with merchandise companies, fan shops and Internet chatting around football. And they boosted their revenues by giving their football fans a virtual home.

An entrepreneur realized the problems in her neighbourhood for the families of professionals working abroad. She started a network to help the professionals and the families with all aspects of day-to-day life in a foreign country. In only six months her company was so successful that she could employ a dozen full-time counsellors. This company is virtual in its presence to the customers – and also the "back-office" is virtual: the employees are scattered throughout the country, they collaborate through the Internet.

So, you should be able to find similar opportunities in your prospect and customer environment!

Recommendation:

- Describe your target segments as precisely as you can, identify the best suited channels and approaches – and internalize this definition.

3.2.2   Retention of existing customers and cross-selling

Don't let your customers trickle away!

The traditional sales cycles to win a new customer are pretty expensive. In the retail market, the marketing and sales costs for new customers eat up the profits of a long duration of engagement: for example, mail-order companies and banks need the first half year to offset those costs with the ongoing profits – and insurances even need up to two years. For one-off product sales, the ratios are slightly better, but you have to set aside more than ten per cent of your revenues for marketing and point of sales costs in order to attract the necessary attention.

In order to reduce that cost impact, your only possible strategy is, to make your customer happy enough, that he buys from you again when his next need arises. If you implement some customer retention programmes and keep your customer informed about your new offerings, you can expect a resell rate of 20 to 50 per cent annually depending on your offerings. But there's a much better thing, namely pro-active cross-selling. Global research in different market areas indicates a 50 to 200 per cent cross-sell rate. Thus you can support tremendous growth with only little additional sales efforts.

In Figure 3-9 below, the three-year extrapolation of a customer retention programme and cross-selling is shown graphically:

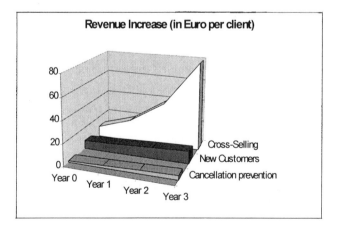

Figure 3-9: The benefit of customer loyalty over a three-year period

As such tremendous sales figures for cross-selling have been observed in most industries – how can you achieve it? Well, the Internet is a good channel to use at low cost and the electronic support you need to build up allows a permanent tuning of the offering. The loyalty effect can be supported further by the creation of user communities. Thus, the community members don't experience a visit on your website as shopping, but they meet virtually with friends and eventually buy something from you, anyway. We'll discuss the community aspect in more detail a few paragraphs further on.

What you need additionally, in order to align your cross-selling proposition with the updated customer needs, is regular market research to find out the additional demand and you need to monitor the behaviour of your customers in order to find the right moment for a proposal. These ideas are further elaborated in Part II of this book. The underlying assumption is that the entrepreneurs will listen individually to their customers in order to understand their needs, as they have a close relationship with them. Larger companies will run various analysis of data to find patterns in the customers' buying behaviour. Several statistical approaches, e.g. Data Mining (Exploratory Data Analysis, Predictive Modelling) exist for the mass market. Data Mining was invented in the traditional retail business and by mail-order companies in order to optimize their supplies and to position their products in the way most effective to trigger customer sales (e.g. separate mail-order catalogues for different customer profiles like fashion, home and garden, do-it-yourself). Often it's assumed, that you also need lots of data for such an analysis, but that's not really the case: some thousand transactions are sufficient to derive key conclusions for an improvement of the cross-selling.

Once you know which customers to target with your specific offerings, you should use the great mechanisms of the Internet to raise your customers' awareness of them and to convince them to buy.

Mailing Lists (*e*Mail and SMS): Invite your customers to subscribe to Mailing Lists. You can keep all people on those lists informed about your latest offerings. To get your customers on the mailing lists, you can ask for their *e*Mail addresses when you close the first deal, you can offer them to explicitly subscribe and unsubscribe on the mailing lists and you can get even non-customers by making some raffles. Once you have the addresses and can map them to the buying behaviour, you can trigger the appropriate information. You could mention only your propositions, but then you'll probably experience your customers unsubscribe quickly from your mailing list. So it will be better, if you complement your offerings with information interesting for your customers, e.g. the latest racing results for the car fan club, the football hit list and maybe some lotto games for the football bank.

Personalized information: From all the information you have available, show only the areas relevant for your customer. Take a book seller like amazon.com. As long as the consumer is still unknown, the reference to all available books and music is displayed at random. But as soon as the consumer's profile begins to emerge, for example professional books or travel books, those are highlighted by showing them at the beginning of the website or in the little box with the current special offers. Even if you don't have huge analysis systems, you can make initial assumptions, e.g. just take the category of the last book ordered to highlight in the next customer interaction.

Banner advertisements: Similar to the personalization of information regarding your own offerings, you can place banner advertisements on behalf of your advertising partners. With a good personalization of advertising the customers shouldn't feel overly bothered by the banners. The only impression you should avoid is that you are more into advertising business than in the core of your offerings.

Recommendations:

- Use the possibilities of electronic communication like eMail and SMS for your marketing.

- Prepare entry offerings targeted for new customers and follow-up offerings in order to keep your customers interested in your company.

3.2.3   Packaging your value proposition in order to match the customers' needs

What's the value the customers get from you?

Your customers will like to think, that they get more value from you than they have to pay – then they'll easily decide to buy. Prepare your offerings while having the customer's perception in mind. Let's discuss some examples:

Basic needs: In order to survive, everybody needs to eat, drink and sleep. Compared to that purpose, any price for the basic products would be ok – but only if there wouldn't be a competitor. As this market is pretty well covered, you evidently need to factor in the competitor's value proposition. What is it that makes your product serve the basic needs better – what's your added value? Do you only support survival or will your customers be more healthy, more powerful, more beautiful?

Professional advantage: Everybody and every company needs to gain as good a skill base as possible in order to survive in profession and in business. These skills have to be applied to generate revenues and to provide the targeted products and services at the smallest cost possible. How do you support the professional needs of your customers? Can they produce quicker or cheaper? Can they gain additional market share? Will they get a better reputation?

Entertainment and fun: Once the basic needs and the base for future wealth are supported, people like to be entertained, engage in social groups and activities and look for fun. How does your offering support this desire? Are your customers guided to your offering by a game? Can they win something? Do you offer multimedia attractions?

One risk of marketing on the Internet is, that those core offerings will be offered by a competitor for slightly lower prices. The Internet is pretty close to a "perfect market" where the prices are negotiated and agreed on the spot based on supplies and demand and where most of the products are just commodities, i.e. items of a defined quality that can be purchased from many suppliers. Also, a good transparency of the offerings exists on the web where the consumers can use agents to compare prices for selected products. Well, it's probably not your interest to engage in price fights (unless you run a very large enterprise and your competitive advantage is centred at handling large quantities of items with big economies of scale). So I assume, that your offering won't be the cheapest listed on the findings of such an agent. Instead, you need to add features to your core offering, that provide some value added (at least perceived value added) in order to pull your offering to a higher level than the commodities around it.

This needs to include the appropriate amount of packaging – in the end your customers must see that it nicely fits together. I remember a story from traditional business. When Black & Decker introduced the new high end product line "DeWalt" that was targeted at professionals like the plumbers and electricians, they didn't succeed in gaining the expected market share. The price was right, the product was terrific, but people didn't buy it. Well, their market research folks found out, that the product line resembled too much the low end equipment for the do-it-yourself amateur. Once this was found out, they changed the colour from Black & Decker blue to heavy duty Caterpillar yellow. And they added a nice aluminium case also suited for additional tools and materials the professionals needed. After that re-packaging the new product line boomed.

Maybe you also want to provide some offers for the smart shoppers looking for the "best buy" or for people on lower budgets. I recommend to do this only from time to time as a special offer. Currently the users of Internet are still those people with higher income – they may occasionally go to the discounter as well, but in general do accept decent prices for decent offerings.

For the discussed packaging it will often be appropriate to bundle your own core offerings with complementary offerings of your partners like the aluminium box producer in our example above and thus create a value network for your customer communities. We will look for the equivalent of those "aluminium boxes" in the virtual world in a minute: these are the communities and contact zones.

Recommendation:

- Complement your core offering by added values in order to avoid a commoditization of your offering and to make price comparisons more difficult.

3.2.4   Communities and contact zones

Keep your customers engaged!

Some of the benefits of customer retention is explained above. But what can you do to keep your customers so happy, that they won't test the offerings of your competitor?

The answer was already indicated in the chapter above: make them more engaged than just as a one-time buyer of your services by supporting them in their whole personal situation. For the consumers this sounds like paradise and I do indeed believe, that we will experience a dramatic improvement in the services for everybody.

If you look to the US some 15 to 20 years ago, the enterprises behaved arrogantly and the consumer felt like he needed going through a tedious application process to receive the honors of acquiring a certain product. Today, the situation has completely changed. To mention some examples:

- supermarkets are open around the clock throughout the year and you get help to transport your sales to your car;
- banks compete for your deposits and borrowings by offering to test their rates, services and staff;
- and for books you don't need to go to a dusty store, but you can flip through the books on the Internet and get the ones you've selected delivered to your home.

In Europe, a similar trend towards the service-society has started now: Crispy Pizza is delivered to your house, you can manage your bank accounts from home, and you can go shopping in US based Internet malls.

In order to keep your customers happy and loyal, you need to enrich your offerings. To distinguish yourself, a good service concept is the starting point and the delivery of a meaningful service is the target. An interesting example is Cabana (www.cabana.com). The source of their revenues is the commission they get for making travel arrangements – like a travel agency. But they do it on the web, and they do it just as the last piece of service. In fact, they've created a community of travellers.

The community members write articles about their adventure trips, they give recommendations for hotels and where the best shopping and entertainment is available. An environment of trust is created: Wouldn't you find the holiday photographs of a friend more credible than those in glossy travel brochures? The customers volunteer to be the location specialist who can help out in case of problems, and even companions for the travel can be found via Cabana's offering. Then a desired travel can be configured by the community member (now becoming a customer...) – and due to this specific customer driven configuration a price comparison isn't so easy any more. Of course Cabana buys their air transportation and hotels like any other travel organizer or travel agency, but with the innovative, customer centred approach they make a better margin.

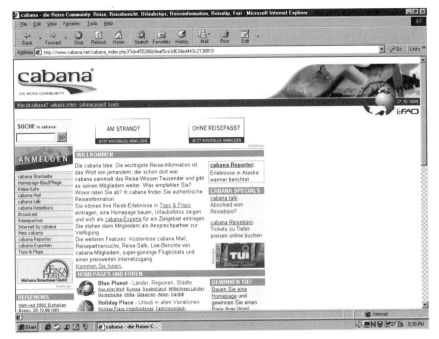

Figure 3-10: Travellers community – www.cabana.com

Create "meaningful" services for your communities!

If you remember the empathic understanding of your customers, it should be conceptually easy, to describe the targets of your customers.

Let's revisit some of the examples mentioned in the section about customer segments:

- the car manufacturer created a fan club for his cars;
- the football fans were already organized and appreciated the additional recognition of the bank;
- and the expatriate families had shared interests and were happy to engage in a network.

So, how often do you think the people active in those groups are going to drop their engagement with the company behind those offerings?

The principle of communities is based on the basic psychological facts, that humans don't like changes and don't like decisions. Once they look after some bigger targets and are engaged in a group, they won't be willing to drop that quickly. And given how hard it was for your customers to decide for your offering the first time, they'll appreciate if you make the buying hurdle as low as possible for them the next time.

The car manufacturer has an easy win selling some special spare parts to his fan community. The bank can have some special offerings (even higher priced offering) to the football fans – provided they find the logo of their club in the right place. And our expatriation specialist can be sure, that new customers are referred to her.

Organize contact zones for your customers

You need to create an environment, where your customers feel well, realize that they are understood, and become members of a strong group. A call centre alone won't be enough for such an environment. Rather, the content of the contact zone, your offering, the people participating in the chats and forums and the "wave length" of your staff in the call centre must be well aligned.

This of course means, that for each of your customer segments you may need slightly different scripts in the call centres and personalized websites with different contents:

- the prospective buyer of a city hopper car will prefer a rational approach;
- the pony car buyer wants to be seduced by some macho statements and rock music;
- and your family van customers should be engaged with some information regarding garden, pets and children.

Avoid unnecessary costs and let customers help themselves

Those ideas sound awfully expensive. As you wouldn't have enough worries to get your core offerings organized! The real expense, though, is creativity and a good arrangement of the contents. This arrangement has to include the partners you select that help you come up with the content your customer communities like. You could create those contents yourself or you could buy them, but that would be wasting money. Your focus has to be on the core offering, the creation of the additional contents is to be outsourced. And the best outsourcing is where you get it for free or almost for free. Your customers (a.k.a. communities) will be the volunteers to create those contents. And they will love you, because you allow them to publish their experience. Now you can add some additional gimmicks, i.e. some items the customers can carry away as a reward; at Cabana for example the writers and photographers amongst the customers can earn some "stars" and once they've compiled enough they get sun-glasses, backpacks or caps as an incentive. Of course with the community logo on it…

The right channel

Let me share the initial understanding of the key characteristics of the different Internet channels using an initial breakdown of target segments. Given the current exclusive use of PCs, we need to wait for quantitative research data of the actual buying behaviour of those segments.

Table 3-5: The right marketing and sales channels for your offering

Target segment	Primary equipment	Constraints	Strengths
Young consumers	PC hooked up by modem with fix telephone wire	Bandwidth Restricted Market penetration: approx. 10% (Asia), 20% (Europe) and 50% (USA)	PC power, e.g. to process information further (text files, calculation data, electronic interaction) Full function keyboard Currently widest accepted device
Big spenders business people and professionals	Mobile phones with WAP display	Small display Expensive connections Dropped calls, i.e. abnormal termination due to bad radio connection Gaps in net coverage	Can be used to provide value added services by sending SMS news to the customers, e.g. financial updates of stock performance, buy/sales triggers, special offers, airplane delays Mobility and (potential) ubiquity
Complete mass market	TV with Internet set-top box; connected via TV cable or telephone wire	Convenient feedback/ data entry missing: only numbers can be entered via remote control.	Large screen Very high bandwidth for realtime video transmission

Don't forget the two most traditional channels for your marketing activities, though! These are the print media – from time to time you should alert your customers of your offerings by standard print advertisements – and the word of mouth, i.e. invite your customers to actively refer prospects to your website and prepare incentives for such referrals. If you go for the real mass markets, you also should place TV spots to pull your customers to your offerings.

Explicit clarity and transparency

In addition, one more prerequisite exists for a successful interaction with your customers: you need to provide transparency to the customer on where he is in the ordering process in order to facilitate his buying decision. It must be very clear to the customer when he is about to order, once he has ordered anything, and for what price. This clarity has to be provided

- Before the purchase decision: look at the "shopping cart" examples on the web – the customer puts something in his virtual shopping cart as if it was real, he can take the items out again, if he finds better suited offerings, he should know the overall cost of all items in the shopping cart.
- At the time of the purchase: check how the "cashiers" are organized – the customer pulls his wallet and gives you his credit card, or you authorized him to use a credit line with you, or he pays with (virtual) cash.
- After the purchase: as the customer can't carry his purchase home, you need to provide the best approximation to that – regular information regarding the status of supplies and delivery is the current standard.

And this clarity must be provided in the way appropriate for the channel – on the TV screen for example, I imagine the real picture of a shopping cart filling up and the friendly person at the cashier accepting the credit card from the customer.

Recommendation:

- Establish customer communities and let them help themselves and help you in creating the contents they want to see on "their" website and provide your appropriate offerings embedded in those community interchanges.

3.3   TOOLS

Use the experience of others!

Practical experience exists in enterprises that are similar to your *e*Venture. You can try to talk to them, but probably there are too many competitive conflicts to get out much of such a discussion. An alternative is to hire some key staff from them, so you win the experience and the insight into your competitors' activities. Additionally, it's possible to leverage the experience of a similar subject area, but from another industry. Examples like the football fan clubs used by a bank can be transferred to similarly organized clubs for other industries.

The industry's experience is also reflected in various tools that are available on the market. In this section, I want to give an overview of the various tools and recommend to you, which type to use at which stage.

3.3.1   Planning

Define where you want to be soon: the next iteration of your business plan

Planning is essential before you launch your operation. You prepared the initial business strategy a few pages back, now we should start looking at the financials. The basic planning can be done "on the back of an envelope" – well, today you probably use a spreadsheet program. The initial considerations should cover the sales forecast and your cost forecast for the first one or two years. A range of revenues for your sales forecast can be derived from the market analysis undertaken before. Regarding the costs you should have an impression from your discussions with the suppliers. So far, that's as in traditional business.

A specific strength of doing business online is now, you can come up with a smart organization of your order handling and inventories. Inventories would eat terribly into your margin due to the fact, that you have to pay for the goods up front, probably by a credit and you need to pay interest fees to the bank while you wait for customers to buy your goods. Moreover you run the risk of having too many outdated products that you can't sell any more. In fact, with the proper supply chain management you can reduce inventories to almost zero. You should also start to think about the size of staff you assume at the various growth stages of your enterprise. For your eVenture and its smart organization, several investments into the appropriate infrastructure are necessary. We'll discuss possible organization structures and IT configurations in the implementation part of the book; at this stage you should focus on your expected sales figures with the respective revenues and costs and with some high level staff plan.

My advice regarding the costs: the leaner you can start your initiative the better! You should focus your activities on your core competence and core offerings. For everything that's not your core activity, you better use outsourced or third party services. This reduces your burden to organize all those things you're not so interested in and you don't incur big investments before you actually benefit from them. Thus you only have to include the lease or rental prices for those services in your initial forecast instead of carrying the investment and paying interests on the necessary capital.

Once you have the first plan together, challenge it. What could go wrong: what if the market doesn't react as you were expecting, what if the costs grow tremendously, what if there are delays in the delivery chain?

Document all the assumptions and risks – and then lock the plan in a drawer for the next month or two, because this plan is just the manifestation of a dream. It doesn't help if you reshape that dream every day. You need to wait until you can check your achievements during the first period of business.

3.3.2   Controlling

Monitor your progress on your way to the defined goal

After the first one or two months are over, you should open the drawer with your business plan again and compare the actual figures with your initial plan. So you will recognize early where something may go wrong, if you need to increase your sales or order your supplies more quickly. You also can check your assumptions and get evidence, where in the range of the best-case scenario and worst-case scenario you navigate. Thus you can update your forecast.

Depending on the size of your initiative, you will need different levels of detail: for a small business, the spread sheet approach might do. But I recommend again, to outsource that reporting to an accountant provided they can set up the reports with a focus on the customer value. A larger enterprise will use the existing ERP system, but also here, it's essential to reflect the value contribution per customer and customer segment.

I strongly recommend you include not only financial aspects in your regular reporting but also the customer perspective, staff perspective and innovation should be monitored. In Part two we'll discuss tools to plan and monitor such aspects, like the Balanced Scorecard, in more depth. In this place I want to give some ideas regarding the non-financial measures you could take every month:

- Number of new customers, number of lost customers
- Average number of sold products per customer
- Hits on Internet pages
- Number of complaints and number of positive comments
- Number of new staff, number of staff who resigned
- Number of new ideas from staff
- Average age of products.

After the first few months of actual business, a refinement of your planning and controlling will be advisable, e.g. you can derive the probability of a sales closure from the number of Internet hits, get a better understanding of the types of your customers and monitor the trends of your customers' behaviour.

Depending on the volumes and design of your data you can use different approaches. You may keep those data on a stand alone PC, or you can create a data warehouse to keep track of the various months of historical transactions. While the entrepreneur should personally monitor the performance, the technical availability of the data should be handled by an outsourcing partner as soon as the indicators can't be kept on a standalone PC any more.

You should highlight the progress against plan in a way to identify where to improve your overall performance (i.e. the financial bottom line), your offering (i.e. the relative performance of various segments) and your Internet presentation (i.e. the website hits and the closures triggered by your various web approaches).

3.3.3   Behaviour and transaction analysis

Use the transaction data for analysis no competitor could perform

Once your initiative has reached a reasonable size, you can use the available transaction and buying data such as the hit rates on your website or the probabilities of closure at certain times, for statistical analysis. This analysis then can trigger a better personalization of the website for one-to-one marketing or dedicated mailings to specific customers.

The first start-ups are now adopting the experience from larger enterprises. For example the Los Angeles food delivery service Pink Dot (www.pinkdot.com) has tremendous success by suggesting additional sales to their customers. Some of the automatically found patterns are trivial (like suggesting milk on top of the ordered cereal) and others are surprising, e.g. sleeping pills go well with coffee. No matter how trivial or surprising – with the additional suggestions the revenues increase each time. The most advanced approaches will be discussed in the Best Practices section (Chapter 7); as long as your customer number isn't large enough for automatical cross-sell suggestions and behaviour analysis, you should work with assumptions. Those assumptions should be documented and checked in order to adjust or refine them and thus also get to a better targeting of the marketing activities.

3.3.4   Benchmarking

Compare your own success with the one of your competitors

To assess how good you are doing, an easy-to-use tool has found more and more users in the last years: Benchmarking. It was developed by consulting companies to get a neutral reference for the performance of a company while avoiding to disseminate confidential information from one customer to another.

In the meantime, the consulting companies often are no longer needed to anonymize such benchmark figures. More and more, the managers in the industry are realizing, that many items that were earlier considered confidential have become public knowledge. The real competition is often in another country or even from another industry. Therefore, the willingness to exchange some key figures with another player in the same market has grown. With this openness, the managers expect to gain a better quality altogether and to improve the customer satisfaction. Of course, you have to be very sensitive to protect the core of your offerings. As an example, for some providers the ratio between closures and hit rate might be top secret, while others can share this information with the other players, but they may be restrictive about the payment morale of their customers.

Key figures you should compare include:

- Overall sales figures
- Relative closure rates (of website hits, of proposals made, of call centre interactions)
- Effort per sale
- Profitability as per centage from revenues
- Risk mitigation approaches.

Different independent organizations exist that can perform such a benchmarking for you, e.g. in the UK you find the PIMS database (product impact on market strategy), in Italy Janus Enterprise International (a.nathanson@flashnet.it) supports such product, price and positioning assessment. This analysis is very specific for each country, so there's no general worldwide recommendation, but you can check for similar benchmarking providers on the web.

Recommendation:

- Monitor your success with a controlling tool reflecting market targets, website acceptance, innovation and staff attrition.

3.4   CHECKLIST

In this chapter we've discussed many concepts available to you to understand your customer, his or her needs, the buying preferences and the ways to approach your customers. To bring it all together and to allow you to document your analysis, please use the checklist below. Let me remind you, that templates can be downloaded from my website, so you can use them as your work sheets.

Table 3-6: Checklist for understanding the market

Item	To check	Recommendation	Self-assessment
Key questions	• How big is your market? • Who are your customers? • What's the benefit of your business idea for your customers?	If you don't know the concise answers by heart, you aren't ready for your *e*Venture!	
Market	Size of the market, size of segments	Include • Actual size • Current growth • Expected future growth	
Customer Value	Do you know the actual contribution per customer?	At least monthly measurement of contribution per customer	
	Do you know the potential contribution per customer?	Regular, e.g. quarter yearly assessment of buying potential and cost expectation per segment Classify A, B, C segments	
Customer Segments	How many segments do you have?	Depending on purpose, e.g. 5–10 segments to differentiate service attention and organization responsibilities	
	How big are your segments?	Depending on purpose, e.g. • as small as possible for direct marketing • a few thousand customers for statistical comparisons	
Customer Retention	Do you have active customer communities?	Communities should be established in the most profitable customer segments to prevent them from engaging with competitor.	
	How successful are your retention programmes?	Success should be monitored by segments and over time. Benchmarking within the industry is advisable wherever possible.	

Table 3-6 (continued)

Item	To check	Recommendation	Self-assessment
Customer Surveys	How often do you examine your customer needs?	Within each major segment, one or two surveys per year are advisable.	
	How big samples do you need?	With the appropriate statistical support, a sample of 50–500 customers should be sufficient.	
Model support	Do you have • Life cycle models • Buying propensity models • Behaviour models • Pricing differentiation model • Exploratory Data Analysis (EDA)	After a cost/benefit analysis, models should be implemented. Recommended focus: • For the segments with high profitability expectations, cross-selling should be the target. • For the segments with small profitability expectations, cost reduction and price adjustment should be the target	

For a softcopy of the checklist see my website.

3.5   DISCUSSION POINTS

Your customers are the key to your success, so be very thorough in understanding their needs. If you want to exchange your experience with other entrepreneurs in similar situations, please do so on my website www.success-at-e-business.com.

- How can you approach your primary customers systematically?
- How can you create communities and how do you keep the members interested?
- How do you personalize the offerings to your customers?

> **Recommendations:**
>
> - Create online communities, where your customers discuss their concerns and desires.
> - Match your offerings with the customer needs and refine the offerings according to the instantaneous feedback you get from your customers.
> - In a start-up eVenture, engage yourself in the interactions with the communities and support framing them; in a larger corporation, implement automated processes for the statistical analysis of your customers' behaviour.

4

Know yourself

Strengthen your core capabilities and complement them with the offerings of partners you are electronically interacting with. Package this combination into a unique offering and provide an end-to-end integration into your customer facing processes:

- *marketing*
- *order entry*
- *quick delivery or if possible electronic delivery*
- *proactive information of delivery status.*

The old Greeks found that it's very hard to "Γνωθη σεαυτον" (know yourself), because people are not used to reflect regularly about their specific strengths (and weaknesses…). But as you now have the mental picture and the documented facts of your customers, you should be able to identify what in your person and in your company it is that matches with their needs. Porter gives some guidance in writing:

> Competitive strategy is about being different. It means deliberately choosing a different set of activities to deliver a unique mix of value. (Porter, p. 45)

Like with the question discussed in the chapter before, you need to be crystal clear about the answers to a few key questions:

- What are your core capabilities?
- Why should customers buy from you and stay loyal?
- How does the electronic interaction on the web improve the quality of your offering?

Again, some more questions are important and you have to do the appropriate homework, but the answers to the questions above must be burned into your mind, into the mind of your staff and into your marketing statements.

Your products and services should combine in a unique way your strengths and experiences with the possibilities of electronic interaction between you and your customers as well as with your suppliers. Analyse thoroughly your value chain for the generation of your product or offering: where do you have unique skills that can be transformed into an online offering beneficial for your customers?

- Did you make a great invention – like the new standard MP3 by which music can be digitized and downloaded from the web, but it can't be copied any further from the customers PC to another PC?
- Or have you developed a software package that could be run on an application server and be made accessible to users around the globe for a little fee – like a next generation text processor? Be careful, though, Microsoft is planning as well to offer their office products on a rental basis, so you may better look for another market niche – what about games people can play via the Internet?

In addition to analysing your value chain, you have to analyse the value chain of your target market according to the life stage model and buying preference model discussed above:

- What do your customers need to further their career? Can you combine your offerings with some professional education for your customers? Can you use the capabilities of the web, e.g. multimedia, to deliver this education very effectively?
- What do your customers need for their family life, e.g. day care or special education for their child, or savings for the university time, or special diet meals for a sick child? How can you satisfy such needs with your offerings? Can you create the community environment for the interaction of many users on the web, e.g. in order to allow baby sitting at very short notice?
- How can you increase the wealth of your customers? Do your offerings help them exploit additional opportunities? An investor is happy, if you publish specific online stock analysis to help him decide what to buy or sell.
- Can you decrease the burdens in the life of your customers? A frequent flyer may be happy if you keep him informed via messages by SMS on his mobile phone about delays of the plane he is planning to use – and you can organize him a limousine with a chauffeur picking him up at the destination airport to make up for the lost time. A challenged professional that needs to also take care of his or her child may be happy, if you make cooking suggestions – and have a package with all necessary ingredients

for the recipe ready to be picked up at the grocery store right at the way home.

- Can your customers save effort or money if they use your products or services?
- Do you add to their entertainment or social recognition and status?

4.1   OBSERVATION AND ANALYSIS

4.1.1   Beliefs and values: your mission in life

Document who you are

Before you look out to the future and the vision of where you want to get, you should look back and consider where your initiative is coming from:

Are you running a start-up company and the initiative is based on your enthusiasm and belief in your business idea? Then you need to prepare yourself for times of possible frustration and you need to convince yourself that your enthusiasm will stay unchanged even in case of unfavourable evolutions. Examples of successful Internet start-ups are manifold – keep your courage, and don't forget to tune your marketing approach or back office processes if necessary.

Did you get together with some friends who share your dream of a customer-oriented service-friendly proposition to launch a highly profitable company? Then be ready for the different interests of the persons running your effort that might lead to personality battles once you get to the next stage of maturity of your company. If anybody in your entrepreneur team believes he can make money on the Internet without a serious investment of time and overtime and weekends, ask him to leave because each of you needs to commit his full dedication to the project.

Is it founded in a large institution that tries to modernize its presentation in the public and its interaction with the customers? Then you will be probably confronted with much of the traditional thinking of that institution and you need to identify the areas where it's important for the success of the project to change some of the old mental patterns. Get your inspirations from large companies like Charles Schwab. They managed to maintain the economies of scale of a large company while throwing out their inflexible traditions. Now they are one of the largest online discount brokers in the US after they have torn down the borders between the former departments and have redefined the business processes in order to create a customer focused organization.

Most of the answers you should seek cover the areas of interests and pride:

- What are the stakeholders in your initiative proud of?
- What success did they have in their professional life?
- What's the motivation for the key players in your team?
- What keeps you together?
- What "war stories" do you share with the other stakeholders?
- How can you use that experience for interactive business?

Once you have this understanding, you can look ahead and define the vision for your *e*Business initiative for the next time frames, e.g. in one or two years. This exercise will help you to break the key aspects of your business plan further down into measurable targets which you can communicate internally, with your other stakeholders and with your staff, and externally with your customers and your investor or bank. In the implementation part of this book, we'll address the tools to regularly monitor your actual performance against those targets.

In your vision you should address:

Your product and service offerings: How you leverage the capabilities of the Internet.

- Which offerings you have that can be marketed, sold or delivered via the web.
- How your prices compare against those of physical shops or other online shops and how the value for the customers is different in each case.
- Which partners you engage with and which of them to link with online in your marketing and sales activities.
- What development cycles you need for the products.
- How you can leverage one service offering in order to cross-sell another offering.
- At which stage of the cycle marketing – order – production – delivery you want to interact with the customers.

Your market penetration: How you will be able to quickly gain market share.

- Which customers you will be able to address.
- What electronic interactions you will use to win new customers and to keep the existing customers, e.g. Search Engine entries, *e*Mail, SMS, web personalization, links from other websites.
- In what regions you will market your products – and which languages you need to support on your website and in your call centres.
- Whether you intend to step out of your start-up region and maybe launch your offerings in another country.
- How you can organize your customers (e.g. in communities or business user groups).

Your organization: How large you will be in terms of staff and places you operate, how you can keep the management overhead small, how to maintain the pro-active pioneer spirit in your team, and how the "supply factory" for the products and services will be organized (e.g. if you need a lot of third party materials, or if you need people with specific skills).

Your financials: How large your revenues and profits will be, how they break down into various customer segments, to what extent you will be financially dependent on a small number of products, where your largest cost areas are (e.g. hardware or telecommunication or staff).

Your key processes: What key areas you will support yourself and what by your partners' offerings, e.g. marketing, sales, order entry, delivery.

As a side effect, you get good indications, where you should focus your management attention to grow your business and you get an initial risk assessment of the areas to keep on your regular monitor. It also indicates the measurements you have to implement.

Recommendations:

- Define your vision by addressing what benefits the customers will gain by using your products and services.

- Be explicit about which aspects of the web technology will be useful for your customers and for you.

4.1.2   Your strengths and your offerings for the web

What are your core capabilities?

With your market targets in mind, check again honestly the strengths and weaknesses of your initiative. What are you good at? And who besides you believes, that you're good at it? Did you get rewarded by market recognition, e.g. do you have the first customers for your service idea? What makes you so strong in it? How can you organize the leverage of your know-how in a way, that you maintain an entry barrier against your competition?

A necessary core strength is understanding your customers – this aspect was covered in the last chapter – and being experienced in an area your customer seeks support. In the web age, this experience requires careful management. The consumers share their experience quickly via Internet chatrooms, focus group forums and information obtained by mailing lists. Your knowledge management has to be at least as good as the one of your customers. All your research staff has to share their insights via a documentation of their findings accessible by all of them, e.g. in an Intranet. They need to meet regularly as special expert groups, e.g. in video conferences run via simple web cameras, and they need to allow their marketing and sales colleagues to early massage their findings into product offerings. With such an approach of knowledge sharing, Eli Lilly, the large developer of pharmaceuticals, was able to cut back the creation of new drugs from five to ten years to three to nine months!

For the areas you are good at, you must make sure to use them in your marketing messages and campaigns. It will make a big impact, if you can use references that convince your prospects. For a book buyer, the best is to see how other readers liked the book. A prospective software buyer will decide more easily when he hears enthusiastic recommendations of other users who have gained lots of profitability with that software.

You permanently should strive for excellence in your field in order to leave your competitors behind. But, how can you become better? Will you have the time to improve your offering once your business is in full swing? How can you manage the know-how, in particular the product and service components, the "doing" experience, the understanding of the market dynamics, the view of the competition's moves?

On the opposite end, where are your weaknesses? In my experience, it's much less effective to try improve yourself in the areas of weakness, than to build upon your areas of excellence. I've assessed many business scenarios as a consultant for large and medium enterprises and I have matching private experience. One Euro spent on fighting your weaknesses just contributes to catching up with your competitors, but one Euro spent on further improving your core competencies makes the distance between you and your competitor even larger. Therefore, rather than to fight your weaknesses, look for partners that can compensate those weaknesses. Answers for this compensation can include to outsource this area – the entrepreneurs often don't have the patience for doing the book-keeping, so give it to an accountant BUT monitor the progress against plan yourself. Another answer for an area of weakness may be to hire a person with the strengths you are missing – entrepreneurs are often focused on the technical solution, but they lack the marketing and sales skills, so hire a sales person BUT get in touch with your customers yourself to keep your ear at the market.

Recommendation:

- Build knowledge centres to expand your core competencies. There, your staff has to share insights and success stories and work jointly on the next opportunities and challenges.

Let's look at one of the famous examples of eBusiness: Cisco. They went through a similar analysis like we are discussing here and found out, that they have more experience than just building hardware. So, they re-configured their value chain and now offer integrated services that can be depicted in a chart like the following:

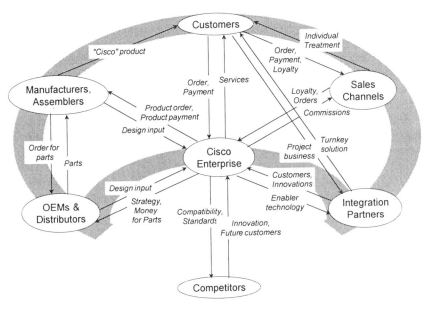

Figure 4-11: Partnership network of Cisco

Their web presentation underlines the integration of the offerings of all partners:

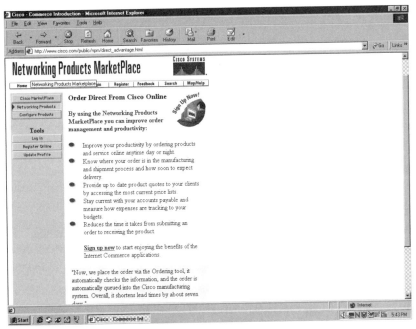

Figure 4-12: Usage of partner network – www.cisco.com

These figures show that Cisco is no longer a company mounting computer boxes. Instead, they have created a network of partners where each partner concentrates on his core competencies and shares the strategic knowledge with each other. Together, they deliver as one brand the best value for their customers and they are handling the competitive know-how of the Internet communication business.

With their self service approach, Cisco has reduced the error rates from Order Entry to delivery from 25 per cent to almost zero! They have accelerated the speed of delivery, cut back inventories, increased customer satisfaction, estimate to make 6 million US $ revenues in 1999 with 80 per cent of the customer care web based – and they have a well performing stock. Bundling the specific strengths of each of their partners, they now perfectly leverage the possibilities of the web and they have created a unique set of cooperation that will be hard to copy.

Recommendation:

- Define your offering in cooperation with a group of partners leveraging the core competency of each partner in order to come up with a "best of breed" proposition.

4.1.3   The changing role of intermediaries

The term intermediary is used for companies in between the original producer of a product or a service on one hand and the end customer, i.e. consumer, on the other hand. Traditional intermediaries are wholesalers and retailers, because they are in the middle between the manufacturer and the consumer, as well as travel agencies or consultancy companies. Direct sales have been possible in the pre-Internet era only if the manufacturer provided a factory outlet store or other direct sales activities limited in number and reach. Now, those direct sales possibilities are at any place where an Internet access exists, i.e. in the homes of the customers! Thus, the Internet is the enabler for the new types of intermediation while the old intermediaries are challenged in their business propositions. Please see Table 4-7 below for some examples of new intermediaries supported by eBusiness and the old ones challenged by it:

The traditional intermediaries need to define new ways of adding value, otherwise they'll disappear once larger and larger numbers of customers prefer to do online shopping; in particular once more and more "free" offerings pop up on the web.

There's a conservative tactic for the traditional intermediaries to slow down the impact of changes: they can frequently adjust the packaging of the products and services. They can offer pure commodity products (e.g. a flight from London to New York, but on a small seat, no food, minimal service, stops in one or two places) or a luxury package including pick-up service, a sleeper seat, shower upon arrival and five-course dining. Plus everything between those extremes, so the consumer will be forced to be either more educated and explicit regarding his needs – or, he can just fall back to the company he has the biggest confidence in. If the service provider manages to balance his offering with the needs of each customer segment, both sides win: the customer gets exactly the product and service he wants and the provider has generated revenues from a happy customer.

Table 4-7: Former versus emerging intermediaries

Former customer demand	Former intermediaries	New customer demand generated	Emerging intermediaries
Airline transportation	Travel agencies	Cheapest airline transportation	Online auction, e.g. www.tiss.com
Classified advertisements	Newspapers	Automatic support for finding offerings	Search engine providers, e.g. www.yahoo.com
Browsing for leisure articles (e.g. books, music, games, wellness)	Retail stores	Virtual browsing and convenient mail-order for leisure articles	Online "mail-order", e.g. www.amazon.com, www.mcgrawhill.uk, www.tvshop.se
Financial services	Large banking and insurance institutions	24-hour banking and insurance service from home	Flexible online providers, e.g. www.bmo.com, www.bank24.de

If the traditional intermediaries allow for such frequent repackaging, they can also go to the next step and redefine their value proposition, by looking for examples how new intermediaries do generate such added values. Let's again look at examples for the enrichment of offerings.

Broadening the product base: In a traditional retail store, limited space is available to display the goods – and even if you have a high diversity of items, you need to guide the consumer physically around in order to give him an impression of the choice. On the web, you should have a completeness of offerings at least as large as your competitors and you should store them in a database with the product descriptions, images or videos of their application as well as the experience from other customers about the use of the items. The database has to allow an easy access for different types of customer demands. This can be handled by well organized online catalogues (see Part III of this book regarding providers of catalogues). This means also, that you need to extend the number of partners, e.g. suppliers, you are dealing with in order to make a complete offering to your customers. This "completing" of the offerings is the value generation process I'm referring to. Look at amazon.com: they have more books in their offering than any traditional retailer – and even more than many wholesalers.

Convergence of "product" and "services": In a traditional setting, the focus is narrow. Either one is in the "product" business or in the "service" business, e.g. he is either a retailer or he's doing repairs. On the web such activities converge. The providers of the basic service also offer hotline service (more often than not around the clock, throughout the year) and can send a field service person to fix a problem with the product. Some examples:

The traditional TV and radio retailer should partner with call centre provider and field service providers. In this bundle of services the customers might get help to configure the loudspeakers according to their living room acoustics or they could get a backup TV set in case they need repair for their normal one.

A real life example from the web is a car rental agency, that now also offers fleet management for corporations (including purchasing the cars, insuring them, and re-selling them when the demand changes or the car is used up): Sixt (www.sixt.com). For the professionals in particular frequent flyers, they offer a neat mobility service. This includes the possibility to reserve a car by a few clicks on a mobile handset (that uses customer preferences entered once at the beginning of the relationship via the Internet). Then Sixt gets everything organized while the customer is on the plane to his destination. When landed the customer receives a brief message on his mobile handset indicating a post box (together with a PIN code) where he can pick up the key. No more hassle with waiting queues or forms, just fly and drive! And of course, also professionals and consumers can now buy cars with their rental agency via an auction, because this works so nicely on the web – every Tuesday at 7 pm:

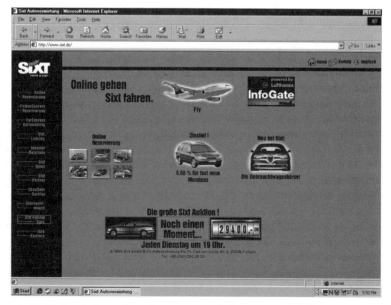

Figure 4-13: Extended services from car rentals – www.sixt.de

Customer configured offering: With the realtime communication features, you can achieve the "buy-in" from your customers by making them configure their product of desire. Examples are manifold and have been mentioned in this book. With Dell (www.dell.com), the consumer can configure his computer in more than 10,000 possible ways:

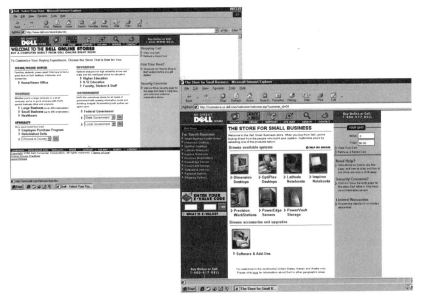

Figure 4-14: Product configuration in self service - www.dell.com

At Books-on-Demand (www.bod.com), the consumer can compile his private book, include a special dedication to a friend and get it printed individually for himself. At Cabana (www.cabana.com), the consumer can configure his individual travel and at Bank of Montreal (www.bmo.com), the consumer can configure his individual mortgage loan. With such a personalized sales preparation, it should be relatively easy to convince the customer to finally buy – actually, he probably won't go through the effort to do such a configuration with a lot of suppliers. If he still wants to, you can keep his configuration on store, so he can check back a few days later and can order it.

That looks great at the surface – it does require a whole lot of integration with other companies. Such integration means political agreements who owns which part of the customer relationship (i.e. where to co-operate and where to compete), it means a business integration (i.e. how to share the revenues), and it means process and IT integration. Please revisit the example of Cisco discussed above to see once more what intensive work is necessary to redefine the value proposition.

So the consumers and professional customers can use the services of new (and improved traditional) intermediaries to get the recommendation of what and where to buy. This is an ideal market for start-up companies: take the example of www.tiss.com, where 40 million discount airfares are listed and can be booked online – just from a little office with less than ten employees.

Recommendations:

- Clearly identify where you add value for your customers in the orchestra of your partners.

- Clearly identify your pillars of revenues versus the areas you can make "free" offerings.

- Achieve your customers' buy-in to your offerings by allowing them to help themselves via self service and customized configurations.

4.1.4   Your suppliers and your interaction with them: SCM

Interact electronically with your suppliers

Companies that often need to re-order specific items, can streamline their operations by agreeing on general frameworks with their suppliers. If you handle those frameworks and interactions with electronic data exchange, we call it Supply Chain Management (SCM). Within these frameworks, specific employees or IT systems can be entitled to order supplies on behalf of the company. Thus, the overhead of contracting can be eliminated from the day-to-day operations: the frameworks are agreed once and the ordering within this framework can be handled directly by the staff and/or systems in charge of keeping the inventories at certain levels. There's a whole chain of supplies that needs to be re-integrated.

Let's quickly discuss Figure 4-15 from the right to the left. The customers discuss their needs in their communities; emerging needs can be monitored there by the facilitators of the community. Then, they order their goods with the retailer. With the discussed data mining activities, the retailer has a good picture on the most demanded goods. He in turn should share this information with his partners participating in his marketing cooperation, in particular the manufacturers of the goods. With the early information regarding the customer demand, the manufacturers can increase their production in time in order to have quick deliveries of their products. They need the necessary components to fabricate the goods and thus need to share the early order information with their partners in the production cooperation, in particular the component providers. They in turn give early notices to their respective suppliers. For all the interfaces, the sales representatives of the vendors and the procurement group of the buyers should agree on standard terms and conditions, the agreed items can be put on an electronic catalogue, and processes and systems are to be put in place to quickly order the items by the exchange of electronic messages.

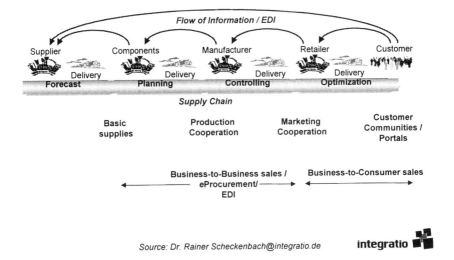

Figure 4-15: Streamlining procurement electronically

These processes can be automated, e.g. ERP systems triggering an order when certain thresholds are passed, or they can be handled manually by the business people of the recipient just ordering the needed quantities without going through new procurement processes again and again. Even better is an approach, that a customer order triggers immediately all activities back at the last supplier. This is the most speedy process to build according to the customer's order – and it saves all inventories and redundancies. Key asset of such an organization are the IT systems allowing such an end-to-end access plus the delivery logistics to pick the goods up exactly when they are ready and transport them to the next company.

Recommendation:

- Engage in flexible agreements with your suppliers that allow to easily scale up (or down) the volume of goods you receive from them and organize all the procurement electronically.

4.2   SYNTHESIS: LIVE YOUR DREAM

Live your dream by enriching basic products with web enabled additions

After those considerations, you can package your offering. Find the match of your customers' needs and your areas of excellence and expand that match.

Define your presence in the market; start in a region and then grow. Define your products and services with the appropriate marketing and sales support, and the production based on the necessary supplies. Will the Internet be your only sales channel or do you envisage other sales channels as well? Can you use the Internet as well for delivery or do you need to build up or hook into a delivery and logistics organization?

Finally, package your offering in a way to avoid commoditization. This means, you should enrich a basic product by features only you or you in conjunction with your partners can provide. The purpose of this bundling is to prevent a competitor from just copying your idea and then starting a price fight.

Table 4-8: Examples for service and product enrichments

Basic idea	Possible enrichments
Mail-order support	Include items that are not covered by traditional mail-order, e.g. grocery
	Add pick up and delivery services, e.g. to take care of your customer's laundry cleaning after picking the items up at the time the customer asked on the web
	Support the selection process by providing samples of the items you are selling, e.g. photographs of wallpaper together with completely decorated rooms, three-dimensional presentation of furniture, video tour through real estate
Electronic delivery of services/ ASP	Provide online access to specific software, e.g. games, text processing, ERP
	Provide news tickers (e.g. stock price quotes) via the web or mobile phones (SMS) triggering buy or sell transactions
Supply chain support	Integrate yourself electronically into a variety of supplier networks
	Partner with companies to jointly present a full service offering

These are highly strategic considerations. You need someone to discuss the ideas and to challenge your thoughts. I recommend to look for someone as your sparring partner and coach. This person should have experience in that area of offering you intend to launch such as a Business Angel or a counsellor for foundations. You have to have confidence in that he won't abuse your ideas to compete against you. And he should possibly stay in touch with your initiative to give you some guidance throughout the first critical years of your activities.

4.3   TOOLS

Use best practice business approaches

The best "tool" to compile the information necessary for your decisions are informal discussions and formal interviews: ask your customers, ask your staff, ask your competitor. The entrepreneur should personally cover a good part of those discussions, but if your markets are getting larger, you may involve some of your key staff (in particular sales people) or you can use a research agency to support such interviews.

You also should take the time to think. Reserve a few minutes every day or a few hours every week without disruptions to reflect about the past events and to prepare your next moves. Consider your principles: what is it you always want to portray to your customers, to your staff and to the competitors? What will you never tolerate from your customers, from your staff and from the competitors?

The next best tool once you've grown a bit is data mining. You may be surprised, how little data (e.g. a few thousand transactions) are sufficient to draw valuable conclusions from your customers' buying behaviour.

After that observation and analysis, compare the recent evolution with your earlier findings and assumptions and prepare your conclusions considering the impact on the market, on your staff, on your financials. Before you take big steps on those conclusions check with a sparring partner or coach.

4.4 CHECKLIST

Again, I want to emphasize the importance of documenting your ideas and plans and measuring the actual progress against it; here in the context of process performance.

Table 4-9: Checklist for developing the strengths of your organization

Item	To check	Recommendation	Self-assessment
Beliefs and Values	What are you proud of? What's your vision? What's your mission? What are your principles?	Compile some "War Stories" Express Vision and Mission on one to two pages What will you never tolerate?	
Strengths and Offerings	What are the core products? How are they embedded in servicing?	Identify the first offering package and a possible second offering (or fallback offering) Create a unique brand reflecting your strengths	
Partnerships	Who do you cooperate with?	Prepare a unique blend reflecting the strength of your network Integrate closely (i.e. via an Intra- or Extranet) with your partners	
Diversi-Fication	Are you dependent on a cash cow? Do you have so many product lines, that you loose the overview?	Balance the per centages per product line of revenues and contribution Keep focus, i.e. not more than three product lines for launch	
Staff	How can you provide focus for the staff and how can you leverage the combined experience?	Identify and nurture stars/ champions in your organization Engage in scientific alliances Identify key knowledge areas and implement centres of excellence	

For a softcopy of this checklist refer to my website.

Those companies who have become excellent have started to measure the aspects of process quality they are really after. Examples include:

- Software vendors warrant for a development quality producing software with a defect rate of less than one per thousand lines of code.
- Many mail-order and *e*Business resellers have a delivery commitment, e.g. 95 per cent of the orders are to be delivered on the next business day.
- When a big US telephone carrier re-focused on the customer needs, they established call centres and committed to answering >99 per cent of the calls within 20 seconds and to resolve the customers requests within 24 hours.
- GE is currently rolling out a "Six Sigma" initiative in order to push quality from 99.999 per cent to 99.9999 per cent.
- Communication providers commit to 24-hour availability throughout the year = 100 per cent quality.

The plan and the measurements have to support all key aspects of your strategy. The outline I give in Table 4-9, follows the Balanced Scorecard approach, which we'll discuss later in this book in more detail.

Table 4-10: Areas for strategic planning and monitoring

Item	To check	Recommendation	Self-assessment
Customer interactions	Implement Measurements per customer segments	Measurements: • How many hits on home page? • How many calls in your Call Centre (and with which response rate)? • How many new customers per month? • How many orders and fulfilments? • How many complaints (and resolutions)?	
Development of assets (products and services, skill profiles)	How can you leverage the initial success – Define targets and implement Measurements	Measurements: • How many products on the market? • What pipeline of products? • How many patents and trademarks? • What centres of know-how and excellence?	
Readiness for Change & Speed of Innovation	Don't allow to stand still – Define targets and implement Measurements	Measurements: • Average age of products • Per centage of products younger than twelve months • Age of Cash Cow	

Table 4-10 (continued)

Item	To check	Recommendation	Self-assessment
Financials	Don't disregard them, but spend equally much attention on the three areas above.	Measurements: Revenues and contribution per • Product segments • Customer segments Dependencies (Cash Cow, customer clusters)	

4.5   DISCUSSION POINTS

Your strengths and core capabilities together with the targets of the key stakeholders of your *e*Venture will drive your interests and offerings. So you need to match the market needs with the areas you enjoy. Let's revisit the key questions discussed in this chapter. Some answers and additional help from your fellow *e*-entrepreneurs can be found on my website www.success-at-e-business.com.

- What are your core ompetencies and your main interests? See Section 5.1.1 addressing the vision.
- Who can you partner with to come up with best of breed offerings? Describe your partnering need on my website and invite potential partners to get in touch with you.

Recommendations:

- Provide a unique offering based on your core competencies and bundle it with complementary enrichment of a variety of partners.

- Strive for high quality in your offerings – and measure the quality in order to make everybody proud of it.

5
Know your competitor

Watch the web to identify your competitors early and to monitor their action:

- *find the entries in the search engines using the index words you plan*
- *check their marketing updates and pricing frequently*
- *try their electronic interactions and performance by test orders*
- *to come up with and maintain a good positioning against them.*

In order to design the appropriate offering, it's essential to be aware of which competitors exist and what their key sales arguments are. Such considerations are very similar to those in traditional environments; given the speed of changes in the web age and the ubiquity of competitors, though, even more emphasis has to be put on a proper analysis and competitive positioning. On the web, a mistake will make the risks materialize quicker than in traditional business. On the other hand, this quicker feedback on the Internet allows you to experiment with specific strategies in very controllable market segments – you only need to design those experiments with a clear target in mind and carefully monitor the results. Let's discuss the analysis necessary to set up such strategy experiments.

As in the last chapters, there are a few questions that you must analyse until you know the answers by heart:

- Who are your competitors?
- What's their value proposition?
- How fierce is their competition?

Additionally, there are web specific questions with a big strategic impact. What regions are covered by your competitor? Which languages do they support in their online offering? What multimedia presentations do they provide? Who do they partner with, e.g. what links do they have on their website? Which customer interaction and self service is possible? What cost structures do they carry with their ISP and call centre? In brief, how can you stand out against their offering?

In order to understand each of your competitors, you need to go through a similar analysis to the one you went through for yourself. Who are the customers of your competitors, i.e. in which segments is he marketing? How large is his market share? How large are his departments for R&D, marketing and sales and his budgets? What next offerings does he have in his pipeline? Why are the customers buying from him? Where are his strengths and weaknesses? How does his proposition differ from yours?

Are you planning to copy a competitor's approach as a "Me Too" provider or will you challenge his approach with an improved value proposition? Examples of either approach in the Internet "classic" of book business are www.buch.de as a me too provider who uses a similar sales concept like amazon.com – only adapted to the local market versus www.bol.com in conjunction with RocketeBook with the vision that the consumers can download whole books to their computer thus experimenting with a new business model.

Examples for different strategies are given below to help you come up with a concise answer to these positioning considerations.

5.1   OBSERVATION AND ANALYSIS

Use the possibilities of the web – and defend against the challenges of it

For our analysis, we have to look at the various dimensions of competition – and how the Internet puts a specific twist on them.

Speed of communication: At all times, sales have only been possible after a variety of communication (in a broad sense) has taken place. The consumer considering to buy something was talking first to some friends for advice, was then looking around for the various options on the market, tried some of the options and finally decided after more or less profound price comparisons. He did some negotiations and bought the item. This could take him a few days or weeks, and the information obtained wasn't complete, because it was a huge effort to compile it from the various sources. In the web age, this all happens within minutes with a higher quality and a much bigger transparency. The advice from friends is extended by reviews from user groups. The physical window shopping is replaced by a quick surf on the web covering potentially all providers of the respective offerings. The price comparison is done by some automatic agents ("bots"). The offering can be configured real time. Closure and even sometimes delivery, e.g. for music, software code, or software services, is handled immediately as well. *If any of your competitors is faster, more convenient or more complete in* *any of the mentioned dimensions of speed, you are in danger of losing customers to him!*

Cost pressures: Cost reductions have been a favourite for consumers and business people all the time, but usually the targets were ongoing marginal improvements. The web age forces us to think in radical changes, though. Whole groups of activities disappear and new groups of activities are created based on the above mentioned new quality of communication. We'll discuss the changing roles of intermediaries in a minute. An example at this stage: the traditional book retailers and travel agencies see a heavy competition by direct sales via Internet with a terrifying trend of the most profitable market segments already handled online. Streamlining of processes will be a major success factor. So you should check how your competitors approach key cost areas, e.g. supply chain management or delivery logistics. *If any of your competitors has a fundamentally leaner cost structure due to re-architected processes you should copy his approach or even improve it to make the same efficiency gains.*

"Free" mania: On the web, you can get almost everything seemingly for free. And people pore in when they can get something for free. A recently started free ISP provider in Europe gained more than half a million subscribers within only one month by offering free services – and by promising stock options in case the ISP should have an IPO (Initial Public Offering) at the stock exchange. Before you offer anything for free, there should be a good idea of how to generate revenues behind a free offering, though. The "free" Internet services make money by the telephone charges plus banner advertising, the "free" service offerings (e.g. a software trial for a limited period or a trial access to the database of an information provider) are meant to be appetizers to prepare the customers to eventually buy or subscribe to the real service. The challenge is now not to offer something that can already be obtained elsewhere for free. Would you pay for your *e*Mail account, if you can get if for free with almost all ISPs? You need to provide added values that cost you little effort, but increase the benefits for your customers tremendously – you may well consider to pay for an *e*Mail service that allows you to efficiently share the insights of stock analysts and thus to increase your wealth. *If anyone offers products like yours for free, you have to quickly expand your value proposition.*

The changing role of industry boundaries: With the change of the activities of intermediaries and the intensifying partnerships between companies of all kinds, the industry boundaries change as well. We already talked about the convergence of product and service business. Also the labels from the traditional supply and delivery chain don't work any more: there's neither wholesale nor retail any longer – it's just online sales, no matter if you are selling books, music, travel arrangements, banking services, PC software or hardware or "anything" like eBay or Yahoo. I personally have a hypothesis, though, regarding the future industry clusters and boundaries. In my view this will be linked to the customers you are interacting with and to their life stage needs. So there will be clusters of providers around special events like marriage, birth of a child or moving – and possibly even different clusters for different customer segments. And there will be clusters of providers for special life phases like entertaining and educating the pupils while they are growing up, or supporting the family life in all aspects, or taking care of elder citizens.

Following that new definition, you should check who your are competing with. Let's revisit one of our examples: TISS. In a way they compete with the airlines themselves, with travel agencies, with airline reservation systems. On the other hand, they cooperate with each of those "competitors". So the mental concept of competition is to be replaced by one of networks that either contribute to your propositions versus networks that are adversary for your success.

The quality of your answer to this positioning question will be a key for your success. And the answer won't be static – in one constellation you will share your forces with a company and be their ally while in other constellations you will have a joint proposition with other allies and compete against a proposition where your earlier partner is participating.

It won't be enough to revisit your partnerships and plans every other year or every year, as we have been used to until very recently (at least even in important economy regions in Europe). Instead, you need to establish a competition watch that's capably of raising the alarms almost real time. In particular, they should watch out for non-traditional competitors and screen, how dangerous they can become for your business success. In particular the small and unknown companies have an advantage in picking the cherries from the monolithic offerings of the large established enterprises.

To perform an assessment of your position vs. your competitors, you have to go through a thorough process covering the marketing, sales and controlling perspectives. Let us refer to the plans and targets we have defined so far and let's make a step-by-step reality check driven from the competitions' momentum.

As the entry barriers are getting lower and lower – the only device a virtual company needs is an Internet connection – the immaterial factors such as relationships with customers and suppliers and knowledge are getting more and more important. To distinguish yourself from the competitor, you have to be ahead of them – at least a little bit. Being ahead of them might also mean, that you are second with an invention, but you are better in the overall bundle of your offering, e.g. by service, price or quality.

With electronic business, also a very high market transparency does exist. Price finders support the consumers – but they can also support you in defining the appropriate packaging and pricing for your offerings. I'm sure, that specific agents for your industry exist somewhere on the web, just check them out! The most aggressive example is PriceLine, where the consumer now can even "negotiate" the price for his groceries at the local supermarket:

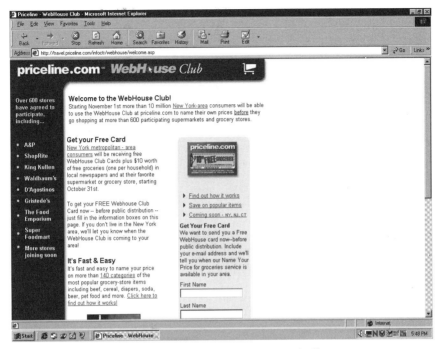

Figure 5-16: Price negotiations on the web – www.priceline.com

The list in Table 5-11 is to give you some impressions across the industries.

Table 5-11: Agents finding best offering on the web

Company	Website	Coverage
Ariba	www.ariba.com	Enables catalogues for electronic procurement and supply chain management
Best Rate	www.bestrate.com	Comparison of mortgage interest rates
BotSpot	www.botspot.com	Provide a magnitude of price agents for various industries and demand profiles
Cendant	www.netmarket.com	"Best buy" reference to eight superstores and direct sales; broad coverage of consumer items
ComputerESP	Shopper.cnet.com	Have more than 100,000 PC hardware and software items listed with > 500,000 price quotes plus links to retailers
Ebay	www.ebay.com	Auction: Buy anything, sell anything for a freely negotiated price
Hotbot	www.hotbot.com	Combination of Search Engine and price survey
Preview Travel/ Farefinder	www.previewtravel.com	US domestic flight tickets; price comparisons; hotel reviews
Priceline	www.priceline.com	Offering made by consumer; then priceline looks up merchants and checks if they want to make a proposal
TISS	www.tiss.com	International flight tickets; in particular. Last minute offerings and discounts

If you want to find the "bot", i.e. the agent relevant for you industry, you may check with some generic providers such as botspot.com:

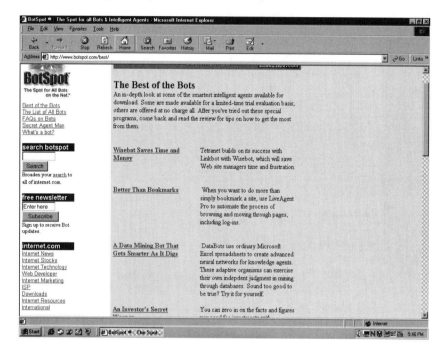

Figure 5-17: Agents to find the best offerings for your industry

---

Recommendations:

- Check the web for the experience of all industries related to your offering and leverage their examples.

- Test their services and offer something better!

5.2   POSITIONING

5.2.1   Your unique selling points

Why should customers buy from you?

Identify the aspects that differentiate you from your competitors. These may be:

- The electronic presentation of the offering (like for all *e*Ventures) – so be more specific, e.g. what in particular you offer for your communities. Like the travel information we were talking about in the case of Cabana or the football information in the case of the fan club handled by the credit card company.

- The immediate confirmation of availability and delivery time – again, the best practice eBusinesses provide that as a normal feature – so clarify how you integrate with your customers' needs such as production cycles for business customers or the birthday gift to be handed over nicely wrapped the next day[10] for consumers. You may need to go a step further: inform your customer about upcoming events like birthday of spouse, child, colleague or client, make suggestions for a gift according to a customer defined profile.
- Quality of the offering only you can provide, e.g. pro-activeness of your call centre, flexibility for add-on features like a greetings card on top of the nicely wrapped birthday gift.
- Specific added values and services for your particular communities.
- Targeted loyalty programmes, e.g. similar to the airline frequent flyer programmes.
- And of course speed, convenience and price.

For your presentation in the market, you should also be aware of the possible prejudices your customers may have. For example, a US based company will be viewed as modern and progressive in Europe (even if it's public knowledge in the US, that the company is not dynamic and has dinosaur attitudes). A German company will be viewed as solid in the US (despite the fact, that some German car manufacturers have started to challenge the prejudice by delivering cars after only sloppy quality controls). Therefore, the decision for a brand that's aligned with your strengths and targets is also important. For the eBusiness initiatives of large enterprises, the connotations of the large enterprise brand should be checked: will it be positive or negative for the customer's perception to stick to the traditional brand? For the small start-ups the opposite consideration applies: is it good to show, that you're an aggressive (but unexperienced) young and dynamic group of people or do you want to create the perception of a more solid enterprise? Your answers to those questions must again be reflected in your marketing statements and marketing campaigns.

Recommendation:

- Provide specific values for each of your customer communities.

---

[10] Actually, I'm surprised that the electronic booksellers have only started gift wrapping in the Christmas season of 1999. www.bol.de and amazon.com were the first to offer this service which is a standard feature in most of the department stores. The results were still mixed, because the service was well accepted by the market, so bottlenecks in the wrapping lead sometimes to delays of the delivery. Also some of the logistics providers start testing the market receptiveness. I guess, that we can see this as a standard for most of the online shops soon.

5.2.2   Gaining market share

Prepare for growth

The concept of market share is trivial, namely what piece of the business is yours compared to all your competitors. But the tricks are in the details: How do you define the overall market, e.g. do you look at the overall mail-order market, do you focus on electronically supported order entry or are you in the call centre business rather than in mail-order?

These are nice academic considerations – but success in real life knows only one answer to it: GET BIG FAST! Due to the discussed pressures to streamline your costs on one hand and due to the global reach of your offering on the other hand, you can be very successful, if you use the economies of scale of a large enterprise. If you miss to grow, though, soon there will be a competitor who actually will challenge you with his economies of scale.

Internet tools can win you customers

Let's now discuss how your prospects can find you. Most importantly, you need to raise the awareness regarding your offering.

Search engines and bots: On top of traditional marketing, e.g. newspaper ads or TV spots, you need to be present in many search engines and bots (i.e. the agents comparing prices) – and in each of them in a top position. It doesn't help much if your website shows up as number 9,510 of 11,000 entries on the findings. And even worse, still more than two thirds of all websites aren't listed in the search engines at all. You need to design the website accordingly, i.e. with the appropriate key words describing your offerings both in the text and in HTML meta tags, you need to register with the search engines, you need to engage with partners providing links to your website and you may need to pay some fees for advertising.

Mailing lists for *e*Mail and SMS/Special offers: Get your prospects and customers on mailing lists (*e*Mail for fix wire Internet or SMS for WAP Internet) and keep them posted about special offerings – like the dealer of historic cars is sending me regularly his offerings for historic Porsches. They are still too expensive for me, but eventually I may fall over the affordable car of my dreams. The great advantage of the *e*Mails is that they cost you virtually nothing (very different from paper mail), you can include a direct feedback, and you can monitor the effectiveness in order to strike people from the mailing list that never buy with you, anyway. With SMS, you can also address specific customer groups directly and still at lesser cost than with paper mail. In both cases, i.e. for *e*Mail and SMS you should include a reply function by which the customer can immediately order the special offer.

Free offerings: Check if you can reasonably offer something for free – you'll be listed in the top section of the bots (price comparison agents) and you can attract the customers most easily.

Infotainment/Games: Check how you can bundle your services with some games. Invite the consumers via traditional media to play a game with you, provide some prizes, collect their preferences while playing the game by answering some questions, and guide them through your website in order to educate them about your offering.

Compiling competitive data

You have to find approximate answers in order to do your planning: you can approach the question top down or bottom up. For the top down approach, you can refer to publicly available information and pragmatically pick the available data that come closest to your information need. For the bottom up approach, you should focus on a small number of direct competitors and estimate their market share. Probably you get some indication of their revenues, e.g. from staff you hired out of them, from annual reports if they are listed at a stock exchange, from market observers. Thirdly, you can use extrapolations for the financials, e.g. based on their staff size or based on hits of their home pages.

Those derived figures frame the overall market size. With the bottom up approach, you have also identified the key players and you have an idea of their coverage of the market. With the plan you have prepared so far (see Section 3.3) you can identify your relative market coverage.

Then, the starting position is to be extrapolated to the future. Initially, a one- or two-year planning should be sufficient – the actual development will be different, anyway! You should cross-check now, if the revenues you've assumed can be supported by the staff you are anticipating and if you believe, that you can hire enough staff you need. Also, don't forget the supply needs and dependencies (see Chapter 12 for an example of a business plan).

To prepare for your competitor watch, let's check the current trends. Areas with growing market share, i.e. your primary competitors, will be convenience stores (e.g. gasoline stations, train stations, airport malls), specialised dealers and megastores. Areas where you can gain market share from declining business include fan-shops, small retailers, small warehouses.

> **Recommendations:**
> - Start with a controlled subset of offerings for a clear target market.
> - Use the low cost Internet tools to interact with your customers, in particular *e*Mail for marketing.
> - Quickly expand to gain a large market share – "Get big fast".

5.2.3   Market position

Become the best in something

Successful electronic business activities have a unique combination of services and support specifically defined segments of the market. This unique combination can either be based on very efficient processes leading to low prices or on very innovative ideas more appealing than the older propositions. So it boils down to a leader or pioneer position in the market versus a follower position. Well you won't find these clear extremes very often in the market, but it's a good mental model to think your activities through.

Imagine what it means for your customers, your staff and your processes, if either of the extremes materializes: If you would be the

Market leader: The upside is that you can define the contents of your offering according to your strengths and that you can set the market rules – the downside is that sooner or later a competitor will copy your idea and will challenge your prices, your service bundles, and your customer loyalty. For your positioning, you should anticipate how much time it takes a competitor to build up a similar organization. From that point on, you either have to have the next improvement to your own offering ready or your margins will be under pressure. In other words if you decide to be the leader you need to organize to stay the leader.

Second or third entrant to the market: the first player has developed the market, sometimes with missionary approaches. Now the customers have become more demanding, but with the start-up infrastructure, the initial player can't support the new customer needs any more. The new competitors can select some of the new key needs of the customers, can build on the experience of the first player (e.g. by hiring some of his key staff), avoid some of his mistakes, and achieve great business results. Often, it's easier to have the second position in the market, but the time of the easy money and high margins is over. In fact, you have the start-up investments while the pioneer is already making profits. You need to organize very efficiently your financial environment with a clear focus on expenditures, costs and streamlined back office processes. And you need to be ready for price fights.

An interesting example of a late entrant in the market who converted to a leader is Microsoft. Bill Gates and friends could build on user bases of text processors, spreadsheet calculation and GUIs. The initial leaders such as primarily WordPerfect (text processing), and also some other independent companies in the various countries of the world, Lotus 1-2-3 for spreadsheet calculation have vanished from the market or are close to vanishing. Other companies like Apple with their initially innovative Graphical User Interfaces had to create new value propositions before they almost disappeared. Common reason for those changes was, that the software providers were not smart enough or not large enough to support the growing user desires quickly enough. Today,

Microsoft has taken over the lead as the only global provider in the standard business (and household) applications as well as the provider of Windows, one of the most spread commercially used PC operating systems. We will see how this leadership role will evolve following the changes in Microsoft's management and the expected fragmentation of the enterprise.

In the following synopsis, I want to give an overview of the recommended focus areas for the initial player and for the followers.

Table 5-12: Market positioning considerations

Position of market entry	Upside	Downside	Recommended focus for management
First player/ Pioneer	Can define the offering	May get distracted by technological features and constraints Needs to protect his customers' and staff's loyalty Lack of best practices in the particular online business	Listen to your customers Drive innovations in order to have permanently new products on the market Grow quickly! *Has worked for amazon.com, eBay, Dell* *Can be tried in similar mass market areas, e.g. music, software, grocery*
Second and third player	Choice of the most interesting product niches and customer segments. Or: Possibility to bundle the basic offering with additional features.	Will be compared with the first player as long as no own reputation is built up Don't assume that the initial margins of the first player will be valid for the second and third player, too – the prices will get under pressure	Use such areas where the first player is not responsive to the markets to your advantage Clear differentiation from first player Have better ratio of quality/price than first player (either by quality improvement or by price reduction) *Has worked for TISS, Ricardo.de (auctions in Germany)* *To be observed for BOL (books on line)* *Can be tried by adapting and improving pioneers' offerings, in particular US examples, to Europe and Asia*
Followers	Clear picture of the market	Need to have a very distinctive offering	Exploit cost advantages and economies of scale Boutique offerings for specific market segments *Will be a challenge when many competitors exist, e.g. in the online care sale where many companies start simultaneously*

So far, the Internet experience shows, that a global positioning is possible, if you can quickly grab the majority of the market – either because you are alone in your market, or because you outperform the competitors. Therefore, an adaptation of US examples to local markets with the different languages, legal situations and payment habits, like in Europe or Asia, can be a good business idea allowing a good launch. If you intend to launch such a service, push to gain similar economies of scale like the US providers, i.e. target pan-European or pan-Asian customers. The business, though, should only be implemented country by country due to different cost implications and legal requirements. For example, delivery of physical goods is only interesting, if you find a logistics partner who supports you worldwide at a reasonable cost, or payment can only be implemented in accordance with foreign currency regulations.

Another valid approach are boutique offerings with very specific value propositions. In this case, your customer number will be much smaller. Therefore the implementation cost should be likewise less.

Recommendations:

- Identify what you can learn from the pioneers in your market – and how you can prevent followers to easily use your experience too easily.

- Cover your target market as completely as you can.

- Get big fast in order to leave the competitors behind.

5.2.4   How quickly can your competitors steal your customers?

Cover your flanks

Table 5-12 above already indicates the dangers for the long-term success of your initiative and outlines your mitigation strategies. In addition to those risks based on your relative position in the market, you will be confronted with challenges based on your start-up situation. In order to mitigate those risks, you should stay ahead of the evolution in your industry and in the markets:

- Check the offerings of your competitors frequently.
- Go to the web and use the services of your competitors and check the responses of their customers.
- Create a culture in your company where permanent risk assessment is preferred over an attitude to only discuss good news – of course you should appreciate good news and support the fun-at-work aspect with a party from time to time to celebrate particular success stories. But the biggest danger would be to put the head in the sands in the face of any risks. So reward your staff and customers also for identifying and mitigating risks.

Consider the examples we used in the Customer section: the car fan could purchase his spare parts elsewhere – maybe even cheaper, but he wouldn't get the additional value of the confidence he has in the particular brand, the value-added information and the community services. The football fan could make his payments by whatever means, but by using his bank fan card, he's entitled to additional gimmicks from his fan club and he feels to be part of the group. And for the relocation service customers, the wellness and sanity of the family is a value much higher than some consulting fees to pay.

In each of the examples, the key risk is that either the competitor unbundles the services, e.g. he sells just the spare parts and convinces the customers that they can run their fan club alone and don't need to pay a car manufacturer any overhead, or he integrates the offerings further as we have discussed in the Microsoft example. The only successful strategy is to have very close relationships with and very good feedback from the customers. Suggestions from the customers should get quickly filtered by marketing, sales and product specialists to check the potential for an adjustment of your offering.

Sometimes patents are discussed as a protection against competitors. If you have a great product invention or health formula, you should indeed register a patent. Most of the other business ideas usually can get no patent, though. If you have the smartest spreadsheet program – improve it faster than any competitor in order to keep the distance. If you have the best call centre approach strive for even better performance to keep the distance from your competitors. Intellectual properties take so long to be properly defined in the legal terms, that the markets have run away until you are gone through the formal process. So the only way out is to organize those properties in a way that the knowledge of your corporation and the deployment of this knowledge by the business processes you are executing is difficult to copy. One aspect are knowledge centres, i.e. human networks between your staff that share the same considerations, concepts and visions. Another aspect is continuous business process re-design in your organization and also for the processes your customers are involved in to achieve a higher effectiveness and a better convenience.

Recommendations:

- Check the web for upcoming challenges frequently, e.g. once a month.
- Be pro-active and drive your innovations based on YOUR strengths!

5.2.5   What can hurt you?

Prepare your defence

You are aware now of your strengths and weaknesses. Let's now anticipate the game plan for mutual attacks:

Who will attack you? How can you defend yourself? Watch out for your weakest point and defend it by a smart compensation. We've already discussed deferred payment schemes for key staff to prevent them resigning. We addressed bonus schemes for key suppliers to keep them supporting you. And we discussed customer loyalty programmes and communities in order to keep your revenue situation stable. There's one thing, though, you won't be able to prevent – and that's a price erosion or a price fight. Therefore, you should regularly compare your cost of doing business with that of similar companies and benchmark your effort levels in order to streamline your operations. You don't need to share the benefits immediately with your customers and staff – but if you are proactive in making your sales and production more and more effective, you have reserves you can use once a competitor challenges you.

With regular benchmark activities in the various aspects of your business, you will get early warning signals from where an attack might start. Identify, who will be in a position to challenge your approach, focus on those challenges that are essential for your standing and profitability and try to outsmart your competition in those areas. But be aware of your strengths as well – it doesn't pay off to fight competition everywhere. Sometimes you may even find, that a cooperation with your competitor allows both of you an ongoing solid business provided that you can complement your activities and serve your customers better by a combined offering.

Don't block your activities by a mere focus on competitors, though. Usually, the market is big enough for many players – rather create some innovative products and better offerings. Or create propositions where you can engage in a partnership with an earlier competitor.

5.2.6   Marketing mix

Make it fit together

In your marketing mix, you have to find the appropriate balance of the product, your servicing concept, the sales story, the sales and distribution channels, the price, and the presentation. It needs to fit together to be in synch with your differentiation from the competitors.

Hand in hand with the question discussed in the last paragraph, you need to decide, if you intend to be a quality leader or a price leader (see Figure 5-18). With the ongoing productivity increases and organizational effectiveness gains, you can choose your position on the always expanding curve of productivity and share the benefit with your customers either by making better, i.e. cheaper prices, or you can offer them a higher quality for the same price. In order to maintain a clear image of the brand, you should not change your once selected position too much. Your customers will either perceive you as a quality provider or as a price fighter (or something in between), but you must not confuse them by changing your positioning frequently. If you want to maintain a choice of various positions, the Internet allows you easily to launch different brands – just use separate websites for your high quality offering and versus your low price offering. Many of the back office processes of course can use the same systems.

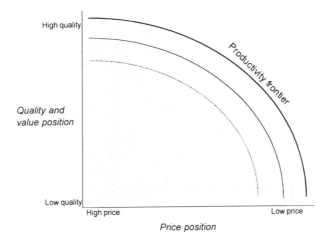

Based on Porter: On Competition

Figure 5-18: Productivity frontier

Depending on the size of your initiative, you may want to use one of the professional marketing companies for a professional presentation of the selected image – by the way, your head will be dizzy after seeing some of their pretty different presentations. Or you may use the help of a start-up counselling or Business Angel organization.

The additional pragmatic approach is to just test your story with some prospects, initially in the way of interviews. How do they like your proposition compared to those of your competitors, what do they recommend to improve in order to make you best in the market, when are they willing to pay a premium price, do they perceive a good cost–benefit ratio, what would they change in your offering package?

Wherever possible, pilot your offering in a small test market – you don't need to build up your complete infrastructure and staff. Just do it on a small prototype scale. You will learn much in that stage and can save much unnecessary investment by following the guidance of the market.

Marketing is a fuzzy area, so you will find many opinions about the best approach. My three recommendations are:

Recommendations:

- Trust your instincts – there are many good reasons not to do something, but the *e*Business is a representation of your own visions, so people should have extremely good reasons to talk you out of a good idea!

- Include fun in your offering – film sequences and stories supported with sound make a difference. Would you rather buy a travel ticket when you just recognize the price tag or when you first see the palm leaves waving and hear the sea rolling?
- And in case of doubt – ask your customers.

5.2.7   Watch out for changes

Maintain your awareness

As you have started with a creative new business idea, don't be surprised if others are creative in a similar way. Depending on your product focus and customer segments, you have to watch out for competition from traditional and non-traditional directions.

- Encourage risk identification: Maintain an open information policy – not only on successes and opportunities, but also on threads and risks to your company. If you encourage your staff and your customers to tell you what's going on in the market, you have a great network of allies to prevent attacks.
- Keep not only virtual malls and call centre services under observation, but also the physical point-of-sales. The big enterprises now launch their *e*Commerce and *e*Venture themselves – and they can work with better economies of scale. So the positioning in each market segments needs to be clearly distinct from the other players.
- Implement loyalty – for your suppliers, for staff and for your customers: A small start-up company should engage their customers in development cycles for permanent offering improvement and make them subscribe to the improvements, which is another way of cross-selling. By that, you can leverage the existing customer relationships saving a lot of money for the acquisition of new customers and you show more value to the customer by not being just a niche provider. A cost-effective way for such loyalty programmes is to allow only your good customers to access some specific added value information. This can be done via a website with a specific password, e.g. for "gold club members" only.

Recommendation:

- Perform a regular assessment of the competitors – just check their websites monthly.

5.3   CHECKLIST

To wrap up this section, let me highlight one key business process. A good indication for a company's ability to survive is the attitude towards customers' complaints. Some companies may consider such complaints as a disruption from the beautiful straightforward work. Or they may have them treated by a team experienced in downplaying problems. That would all be wrong! Each customer who takes the energy of informing you about a refinement of his needs is a valuable source of information that probably your competitor doesn't have. Thus you obtain bit by bit competitive advantages. Please don't understand me wrong: this doesn't mean that you have to always fix or extend whatever the customer desires. But be sure to establish a feedback to your product management and sales to check, if there's a market for such additional services.

Table 5-13: Checklist regarding

Item	To check	Recommendation	Self-assessment
Market	Your market share Possible growth of market share	Include optimistic and pessimistic assumptions and consider which is more probable	
Positioning	Pioneer versus Follower	Identify clearly your understanding Identify Unique Selling Points (USPs) and leverage them in your core products	
	Pricing	Check the current pricing of your competitors using bots	
How quickly can you be hurt?	Marketing and sales, e.g. Cherry picking/price fight, Bundling/ Unbundling Operations, e.g. Poaching staff, supply issues Financial or Legal issues	Check what would you dislike the most if your competitor would know?	
Closest competitor	Who do you attack? Who's attacking you? What are the challenges on your core competencies and core offerings?	Identify relative strengths and weaknesses What would you do, if you were your competitor's mgr.? Strengthen your strengths Mitigate risks	
Marketing	Is the product, servicing, sales story, price, presentation in synch and aligned with USPs? Include fun and positive experience in your offering!	Test your marketing mix with your prospects and customers Find a replacement for the point-of-sales experience by multi-media representations (audie and video)	
Pilot offering	What are the key improvement suggestions?	Just do it!	

For a softcopy of the checklist refer to my website.

5.4   DISCUSSION POINTS

Between all your competitors, there must stay enough room for you to prosper. In order to assess if this will be the case we addressed several key questions. For further information on those topics, please check my website www.success-at-e-business.com.

- How do you provide value differently from your competitors?
- How aggressive should you be?
- How can you avoid that your competitors steal your ideas?

Recommendations:

- Identify your regional strengths against the global competitors.
- Be clear who to cooperate with and who to fight against.

6

Innovate – smarter than your competitor

Stay on top of the evolution by:
- *extending and improving step by step your electronic interactions with your customers and partners*
- *making regularly new offerings available.*

Innovation – at least successful innovation – cannot be generated off-the-shelf. There are some principles, though, which are not always sufficient, but they are all necessary for success. These principles are discussed in this chapter. They will get very relevant once you are already some time in business when you strive for further growth, but you have to prepare their implementation early in order not to become outdated quickly.

I assume, that your initial business idea is something pretty new – in fact almost all electronic business offerings do still represent a very innovative approach towards the consumers. But it won't stay like that forever: the market will become more mature and the customers more demanding. Competitors will copy your business idea and maybe even add some better features, so some of your customers will be inclined to end their loyalty.

In order to maintain your leading edge, you are forced to continue with your innovations.

6.1   THE NATURE OF INNOVATIONS

6.1.1   Innovation cycles in traditional markets

The nature of innovations is that they come in cycles: Initially there's a new idea. This will be refined to a stage where you can "productize" it, i.e. to a stage you can set up an organization to produce it, to sell it and to deliver the service around it. The initial product will attract people or businesses who are very forward oriented, like to experiment with new things and have themselves some innovative ideas how to use them. Those "early adopters" don't mind paying pretty high prices and are willing to make compromises in the quality – their main objective is to be one of the first users. This is true for all types of products, no matter if you take as examples very complex products like the first cars or the first facsimile transmission devices or if you take less complex offerings like a travel "in 80 days around the world". Actually, as long as not all the components are perfectly understood, each of such offerings had a pretty high complexity to operate it or consume it. Over time, the customers will look for a higher convenience for using the product or service. During this period, the focus for the innovator is an incremental improvement of the processes to build the product, a better quality in its components, standardization and better cost / benefit ratios, adjustments in the sales approach, and establishing supporting services.

Going back to the example of the first cars: The car industry had to improve on aspects like building more robust engines and tyres, Taylorized production, reseller chains, or building up of gasoline station networks. Still, the product was oriented to a progressive clientele that could afford the unusual luxury of a product that still might be considered not essential for everyday needs. In the next step, the product was to change to a commodity, which had a very broad market because it's seen as a necessary support to fulfill your purposes in life. At this stage, the offering is basically the same from many vendors. Those companies who want to stay strong players need to define clear differentiators from their competitors, the need to add little features to maintain their market share. For the cars this means features like leather seats, or four-wheel drives for the quality leaders or very cheap retail prices for the price leaders.

At this stage, you are better off, if you can start the next cycle of innovation. Change the perspective and check what the customer's real need is. Does he want to gain reputation – then offer an expensive looking model. Does he need guaranteed performance – then embed your product in a logistics package (e.g. mobility guarantee provided by some car leasing companies). Is he looking for fun – then offer a Recreation Vehicle of a Beach Buggy. In market segments like that you can maintain a good margin, whereas you must be extremely cost sensitive in the other "bread and butter" market segments.

In the times of product maturity, the companies will disappear that aren't able to adjust to the more challenging markets and that cannot kick off the next innovation cycle.

6.1.2   Electronic business innovations

What does this mean for electronic business? At this time, we are still in the beginning. The whole market is in startup-mode. Your first customers will be the "early adopters". They have a good risk profile and are willing to experiment with your offerings. They may sometimes be ready for compromises if you don't fulfill your delivery promises. But soon this is about to change! So after you have done your homework to make your initial quantum leap innovation work – be ready to make your offering mature enough to defend it against the upcoming competition.

Let me highlight the key innovation considerations for the manager of an electronic business initiative in Figure 6-19:

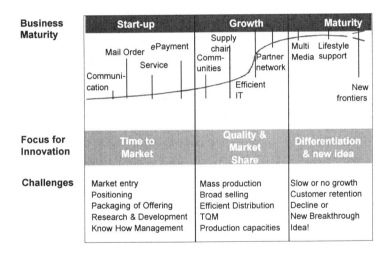

Figure 6-19: Innovation stages in *e*Business

Look for the next change to come in your concrete industry, in the specific channel you use or in the web technology, like now from PC based Internet to WAP and TV based Internet. In our days, the innovation cycles are getting faster and faster and the market penetration of a product idea is accelerating too! Today, the customers are primarily looking for:

Continued improvement in convenience: In the first wave of *e*Business as we have it now in Europe, it may be sufficient to offer 24-hour availability of your call centre at seven days a week and make only a few goods available online. In the next wave, which is starting now in the US, your customers will expect that you can deliver everything everywhere almost immediately.

Individually personalized presentation: The banner advertising will be considered more and more as bothering – but personalized information will become king. Customers will even expect, e.g. that their online bookseller offers them immediately, i.e. without complicated search activities, the types of books they're interested in.

Free offerings: So many things can be obtained for "free" or at least look like being free, that you need to come up with smart packages of free entry propositions combined with a business model of ongoing revenue generation.

And don't forget the speed of change – who acts first will be the winner!

At the different stages of your offering's maturity, you have to balance two main perspectives: lateral thinking on one hand and focus on the other hand, i.e. creativity and creation versus analysis and solidity. In the beginning and to prepare a later Breakthrough Innovation, you should have a preference on lateral thinking; once you reach a higher maturity when incremental improvements are necessary you should provide clear guidance and focus. For such a focused analysis, you have to decompose the issues into managable pieces, e.g. to improve the quality of your components, to improve the production processes, or to boost your sales activities. This decomposition has to go to a stage where you can decide that either the component is one of your core competencies or that it's an area you can outsource.

For your core competencies, you have to:

- Boost your knowledge permanently – pull the thought leaders together, watch the competitors' moves by checking their offerings regularly, talk to professionals working in your business area in other countries, and invite some consulting companies from time to time.
- Leverage those skills for your products and services in permanently new ways of interactions on the web, in particular now by defining dedicated presentations for PC, mobile phone (WAP) and TV based Internet.
- Organize the know-how exchange between your staff in a way further accelerating your corporate knowledge, e.g. by establishing an Intranet with a forum room for thinking about "crazy" ideas that may well become the next offering. Such ideas can be triggered by posting some customer complaints on an electronic billboard and analyse what made the customer complain and what can be done to avoid such complaints in the future.

Innovation also requires a close cooperation between marketing and the "back office". If, for example, your eSales figures aren't sufficient, then you need to break the problem down:

1. Do you have enough surfers on your Web-site, but they don't accept your offering? Then you need to solve it inhouse: repackage, reprice or change other quality aspects.

Or

2. Do people not visit your offering at all? Then you need to position better in the search engines, use additional marketing channels and possibly an external agency to improve your brand recognition in the market, to advertise more (also in traditional media), and you have to engage with more partners to maintain links from their pages and leverage your communities better.

For outsourcable items you may want to bring your purchasing behaviour to a stage where they are commodities and you can purchase them from the supplier with the best quality/cost ratio or the necessary services can be provided by a partner. Evidently, this target is opposite to the interests of the suppliers – they want to complement their offerings with the appropriate packaging in order to avoid that you shop somewhere else. The conclusion of those different interests depends on the type of relationship with your supplier. If you cooperate with them very well and there's no doubt in a long-term partnership, you should integrate your business processes very closely into a neat joint offering and agree only on a high level about the split of revenues. If, on the other hand, you have only an occasional cooperation or you expect that it may end with short notice, you should be ready to get the materials from other suppliers quickly – and you should base you payments on itemized and auditable bills.

6.2   CONTINUOUS IMPROVEMENTS

As the virtual market is much more fierce and changes happen quicker than in the traditional market, you need to consistently improve both the substance of your offerings and your electronic presence on the web in order to maintain and extend your position. Both aspects need to be approached systematically.

The substance of your offerings should be improved and extended by a group dedicated to product management. Their success is to be measured in new products launched per month, the market acceptance of the new products, and their performance. Product management has to:

- Work with internal marketing staff and external agencies to fix responsiveness issues.
- Compile suggestions for improvements from internal sources, customers, complaints, competitors.
- Work with the back office to push for increasing operational efficiency.
- Be faster than the competitors with new product launches – if necessary several product launch teams have to work in parallel to reduce the lead times for new products.

Those activities will be further refined in Chapter 10. For your electronic presence I recommend the phase model of the emerging best practices that will be discussed in the next chapter.

6.2.1   Incremental improvements

For all those improvements, you should establish a cooperative work and information environment with a possibility for your professionals to exchange their ideas. This environment has to allow your creative contributors to keep their mind going. It has to be available around the clock and throughout the year to allow the brain power of your staff to get their ideas communicated, to receive feedback and to refine the ideas – no matter if they are in the office, on customer site or at home. Currently, two good options for such an information backbone are available: either your own Intranet or a Lotus Notes implementation with the appropriate knowledge databases, and discussion forums.

Approaches such as the clear documentation of processes (even in smaller companies), which are now standardized by ISO 9000 or earlier TQM (Total Quality Management) that push you to "say what you do and do what you say" create explicit awareness of activities and process steps you earlier did implicitly. By making the steps explicit, you can then revisit the need for the process steps and can undertake a re-engineering and streamlining of the activities. It makes implicit quality goals explicit and measurable and you can monitor the cost and benefit of quality adjustments. But please be pragmatic with such buzz words – understand the principles, match them with your particular situation and only then invest your staff's time and effort.

Provide a clear guidance and focus. The innovations should be driven by people who have hands-on understanding of your products, the market and your staff. Typically, those people will be your key contributors. Empower them to drive the innovations in some per centage of their time and identify who's responsible for which areas of improvement, e.g. product management, broadening of knowledge base, price policies, staff development. This core group of people should have regular workshops with your participation to synchronize regularly the ongoing evolution.

Recommendation:

- Establish clear ownership for the ongoing improvement of your offerings.

6.3   BREAKTHROUGH INNOVATIONS

In a way, the story about breakthrough innovations is like going through a new business launch again and again. You could go through all the considerations and checklists of this book regularly, but you may rather use an easier approach: You should immerse as much as you can in the customer and offering environment. A nice example Nonaka describes in his book on innovations in the traditional world is the invention of a bread machine for Japanese households. Initially all approaches failed – until one of the technicians went through an apprenticeship with a famous bread baker and realized the subtleties of how to treat the dough during the baking process.

For this total immersion, it's also advisable to have practitioners of the profession on board. If you offer business-to-business solutions, you should seek to hire staff from your customer's industries or to assign them temporarily to an apprenticeship with your customers. If you provide services for small professionals, include their expertise, too, in your staff mix. And if you target private households, get open-minded people on board that have experience in the core of your proposal – for example travel agents or entertainers if you pursue travel and entertainment markets, retailers for the specific goods you intend to sell, or people that can bring a "smile on the phone" across if you are establishing a call centre.

Another important tool is brainstorming. You should have a mix of regular brainstorming, e.g. during annual conventions of your key staff, and ad hoc brainstorming. In case your team gets hung up on a problem, pull a whiteboard in and open the faucet of creativity in the team or with additional contributors from outside the team.

You also should afford to have a few people in the organization that think out of the box. They are often a pain in the neck, because they challenge each and everything. But on the other hand they'll force you to rethink your approaches frequently. If you invest some time and money in strange looking ideas, you get something in your pipeline which might end up becoming a cash cow.

If you have reached a size of more than hundred staff, create centres of innovation, knowledge and excellence. They shouldn't be organized with a lot of overhead, i.e. you don't need physical units for that, but you should point out key people to coordinate ideas, knowledge, conference attendance, publications (internal and external), reference stories and best practices. Those people should also engage with your customers to match their demands with your product evolution.

To keep your product pipeline filled, have always some experiments going: a model and a rapid prototype of a new idea which you let some test customers try out is much better than a glossy brochure. For example, before Amazon launched their music and auction business worldwide, they tested it with a small customer group in the US with a specific website. Or SAP went through a network of certified partners serving a selected small group of customers when they initially launched their application hosting before they rolled it out on a large scale.

You will get instant feedback from the market and from your people responsible for production. You can maintain the financial control of such experiments more easily than of an immediate full roll out. So you can tune your processes in order to generate the next marketable offering.

And finally, you should keep your eyes open, not only in your own product, service and market area, but also in adjacent areas. As you have to do with money (e.g. how are your payment terms with suppliers, how do you get the cash from your customers?), look into the financial industry. As you have to do with logistics (everybody distributing physical products does), watch the trends in Point-of-Sales support, transportation and mail-order. And if you're selling immaterial goods like licences or services, look for the developments on how to enforce your copyright and strive for excellence in order to avoid that your ideas may be copied or stolen.

Even as a start-up company, you should have someone in charge of product improvements or product management. This person has to scan regularly the offerings of the competitors, take some time for skimming through the relevant business publications – and ask the customers what they would like to get improved.

Recommendation:

- Have regular creativity days in order to boost your innovation.

6.4   CHECKLIST

As described, the principles for innovation are just necessary ingredients, but no guarantee for success. On top of those principles you should always ask yourself, what brings them to life in your particular situation.

Table 6-14: Checklist for innovations

Principle	Recommendation	Examples	Self-assessment
Systematic support for Incremental Improvements			
Ongoing Improvements	Establish product management group in your organization		
Information flow and exchange	Provide a physical or virtual pinboard, forum or chat room on improvements	Put an incentive on the "idea of the day" or "idea of the month"	
	Observe competitor's offerings	Customer group discussions and conventions	
	Have a clear information policy supported by information archives	Lotus Notes or Intranet storage of project experience	
Streamline processes	Understand Best Practices and match them to your initiative, but don't blindly apply them	ISO 9000, TQM	
Focus	Establish single point of contact for improvement suggestions	Tracking and follow-up on customer suggestions	
	Establish centres for knowledge and excellence	Tracking and follow-up on staff suggestions	
	Put key staff in charge of improvements	Research centres	
		Active and passive participation on Trade Fairs	
		Internet mailing lists on specific business topics	

Table 6-14 (continued)

Principle	Recommendation	Examples	Self-assessment
Change the perspective	Take outsider views serious Engage out-of-the-box thinking Check industries with similar issues	Hire staff with complementary skill sets: e.g. fire brigade and nurses for call centres, Heavy Industry production experts for software development process improvements Cross-industry disciplines: service, production processes, controlling	
Brain-storming	Organize regular brainstorming workshops Be ready for ad hoc brainstorming	Annual key staff convention Spontaneous Pizza & Beer Solution	
Under-standing of customer situation	Get deeply immersed in your customers' needs	Swap your staff with customer Apprenticeships Solve your customer's problem for yourself	
Experiment	Just do it! Be open and be fast!	First car, first plane, first phone	

6.5   DISCUSSION POINTS

For you to stay innovative in your core competency, let's identify the most important trends you benefit from. Some are identified in the book, some more will be on my website www.success-at-e-business.com and possibly you have identified even another one – that's innovation!

- What's the innovative idea currently being exploited in your industry?
- What can you do to kick off the next innovation cycle?
- How old are your "cash cows" and how old is the idea that led to the development of those cash cows – where does that put you relative to your competitors?

Recommendations:

- Always look for examples you can learn from.
- Be fast!

PART II
Leverage of global experience

Before you begin this part of the book, you should have the materials ready that you prepared in Part I, in particular your high-level business plan and the results of the checklists filled in at the end of each chapter. If you haven't documented your considerations yet, please download the templates from my website www.success-at-e-business.com now, in order to consider your business design in the light of the emerging best practices. You may want to make some adjustments and refinements during the further steps, and the templates are designed in a way to allow you to make the additional annotations.

7

Emerging best practices

Benefit from the experience of Internet pioneers and large consumer businesses by using the accelerated project approaches and the roadmaps to get to
- *eBusiness maturity, with a*
- *customer focused organization, and*
- *efficient operations with your partners tightly integrated, based on*
- *technical architecture for online Customer Interaction, and*
- *secure access to your ISP.*

In this chapter I describe the best practices for *e*Businesses emerging around the globe. We'll touch upon implementation questions based on the experience from other companies, but for concise recommendations please refer to Part III of the book.

7.1 MATURITY LEVELS FOR *e*BUSINESS START-UPS

7.1.1 Characteristics of four distinct levels

The relatively short history of *e*Business shows there are different stages of maturity. In the following, let's discuss a recent study of AMS[11]. They describe the following four stages.

At level one, only static information is provided via the Web. This is like a printed brochure you hand to your customers. No specific interaction with your prospects and customers is possible. Only little investment and time is necessary

---

[11] American Management Systems Inc. (AMS): *e*Commerce in the Telecommunications Industry: Trends and Innovations, Fairfax (VA), 1999, or www.amsinc.com.

to have such an initial web presence – also the costs can be compared with a printed brochure. When you read this book, this is probably a level you have either passed or you don't intend to target for. But it's still a step that needs to be made before you can get to the next level.

At level two, some interaction is possible: customers get some personalized information, the goods and services you offer (or at least some of them) can be ordered directly via the Web and you should be able to give an immediate confirmation of the order back to your customers. This requires already a good integration with your back office. In fact, your infrastructure should include real time inventory keeping, interfaces with your suppliers in order to inform your customers about expected time for delivery, and you should have a support centre or call centre in place in order to quickly answer the customers' eMails. Actually, the majority of eBusinesses are at that stage. And that's a reasonable investment to do – either with some of your own money or with some Venture Capital support. In fact, the nice thing about eBusiness is that you can start small and then grow quickly. However, you shouldn't expect magic; the Internet can support quick growth, but your organization, your partners and your staff won't be that flexible. So start in the right league from the outset. If you plan to stay small, your initial investment can be well below € 100,000; with such a company you can earn your living, but you won't become as well-known as Amazon or Dell. If you want to claim a large market share on the web, you should be ready for an initial overall investment of more than half a million Euro, and have the commitment from a Venture Capitalist to support you with a few more millions once your growth starts. Given that the market is still relatively open and that newcomers can be absorbed as long as they offer some reasonable goods and services, this is a good starting time for your business launch.

The next level now, i.e. level three, offers additional personalization. In particular, it requires you to implement a customer value model in order to follow the one-to-one marketing approach. This means that your website should be supported by decisioning systems:

- To guide the customer through your offerings.
- To highlight such offerings you assume your customer has a high propensity to buy.
- To offer the appropriate price, packaging, delivery service and payment approach you want to use for the particular customer.

If you can launch your activities immediately at this level, you may gain a better immediate transaction profitability, customer satisfaction and customer loyalty. On the other hand, the implementation of this level is much more expensive than level two. It will require an up front investment of several million Euros. Moreover, you need a track record of past customer transactions. Therefore, it's only advisable if you can leverage earlier experience. This may be the case in spin-off situations, i.e. if you branch your Internet offerings off of some traditional business or if you replicate the experience from an earlier launch with some similar new offering. In this case, you also should read the subsequent section regarding the transformation of traditional enterprises.

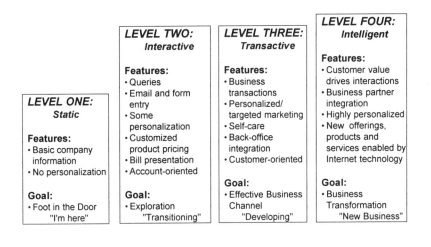

Source: AMS American Management Systems

Figure 7-20: Four levels of eBusiness maturity

The currently final level, i.e. level four, will allow extensive self service. Your customers will be able to configure your services and goods interactively on the screen, they can "negotiate" service levels and prices, and they will get a pro-active and responsive support. If you imagine what desires a customer can get fulfilled in a physical store and compare that with even the most advanced Internet offerings, you see the potential of additional sophisticated support and convenience yet to come. To mention some examples:

- For the cases when the goods you've sold break, you need to establish a field service for repairing or replacing them by a working version.
- For customers who don't manage to get the expected benefits from your goods and services you have to have a "refund" policy – without allowing too much abuse of it.
- You should be able to increase the value perceived by your customer in a way, that you become his "preferred partner". This means you need to understand all his needs and guide him to your allies (who in turn also

refer customers back to you) rather than allowing him to surf through the whole web and be approached by many other vendors.

- You need to innovate your offerings more quickly than your competitors in order to keep the customer loyal.

This vision goes beyond the implementation of even the most advanced current *e*Businesses. Some companies strive for this level, but it's not implemented yet in all facets. One of the few companies that have most of the characteristics of this level is Cisco with 70 per cent of the revenues generated via the web and the whole service culture aligned with the possibilities of interactive customer support.

7.1.2   Focus area by maturity level

At every level, the focus of the activities will be pretty different. Level one companies will go the do-it-yourself way and possibly only seek the support of the ISP. At level two, key consideration will be on getting a good software for the interaction with the customers. Actually both levels, one and two, are still *e*Commerce settings and both are focused on informing the customer about the offerings in a "broadcast" manner. So, classic marketing considerations will drive the design of the website.

At level three *e*Business starts. The business approaches need to be modified. The transactions initiated by the customers need to be performed in an integrated way between front office and back office. The online presentations will be customized by one-to-one marketing. External help will be extensively used, e.g. consultants for the definition of the approach and the IT implementation, and intensive relationships with partners will be necessary to execute the day-to-day business activities. Much emphasis will be put on optimizing the supply chain.

At level four, finally, the focus will be on the newly arising opportunities, on permanent adaptations of the business model and its implementation.

7.1.3   Recommendation for start-ups

Recommendation:

- Be realistic about the desired current step for your *e*Venture. A good starting point for the launch of a niche provider is level two of the model above.

The next paragraphs are not relevant for you, yet, while you are in start-up mode. Please remember, though, to read them once you have grown larger. Some of the recommendations will be quickly applicable for your growing business.

7.2   RE-ORIENTING A TRADITIONAL ENTERPRISE TO A CUSTOMER-FOCUSED *e*BUSINESS

As a leader or manager of a traditional enterprise you need to understand all the information about your existing customers in order to generate a better approach and better profits. In parallel, you have to change the organization from departmental, separate working entities into a joint and strong workforce supporting your customers.

Home for the Customer

- Communities
- Community managers
- Learning organization with increasing leverage of customer relationships

Customer Value Orientation

- Start of Behaviour Analysis
- Profitability Analysis including Potential
- Lifecycle Modelling
- Refined Metrics
- Tuned Marketing

Customer Information Environment

- Metrics Programme
- Customer Information Repository
- Customer Profiles
- Transactions and Behaviours
- Concise Campaigns

Figure 7-21: Roadmap to a customer-focused Business

In the first stage, you should focus on some key tasks that result in the quickest gain of share in the online market while some workarounds to overcome integration gaps are still acceptable. This means to build up a customer information environment and to start acting upon such information. In the second stage you should architect your organization with integrated processes in mind; an operational effectiveness is target at this stage. Finally, you should integrate your internal processes with the customer facing activities into an efficient interaction with your customers.

7.2.1   Customer Information Environment

The most important goal for the Customer Information Environment is to be informed of how you are doing compared to your plans. We'll discuss the key metrics first, namely for your financial situation, for your customer situation, for your staff situation and for your innovations. Those four items have shown to be the pillars of sustained success – if any of them fails, the others won't be able to let you survive. Of course, additional aspects are important too, but for the other aspects you should be able to find work arounds as long as the four mentioned areas are well covered.

Then, we will discuss the best approach for your information repository needed to pull all those metrics together, namely a data warehouse. Those metrics need to be translated into meaningful insights in order to prepare successful actions such as concise marketing campaigns.

Metrics programme

It requires your full managerial attention to define the appropriate metrics for your business. In order to drive your company properly, you have to translate the vision that you generated into key figures. As Best Practices indicate, your figures should cover more than merely the revenues. At least four areas should be on the radar screen of you as an entrepreneur – ideally every day. If one of those areas is not performing as planned, you can take corrective action. Scale up quickly, if the demand is higher than anticipated, or push for additional sales in case of not enough market share, for example. As mentioned, these are:

1. Financials – that's no surprise, you've probably heard that from your bank, from your accountant and from a few other people. Actually, we'll discuss a sample business case in order to help you set up the appropriate measurements later in Chapter 12. Your financial metrics should include your profitability and your liquidity based on the business plan you've prepared.
2. Customer satisfaction – everybody shoots for it, but it's difficult to get the right key figures to monitor satisfaction. A starting point is to measure the number of website hits (your ISP should provide you with the statistics), the number and value of received orders, the number and reasons for complaints, and the number of repetitive customers (i.e. those who place several orders in sequence). My best advice is, that you should immerse with the customer situation in order to understand his objectives, his desires, his quality expectations, his needs for convenience. Once you understand those, you should be able to define a few tangible measurements for satisfaction. In fact, they may be pretty different from segment to segment, but according to my experience you should be able to find some additional commonalities,

e.g. timeliness of delivery, response rate of your call centre, turn around time for eMail requests. In addition, you should run surveys from time to time and ask the customers what you can do to improve your services.

3. Staff motivation – some people may find it obsolete to consider the staff motivation and morale, but in fact the opposite is true. In a world where everybody can copy a business idea, you and the people around you are the most distinguishing factor for your business! So, recognize the achievements of your key contributors, make them proud of their work, e.g. by publishing their success story on your website, and make your employees aware of the benefits they get from working with you. Such benefits include working with a leader in business, it's the exposure to new challenges, it should be a work environment with enough fun and a nice team. And the measures will include your overall number of staff, the (hopefully low) attrition rate, the time you need to hire additional people – and the trends if you compare such figures with your rates in the time before.

4. Innovation and ability to adjust to changes – again, it's imperative that you are capable of being faster than your competitor. Therefore you need to monitor your speed of improvements. Some of the recommended indicators are the average age of your offerings, the turn-around time from an idea to a sellable item, your revenue dependency on products of different ages, the number of trade marks or patents you apply for, the number of your staff actively pursuing new ideas (e.g. in centres of excellence).

These four aspects are also the key components of the Balanced Scorecard. This methodology comes now more and more in use by larger companies. It's about seeing the impact of trade-off decisions and your business dynamics in the day-to-day life in a quantitative manner.

For your launch of eBusiness, the approach can be adopted first of all to trigger alarms when one area is performing below or above plans in order to take corrective actions.

Some examples: If your liquidity and your profitability are below target, you are in trouble and you should overhaul your complete business. Is the number of customers and the number of sold items evolving as planned? If not, which of the marketing activities can be extended promising the biggest success?

If only liquidity is below target and the other areas are performing well, you need to look closer. Are the customers over-using your patience regarding payments? Have you been investing into your growth more quickly than anticipated? If late payments hit your liquidity, strive for early collections – and possibly expand your overdraft lines with your bank as well. If additional investments were necessary, check with your investor, if he can support an additional funding. If your costs are out of control, however, cut them quickly!

If, on the other hand, your profitability is not as expected, you also need to zoom into the badly performing area. Are your margins per sold item as you planned them? If not, can you increase the prices or reduce the sales and distribution overhead, respectively? Are the marketing costs within budget? If not, what are the least effective marketing activities and how can you cut them back and replace them by activities generating more responses? Are your overall staff cost per sold item and per earned Euro in synch with your expectations? Are you maintaining idle capacities (e.g. in your call centre or field service) or have huge inventories built up? If so, rent the spare capacities to another provider or stop buying goods remaining on your shelves by applying just-in-time order and delivery from your suppliers, instead.

You should have positive surprises, either: If the number of customers and ordered items is larger than expected, you can organize your production and service facilities for the quicker growth – or you can softly step away from your initial "special offers".

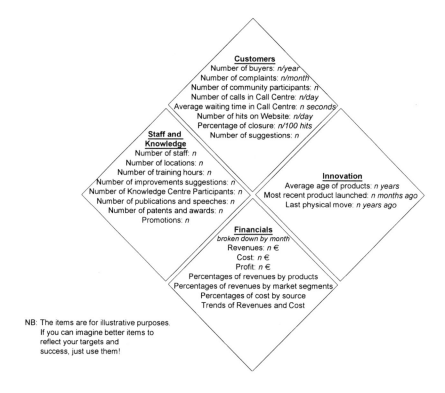

Figure 7-22: Balanced Scorecard example

After a while of compiling the measurement, you will be able to identify trends and you will recognize how successful some corrective actions have been. This allows you to create a "learning organization" where you directly can benefit from the earlier experience. I will explain some of the implementation considerations later in Chapter 9.

Finally, there's one piece of wisdom from all kinds of business which you should never forget: *you won't get what you don't measure.* So:

- if you like to make your customers happy – define measurements for happiness, measure it and report it back to your customers;
- if you want to have your staff motivated – define measurements for motivation, measure it and report it back to your staff;
- if you promise high quality – measure the defects, the number of complaints, the availability of your service or the durability of your products;
- if you want to become rich – well, a measurement is defined, but define HOW MUCH at each date and report it (at least to yourself…).

You should strive for all of those targets, define the metrics and start measuring the achievement!

Customer Information Repository

In the history of your traditional business, you've ended up with several independent computer systems and scattered information – no matter if you have a small business or a large business. In the worst-case, you have several paper files for the various aspects of your order processing, delivery, invoicing and payments. In the best case, you have all information available at your fingertips. This should be your target!

You may have separate processes and responsibilities for each of the mentioned areas, but you should strive for integrating the relevant data into one common repository. This requires

- you come up with a concise process model of all your customer related activities and processes – actually we'll discuss a framework with the key processes Marketing and Sales, Product fabrication and Service generation, Supplies, Distribution, Payment, later in this chapter;
- then you have to identify the relevant data at each stage;
- you need to decide which of those processes you support by an automated solution and which data (e.g. customer profiles, most recent orders and complaints) you need to compile into the central repository. If you use different systems for each or some of the processes, you may end up with redundant data keeping. In this case, you need to define, which system is the leading system, and you need to synchronize the data in the data warehouse from time to time.

The general architecture for your repository can be depicted as follows in Figure 7-23[12].

---

[12] Please note that this architecture only covers internal systems. In case you want to make any of those databases accessible by the customers (or even by your staff working remotely via an Intranet), you have to add a firewall as security mechanism. The general firewall architecture is outlined in the next chapter.

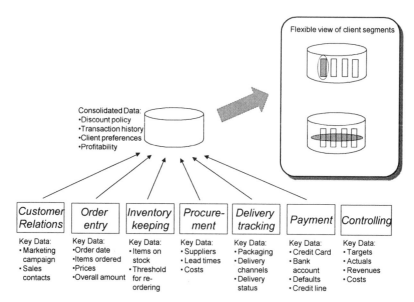

Figure 7-23: Data Warehouse architecture

The key point to consider at this stage is, that the data provided by the various functions (as well as those needed by them) differ highly – that's the reason why it's often a challenge to integrate them into one common view. As you probably have the luxury to create your approach from scratch, look for an early integration of the data models in order to have the flexible view of customer segments available. It helps the design of your flexible reporting greatly, if you identify early the types of analysis you need to run. Some of the needs will become more clear when we discuss the next stages in the evolution to a customer centred company, but let me mention some examples here:

- Profitability of customers by region, by size (of companies), by age, by duration of relationship with you, by types of services or goods ordered from you.
- Success rate of campaigns.
- Impact of discounts on your overall profitability (e.g. increase of demand vs. decrease in contribution by item).

Customer profiles, transactions and behaviours

You will be able to find patterns in your customer interactions. These may be characteristics as defined by static data such as regions or age of the customer, family situation of the customer, education, income and other socio-demographic differentiators or it may depend on the industry and size in the case of business customers. Additionally, the types of products and services those customers actually purchase from you, should be included. Alternatively, and more advanced, is to search for patterns in the customer behaviour, e.g. what website they visited before or how frequently they stop by. The latter approach will be discussed in the Section 7.2.2 below.

Once you've completed this analysis you should assign your customers to specific segments which you can describe by the characteristics found out by you. Due to the discussed quick changes in the market dynamics, some of those segments may require to be revisited frequently (e.g. once per quarter), others may be more stable. In any case, you have to get your infrastructure organized in order to support the analysis and to keep the results in one place, namely the customer information repository supporting your decisions in the day to day business.

We talked about transparency earlier in this book. The customer profiles are another area where tranparency makes the difference. Let your customers know, what you know or assume about them:

- What segment you've put them in.
- How you've experienced their transaction behaviour.
- What preferences you have stored about them.
- How you score them regarding eligibility for loyalty programmes and what they need to do to get to the next better category.

Let them update those areas of the profile that give them a higher satisfaction and convenience without damaging your areas of interest. In other words don't allow them to change their risk profile or the discount scheme directly, but let them know what they need to do to get more discount, e.g. by having higher order volumes.

Monitoring customer responses

Below you see a model, how you can refine the measurements and the assignment of customers to specific profiles based on their past buying (or referral) behaviour.

With the mentioned example of measurement, the probabilities for cross-selling successes can be monitored. For each customer segment and campaign, a probability in per cent can be indicated, if the customer purchases an additional product, if he shows no interest, if he increases the usage of the contracted product or service or if he makes referrals. In mass marketing, it has proven successful to run similar, but slightly different campaigns as a test in parallel, to compare the outcome and then to use the better one for a full coverage of your targeted segments. This comparison shouldn't be only a one-off activity, but you should perform this on an ongoing basis. So you always will have a standard marketing campaign running, which is the current "champion" strategy and a new "challenger" to the existing strategy which may outperform the former champion. Thus you permanently tune your marketing activities.

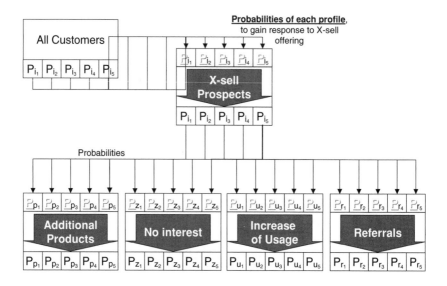

Figure 7-24: Measurement of behaviour probabilities

Recommendations:

- Track the customer interactions in order to identify customer segments with their respective buying behaviours.

- Match your marketing and sales campaigns with the customer segments and monitor the results.

- Monitor your progress against plans regularly.

7.2.2   Customer Value orientation

Start of behaviour analysis

Your analysis should be supported by various tools. Some of those tools are sold as data mining tools, others are referenced as statistical tools.

As Meridien Research defines the more sophisticated approaches and their business application in its report "Data Mining Solutions and Customer Management":

Table 7-15: Sophisticated data analysis approaches

	Data Mining Task	Algorithms	Business problem
Directed Data Mining	Classification	Decision Trees, Neural Network, K-Nearest Neighbour	Which segments do those customers belong to?
	Prediction/ Estimation	Neural Network, Association rule induction, Decision Trees, K-Nearest Neighbour	What if analysis
Undirected Data Mining	Associations and Affinity Grouping	Association rule induction	Which products are purchased together?
	Clustering	Decision Trees, K-Nearest Neighbour, Neural Networks	What are some valid ways to segment my customers?
Directed or undirected	Description	Association rule induction, other algorithms to varying degrees, OLAP	Which variables are important in determining an outcome?

Source: Meridien Research Inc., Data Mining Solutions and Customer Management

With the results of data mining you can "slice and dice" your customer data. You should focus your marketing campaigns, e.g. by *e*Mails, to those customers with the highest expected propensity to buy. You should personalize the websites for each specific customer segment, e.g. the discussed examples of book preferences, and you should have the appropriated prompts popping up on the Customer Care Representative's screen when he talks to a customer within a specific segment. With this approach you can reduce the waste in your marketing efforts greatly, because the response rate to your offerings will be much better than without it. Moreover, the data mining can be set up in a way, that your organization learns from successes and failures. You can run two campaigns, e.g. with two slightly different marketing messages or with two differently selected customer segments, then you monitor the responsiveness to the campaigns and you can improve your predictive models accordingly. You also should perform some market research interviewing your customers – or you may use the first-hand experience from your sales force and your Customer Care Representatives in order to find out what makes your customer buy. Similar to the analysis of patterns in the static data, e.g. buying preferences by ages or regions, you will find transaction events and triggers that support the buying decision. Some of those events and triggers are:

Major changes in the customer lifetime situation such as completion of education, marriage, move to a new home, birth of a child, new job assignment. For those changes, you have the opportunity for successful sales, if you get an early indication of an upcoming change and an offering taylored to the needs of the customer at that change. In order to get those indications early, it may be appropriate to offer the appropriate "consulting" services for such customer segments within their community who may be confronted with such a change.

If you manage to create benefits for the customer when he informs you early, you will be among the first being able to offer him the appropriate additional services and products. So, give him some ideas when he's looking for a name of his baby yet to be born, or support him with getting the child care organized. In either case, you'll learn a lot about your customer's needs. At least you should monitor such triggers as soon as the change has happened. So, don't consider a change of address as a pure administrative task; instead, it offers you the opportunity for additional sales!

Events during the course of periods such as annual holidays happening at certain times of the year, prolongation of subscriptions happening towards the end of the current subscription period, purchases close to the beginning of a month when the customer has received his salary. Such patterns are usually found out by data mining activities, where all your transaction histories are pumped through sophisticated analysis machines and specific correlations are identified.

Passing of thresholds such as for business customers the growth of revenues or staff to a number where additional services become appropriate, for private customers the growth of usage of your services to volumes that allow another treatment. Again, if you can show your customer the benefit of belonging to the "Gold Club", you can create a better loyalty and higher revenues.

I've mentioned some examples for additional sales, but similar patterns apply to the handling of customer complaints (just imagine what valuable information you can create from those customers who challenge your current service and product offerings – they provide you a very concise voice of the market needs); also indicators can be identified to predict (and counteract on) cancellation of customer relationships.

Profitability analysis including potential based on life cycle models

For a profitability analysis, you need to have several ingredients straight. Most important is the top line with your customer, i.e. the revenues with your customers for the various products and services. Then you should be able to assign your internal costs to the products and services in order to calculate the contribution; this should include all costs end-to-end, i.e. the sales costs, the costs of the product as such, the packaging and delivery costs, and the service costs for the specific customer. Much analysis can be done to watch your performance from various perspectives and they all boil down to the basic formula:

$$Profit = Revenue - Cost$$

This analysis can be run for the whole time from inception of the customer relationship until today, or you can check it for specific periods, e.g. for the current month. This retrospective approach is usually taken by your accountant to prepare your balance sheet and tax returns. A key element is missing, though, namely the look into the future.

This additional look can be made by including additionally the expected profitability potential of customers. This usually requires two types of life cycle models:

- the first has to cover the cycle of the relationship between your enterprise and the customer (e.g. initial sales, continuous buying/usage of one product or service, cross-/up-/deep-sales, references to other customers, finalization of relationship);
- the second is a customer life stage model reflecting specific buying triggers at certain transitions of the customer into another stage – as we discussed regarding marriages or child births. If you are aware of the buying behaviour at certain life stages, you can predict the overall customer value and drive the appropriate decisions for your sales activities.

Those models indicate the possible volume of revenues and the probability of those purchases. So the overall value can be calculated:

$$Expected\ Customer\ Value = Cumulative\ Profit\ from\ Inception\ until\ Today \\ + Possible\ Future\ Profits$$

With a sophisticated implementation, you can actually run predictive models showing the financial results of certain offerings or marketing approaches. But even if you have only the web hit patterns and the sales statistics, you can draw the key conclusions, namely decide if it's a worthwhile effort to spend money on specific customers in order to attract their business. The customers with a high expected value should be pursued by aggressive marketing campaigns across several channels (including the more expensive traditional channels like paper mail and calls from sales agents) and they may get some discounted initial offerings (possibly even subsidized offerings). The customers with a lesser value should be treated with highly automated and very efficient approaches and not get discounts that eat your margins.

Refined targets and metrics

With the additional insights, you can refine your targets and metrics. I don't recommend to change your targets on the fly, but to add some specific measurements whenever you find particular areas of interest. These may be measurements for a specific customer segment, for a specific department in your organization or for a limited time of a campaign. Still, if it turns out that your initial targets have been unrealistic, monitor the gap and have some specific stages during your controlling cycles where you officially adjust your overall targets – this may happen once every quarter.

Tuning marketing to one-to-one messages

The traditional marketing approach uses a lot of "broadcast" messages. TV and radio spots, newspaper advertising or broad mailings all have the disadvantage, that the majority of the recipients aren't interested in the offering. But you have to pay for its distribution, anyway. The electronic interaction provides now a tool to send out very targeted information – provided you know who to target. The current one-to-one marketing approach requires the analysis we have discussed above in order to select the different target groups. The vision is, that eventually every customer can get a different marketing message, and that this message is delivered on the most appropriate channel. Thus you can save all the unnecessary cost of sending information to people who aren't interested anyway.

With your initial concise marketing campaigns, you've compiled data about the responsiveness of your customers and prospects to your campaigns and you have observed the performance of different marketing messages. Now you can add the "Value" dimension as described above to the steering and management of your campaigns. This means that you can focus on the most profitable segments according to the decision matrix in Figure 7-25 below.

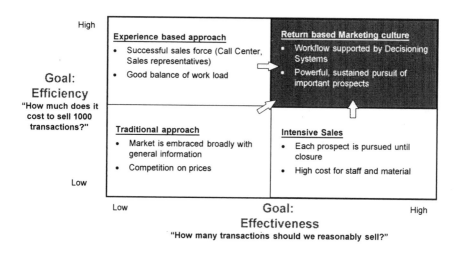

Figure 7-25: Improved effectiveness by experience-based marketing

What you should stop or at least reduce, are the activities in the lower left quadrant: your cost of sales per transaction (or unit) are very high, and you need to compete with price cuts in order to close the deals – so this has been squeezing your profitability from both sides. Your competitors probably also compete with price cuts in this area, so the margins are getting less and less and you may even contribute to losses. Therefore, you have to discontinue this approach in order to free up your resources to do more profitable business.

What you should control closely, are the intensive sales in the right lower quadrant: you successfully sell your offerings, but the sales costs eat into your profit margin. So only do that in strategically important customer segments, where you really want to "buy" market share.

You are already well off, if you are in the left upper quadrant: your sales people are successful. However, they might turn requests from customers down, if they don't see the immediate benefit or if they are not enough pro-active with an opportunity that should have a high potential.

With the appropriate metrics as discussed, and a good integration of those metrics into the marketing and sales decisions, you can focus on the most promising situations. The situations will more and more be considered on a case by case basis. You should target, that your sales agents have permanently an indicator available, if it's still worth to pursue a certain prospect or if it's time to stop the attempt. With this approach, you get the low hanging, good fruits most easily, you stop wasting sales efforts and you engage best with your most important customers. So that's a gain for all parties.

Recommendations:

- Establish models to analyse customer value per product or service and per behavioural life stage.

- Focus on the most profitable customers.

- Use the electronic means like eMail, SMS and web personalization extensively for your one-to-one marketing activities, in particular to approach your preferred customers.

7.2.3   Home for your customer

Communities

Ultimately, your customer should feel at home with your company. As we discussed in Chapter 3, you need to provide the appropriate community for your customers. This means to invite the customer for contributions to a group. For example by providing a chat room, or as Amazon.com does, by inviting their customers to come up with reviews of the books they purchased and to publish those reviews on the amazon website or like the Cabana case with private pictures from holidays.

The general approach to create communities is the response to one or several underlying desires of your customer segment. Let's discuss some examples:

- If you deal with furniture, let your customers exchange their thoughts with interior architects, or seek for the most creative ideas how to furnish specific difficult areas in their homes (like the area below a staircase). This should be even more powerful in specific life stage transitions, e.g. how to equip the room of the new baby, or how to deal with removal issues. If you want to sell wine, create the ambience for wine tasting – with stories from the regions where the wine grows or with nice recipes for good dinners.
- If you are in the finance business and generate your revenues from processing stock orders, you can hook up with your customers by providing them stock performance analysis, retirement consulting or similar services. To create communities, you then can invite your customers to exchange their segment specific experiences, e.g. how to deal with tax issues for high wealth individuals or how to approach health problems for your elderly customers.
- Or look at the various auction providers: they've created a new mentality of "collectors" supported by an entertainer, in some cases embraced by audio and video clips – they buy for the pleasure of "playing" at an auction and "winning" the good they somewhat desire. So completely new needs are created – and if the customer realizes that he didn't actually have the need, he can resell it by an auction thus creating the next commission for the auction company.

Community managers

In order to establish the appropriate environment and content for the communities, you should establish managers for each respective community. They are in charge of organizing the group, creating the dynamics within it and pull additional contributors into the group such as the mentioned interior architects or tax accountants. They also have to organize the materials provided by the customers and clean the contents up.

The goal is to create an attractive home for the customers and at the same time to monitor the financial performance, i.e. the contribution of that community to your company. In a way, those community managers have to behave like a little company within your company.

Learning organization with increasing leverage of customer relationships

Once you are aligned with the needs of your customers in the ways described above, you "only" need to stay ahead of the crowd of competitors. New ideas will pop up every day, but do they promise to increase your profits? New challenges will come, either – will it be more costly for you to counteract or to let a piece of the market break away? You need to consider the short term and the long term impact of such opportunities and challenges. For a quick decision on opportunities and challenges check their impact. What will happen, if you follow the opportunity (necessary investment, distraction of key staff from other important issues, additional revenues) versus if you just let it go (loss of market share, dissatisfaction of some customers BUT maintained focus on existing core business)? Similarly for new challenges. What will happen if you don't counteract, e.g. against a new discounting scheme of a key competitor or regarding the constraints of WAP-Internet compared to PC-Internet (loss of market share) versus if you take the necessary steps (investment, distraction of staff from current objectives, lack of revenues)?

Such reactions to opportunities and challenges are difficult in itself. Therefore, there's one thing you shouldn't have in your way, namely an inflexible organization. Educate your staff to be balanced in their approaches:

- You need to have proper processes and procedures in place BUT you must not have the legacy of sticking to rules that were valuable in another time or in another market.
- You have to have good quality in your products and services, BUT if the competitors eat into your market share by offering less sophisticated products and services, you must be ready to reconsider your complexities in production, service and engineering.
- You need to maintain a high morale in your staff AND you need to expose them to new challenges regularly – so don't pay the price of providing a "cozy" environment by letting your staff fall back into lacking pro-activeness to customer requirements.

Each of those considerations requires everyday judgement. This will only be possible in an open environment, where you allow your staff to come up with constructive criticism, where you put incentives on an awareness of risks (rather than incenting only good news) and where you freely discuss opportunities, product ideas and marketing approaches. NEVER punish a messenger of bad news!

You will soon find out, that this is a much more pleasant working environment for everybody than any traditional approach with hierarchies and command structures.

Recommendations:

- Focus your offering at communities.
- Allow your customers to edit their profiles on-line in self service.
- Learn from customer feedback and improve your offerings according to their recommendations.

7.3   NEW APPROACHES FOR START-UPS AND LARGER COMPANIES

7.3.1   Acceleration of projects

The *e*Business projects undertaken by companies of different sizes and in different regions show some key commonalities. If the key success factors listed below are not followed you run a major risk of not being successful. The most important messages are:

Transform your ideas QUICKLY into an offering and reduce your time to market! Many good ideas can be copied and implemented pretty easily – and you probably want to get some money for your idea and not have the same fate like the inventor of the new standard for digital music MP3. Karlheinz Brandenburg, a researcher at a German university, invented in 1977 the MP3 code for music which compresses music data for quicker transmission on the Internet and which allows to prevent illegal copies of the music data. He failed to exploit the business potential of the idea and thus he isn't even known and famous for having invented this widely used standard. Instead, other companies converted the idea into a business concept, like MP3.com working as an Internet music publisher and having now a market capitalization of two billion dollars or the developer of the MP3 player, Diamond Multimedia Systems, whose business is to sell those players. The inventor even gets some licence fees, but the real money is made by those who converted the technical idea into a service and product usable in the mass market. So, the earlier you can manifest your offering, the better you are off.

Follow an accelerated project approach to support your target to reduce the time to market. In contrast to other businesses where you try to be very solid in order to allow for some extra quality in your offerings, in the Internet business you have to push for quick implementations. This may require a shift in the mind set of the people working with you: more often than not people (and organizations) progress slowly by looking for the next logical step again and again. They are outperformed by those people and organizations who establish a vision, communicate that vision, and implement all the necessary functions by thinking back from their targets rather than thinking forward from their current standpoint. Implement and refine your business by designing backwards from your targets.

This new approach is used in projects of all sizes. Large projects with several hundred team members, e.g. for the implementation of highly complex customer care and billing systems for telecom providers, are successfully executed based on such a target oriented setting. And also small projects like writing this book can only be completed in time, if constraints or issues are solved instead of being accepted as a restriction.

Let me illustrate the necessary change in the approach (Figure 7-26).

A stepwise approach will place you behind your competitors...

...while the more performant approach works from your vision and deduces the necessary activities to get there

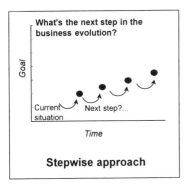

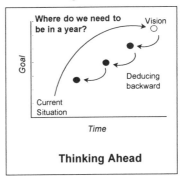

Figure 7-26: Accelerated project approach

Due to the traditional stepwise approach, large organizations often stagnate or make only little progress. In fact, even approaches looking nice at the surface like TQM (Total Quality Management) or BPR (Business Process Redesign) slow such companies further down instead of pushing them forward. So, here's your opportunity when you can establish a lean environment: don't allow your thinking to be driven by constraints; formulate your dreams (or vision) and engage with the people that share your vision. You still need the practitioners and the engineers – and they play a very crucial role, but only after you know your vision. As a second step, you then should do a reality check: what does it mean to implement all the business processes and IT systems, how much staff do you need to support the services, how much money is necessary if you do it according to this initial outline. Then comes the time for compromises and adjustments – but don't get dragged back to the traditional approach. Once you went through two or three iterations of visionary thinking complemented with the appropriate feasibility considerations, you can finalize your project plans, business plans and you can start marketing your ideas. Examples of business plans and project plans are provided in Chapters 12 and 13, respectively, to help you getting started.

This new project approach may make your project more complex – in particular because some activities may go on in parallel – and thus more risky. And it requires the readiness to step away from the "nine-to-five" attitude. This "downside" is offset by the benefits of an earlier launch of your offerings and also by the savings you gain due to the fact that you don't over-engineer your offering. If you don't feel comfortable about managing all the parallel project activities, dependencies, issues and risks, you may consider engaging an external programme manager dealing with such questions. But don't leave him on the long leash – he has to give you the full transparency of all implementation activities very frequently. And he has to escalate everything that creates new risks, e.g. slippages, immediately to you. Don't forget how large projects run very late: day by day by day…

Two tricks help to follow this new project approach. One is to be more demanding – from yourself and from your staff. If you see that you haven't done the day's work, just continue until it's done. This trick works as long as you have only smaller slippages, it doesn't help if greater problems occur. Then comes the second trick: when you realize a larger problem, you should invert the traditional thinking. Don't ask: "How much longer does it take us until completion?" but ask: "What is stopping us from being successful?" If there are external dependencies or possibilities to outsource the solution (even if it is for some additional money), you should resolve that by pushing on external partners. If all this doesn't help, still follow the inverted thinking paradigm and ask now: "What's possible to skip, e.g. which function isn't survival critical, how could we focus on the most important customer segment within the already focused customer segment to reduce complexity, what fallback concept can we use to still make the deadline?" Some of those decisions will be painful – but they will be better than to have the project dragging along.

And of course, you need to follow the traditional project management experience to closely monitor scope creek. Many good new ideas will evolve while the project is running, but if you accept that those new ideas are included in the scope of the project, you contribute to its delay. Therefore, every new idea or "requirement" must be checked, if it's really worth risking the project timeliness for it. For every such change, you should look for another feature you can waive.

Integrate your suppliers and partners early! In traditional business settings with brick and mortar boundaries, the responsibility of each player was clear, e.g. in the supply chain, whose task it was to get a specific item organized. So, the focus was rather on detailed contracts with specified liabilities in case someone failed to deliver. In the Internet age with the dissolving boundaries the objective is rather to look for the partner who can come up with a certain service the easiest (like three shift call centre support, or intraday delivery logistics). Once this partner is identified, you should work with him directly to organize the processes across the companies boundaries in the most effective way, i.e. with the least cost and the biggest outcome for both of you. And instead of investing time in legal proceeds in case of a failure of one partner, recognize that it's usually both companies who have contributed to the failure, so if you can't fix the problem, look for another partner. This means, that you should rather have contracts with easy termination possibilities.

If you are a large company looking for an *e*Business spin-off, this also means that you have to revisit your supplier partnerships and check, if you have processes (and contracts) organized in a way that support the frequent execution of little orders. Your traditional cheap delivery ways with infrequent bulk orders won't do any longer. In this case you also need to check your existing IT infrastructure – the legacy systems with their batch cycles aren't state of the art either. So the asset to leverage in the case of existing traditional businesses aren't the processes, machines and inventories, but they are the knowledge of the market, the knowledge of the products and services, and the knowledge of the suppliers. With this knowledge, you are way ahead of the start-ups and you can re-design the whole business much more easily than any newcomer. You need to implement similar new tools and processes as the start-up. The challenge (and cost driver) will be the integration with your existing back-end systems. Maybe you can't throw your existing ERP system out, because you need it still for your other business areas – so implement a modern realtime ERP for the *e*Business branch in parallel and interface it with the old one. In the long run, probably your other business areas will benefit from that, anyway, because the approaches with quicker turn-around times probably spread out into all your business activities, so you can migrate more and more of your departments onto the new way of business.

Another leverage from the emerging Best Practices are business approaches and IT components. As the "first wave" of Internet business is now settling, we can learn from the experience of the pioneers. The software industry and the consulting companies have put lots of effort into frameworks and offerings to support *e*Businesses. We will discuss those aspects in Part III of the book.

Recommendations:

- Establish a clear vision and communicate it early to your prospective partners.

- Prepare an aggressive, but solid project plan – outlines are provided in Chapter 13.

7.3.2   Streamlined operations for *e*Ventures

Your value proposition breaks down into the value provided to your customer by your respective products and services on one hand and the various steps to get to closure in an online environment on the other hand. We won't discuss the specifics of your core offering here, but we will focus on the interactions towards closure of the sale. Let's now examine the specific differences from a traditional business and an *e*Venture. The differences are primarily to be found in the online presentation of your offerings and the online steps toward the closure of the deal as well as the online post sales support.

Consider how the buying cycle looks like from the customer's perspective – he first wants to obtain general information from the market about the available offerings in general. Once he has an idea about the possibilities, he will start to narrow the options by selecting a specific "product" with some key features. Now he can see some concrete examples of how his request could be fulfilled and he will like to check the experience of others. Once he has bought the product, he will appreciate post-sales support in order to benefit from the product. Let's look at the generally valid steps with an example from the travel industry:

Table 7-16: Example for the steps towards closure of the sale

Steps	Example	Preference/Details
Get a general understanding of options	General travel offerings for the season	Large travel agencies
Narrowing the options	Continent to be visited	Australia
	Price range	Maximally € 5,000 for the whole family
Key features	Transportation	By air
	Environment	Walking distance to restaurants
Check experiences	Chat with people who have been there	
	Watch a video	
Select a product	Click the "Buy" button	
Sales execution	Get confirmation	Download travel vouchers from web
Post sales support	Prepare for trip	Get foreign currency
		Make restaurant reservation for the first evening
		Buy books and toys for entertainment on the flight
		Buy swimwear
		Make reservation for Opera performance

The steps until closure will be similar in each industry. Please note, though, that in a traditional travel agency the selection of "Key features" would need expensive human support or time consuming scanning of all offerings, while a well-designed website allows the quick interactive search. "Check experiences" wouldn't be possible at all, while companies like Cabana have made this a central part of their web presence. The post sales support couldn't be offered by the travel agency, either, while in the online setting the post sales support examples could be expanded endlessly. There's a huge opportunity for additional sales to be performed by any combination of your value network partners and you can get a commission for each transaction closed by you.

Let's discuss now the impact of electronic communication on your organization and highlight the areas where information and communication technologies can be particularly leveraged. In the past, the departments were working independently and the focus was on research and development and in some modern industries also on local optimizations. The focus is now shifting, in particular for *e*Businesses, towards a cooperation of the whole workforce with a focus on marketing and sales and global optimization.

In the figure below I use a traditional organization breakdown and indicate the areas that need to change for a successful *e*Business. In Chapter 10 we'll discuss the new integrated process model resulting from those changes.

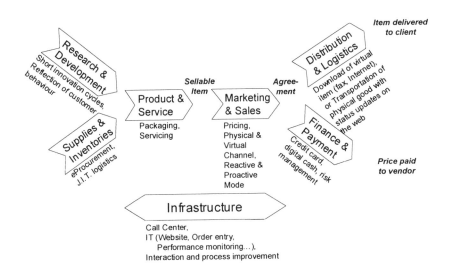

Figure 7-27: Streamlined operations for ongoing improvements

Figure 7-27 illustrates the major activities to get a product or service to your customer. Below each activity, the key impact of doing business online is indicated. We'll walk through it in two cycles: first of all for the initiation of a product or service and the first sales and secondly when the fabrication or service generation and the market are in full swing.

Research and development: Research and development creates a physical instantiation of a new product or service idea. This can be highly complex (like a car or a computer), it can have a less complex physical structure still representing a complex concept (like a book or computer software). It can have no physical structure at all (like data transmission via the Internet), or it can be of little artificial complexity (like natural goods, e.g. fruits, or handicraft products). The new aspect for an *e*Business is that the innovation cycles have been cut back to months or weeks and that the customer buying behaviour needs to be reflected in the next version of the offering quickly. In order to achieve this acceleration, many task forces work in parallel on different versions of the offering. Another impact induced by the web is that you can watch the trends in the market more easily on the Internet than in traditional markets allowing you to respond more quickly to new offerings of your competitors. In turn, this transparency also pushes you to more quickly move ahead because the competitors will react to your new offerings more quickly as well.

As a result of this work you have a concept of how to turn the idea into a product or sellable service.

Supplies and Inventories: Depending on the "ingredients" for your product, the supplies need to be organized. For products, this requires agreements with the suppliers, the appropriate inventories and the logistics to keep the inventories filled. More modern approaches reduce the size of the inventories with just-in-time logistics including electronic procurement of the necessary amount of components. This is one of the key applications for *e*Business. We discussed the Supply Chain Management (SCM) in Chapter 4. The biggest benefit of electronic SCM leads to the just-in-time reception of goods by which no longer expensive or outdated stocks need to be kept thus reducing the financial burden of keeping large storehouses. For the services you want to offer, you need to have the staff, freelancers or partners to actually provide it. They even can work together remotely, i.e. connected by communication devices such as the Internet. In any case, you need to get a clear picture of the dependencies and protect against them with contracts, insurances – and some fallback concepts and partners. You should model the supply and production processes to be implemented in order to clarify and formalize those dependencies.

Based on this activity, you know you will get the supplies you need whenever you need them.

Product/Service: With the concept for your products and services and the necessary supplies, the traditional businesses could fabricate the products and do the maintenance. In *e*Business, the fabrication aspect is reduced and the responsibility expands to an ongoing packaging and re-packaging of the offering. With this packaging I refer to those things you use to drive the customers perception of your product to a high level. This might be a few special features for particular customers, e.g. additional quality, or performance tuning, or additional beauty added to your product. Let's take the example of PCs: Apple is packaging their Macintoshs for different markets. Some have special Desk Top Publishing features to maintain the high reputation in the "home" market of designers and publishers, you can get them equipped with the fastest processors and coprocessors to support private and business high-end users – and you get them in fancy colours. Or let's use the example of Cabana – they have packaged their travel offerings as companion for discoveries. In addition to the actual product, the service concept is to be implemented. This is important for both pre-sales and post-sales servicing. Pre-sales and sales will be discussed in the next paragraph. Post-sales services have to address the customers' needs once they have received the product. It has to include:

- Configuration support (e.g. for software and hardware); as we discussed this configuration can be done to a good extent on the web – like with Dell PCs.
- Warranty work (in particular fixing of defects); in the case of software for example, this can be done by downloading corrected versions of the code from the web – no matter if the original software was also delivered via the web.
- Availability of enhanced versions (as above).
- Communication of experience with the product under specific circumstances, e.g. operating instructions from a hotline service. Such information can ideally be provided on the web or from a database connected with the web. Depending on the licensing agreement, this information can be transmitted for free, or for some payment, e.g. using the Adobe micropayment approach discussed earlier.

At the end of this step, you have an item you can offer on the market. This market can be anything from a big mass market to one specific individual customer requesting the item.

Marketing and Sales: To create the environment for sales, you need to have the appropriate mix of marketing and sales channels. With the electronic business possibilities, you need to decide, if *e*Business shall become the only sales channel, if you want to maintain (or launch) additional physical point-of-sales or direct sales activities, and which traditional marketing means to use. If you maintain different channels, you have to make sure, that your messages and offerings are consistent throughout the channels. This doesn't necessarily mean, that exactly the same products are offered for exactly the same price on the different channels, but you have to make a clear decision and you need to communicate it to your customers, what different options exist.

Let's briefly examine the different sales models: The traditional sales model was primarily to create a positive image for your brand or your shop by marketing activities and to facilitate the customer's decision by some point-of-sales attractions. The pro-active element in this sales approach was the sales person that engaged the prospect into a dialogue leading to closure. In addition to this POS approach, the direct sales approach was invented. The main upside is, that the company doesn't incur the cost for the physical environment and that the focus lies clearly on the pro-active sales personnel.

The downside is, that there are little economies of scale and leverage in direct sales organizations. You can compensate that by mailings or phone calls, but then you just replace the overhead costs for the physical POS by those for your direct marketing activities. With *e*Business now, smartly implemented, you have the benefits of both:

- A great marketing tool where the customer can be actively engaged in finding your offering via search engines and links and where you can inform him regularly via *e*Mail, SMS and personalized websites.
- A (virtual) place your customers can come by to do window-shopping.
- And you can (and should) establish a friendly and forthcoming sales approach.

This online interaction can be implemented for those of your customers who know what they want by just a quick (!) entry into your order form, it should cover as well an empathic consulting if the customer wants to get support and some attention before he decides for your product. You also need to implement an ongoing pricing or re-pricing in order to quickly react to the market trends. Actually, the idea is old. Do you remember the farmer markets where the prices were striked through and the grocery got cheaper and cheaper towards the end of the market time? Nowadays, we see a similar thing in the "traditional" mail-order. Towards the end of the season of the sales catalogues supplementary brochures with the current price reductions ar mailed. And on the web you can define your price at the time of your offering, e.g. once the customer has configured his computer. For a participation in "reverse auctions", i.e. if you want to be one of the suppliers that react to customer price proposals, you need to adjust your minimum prices flexibly in order to be able to cut "last minute" special deals. For such real-time price decisions, your systems need to be able to calculate if it's financially better for you to accept a bad deal rather than not selling at all – e.g. for selling the last Christmas cards the day before Christmas before throwing them away. In this case, however, you need to know all costs related to that specific sale, e.g. delivery, in order not to generate losses by such special deals.

In the end of this step, you have reached an agreement to exchange one of your goods or services against a defined amount of the customer's money.

Distribution: Several of the *e*Business companies will be able to distribute their products or services via the Internet. If this is the case, then you have to carefully check how you can defend against theft of your idea. If it's so easy to be distributed, then everybody can copy it and sell it for half the price or even give it away for free. So it's advisable to encrypt the delivered item in a way prohibiting further copying. For this encryption no standard approaches exist yet, only dedicated developments have been made so far. For example:

- Digital coins can be copied and transmitted, but they have a unique identifier. This identifier (certificate) needs to be approved at each time of transfer to make sure that only one authorized copy of each coin is around. Thus it will be exchanged against real money only once.
- Music is encoded with MP3. This code has a built-in deterioration for the quality of the music at each time of copying.
- A recent development of Adobe and Intertrust allows to view documents only once the customer has paid for it. The PDF documents can be copied as often as one likes, but the reader software checks, if each particular user has paid the price to the documentation provider before opening the document.

If none of those approaches is feasible for you, you need to bundle your online delivery with some physical shipment – be it a CD-ROM, a certificate with some PINs on it or some physical devices necessary to benefit from your product.

For all the physical shipments, you should keep close track of the delivery and keep your customer informed about the delivery status, and you have to have the appropriate network ready allowing quick deliveries. For local distribution, mail or courier services probably are good enough and you can engage them on an ad hoc basis. For international distribution you should carefully check the offered service levels and prices of the large transportation companies.

After completion of the Distribution, the customer has obtained your product.

Finance and Payment: For electronically delivered services, you must make sure that the customers don't run away with your delivery and don't give you the money they owe you. So if you have (virtually) delivered your product how can you make sure to (physically) get your money? In a few years it will be much easier once digital cash will be implemented on a broader basis than just the mentioned Adobe and digital coins examples. Then, you will be able to get a digital payment at the time when the customer opens the purchased document, music or video (in Adobe's approach) or at the time of the customer's decision to buy (with digital coins exchanged at your virtual cashier). But before a broad roll-out of such electronic payments, you need to implement workarounds. The currently most frequently used alternative are credit card payments: the customer has to enter his credit card number, you can (and should) check if the amount is authorized by the credit card issuer and only then you can finalize the order.

And now, at the end of this step you are happy to have received the money you have earned… .

I promised to walk through the activities a second time and here we go. This time we only reflect areas we had to disregard in the first round, because no track record of your success did exist yet. Now we can use the data obtained in the first round of marketing and sales in order to improve the offering.

Research: With some archive of transaction data you can examine the customers' buying behaviour and analyse it statistically: e.g. are there preferences by regions, what triggers the sales success with a particular customer, are there indications to upgrade the product to a higher price version or to streamline and downprice it?

Marketing and sales: You also should implement a good solution to keep track of the interactions with your customer. What are his interactions and buying preferences, how does he use to pay, what did he complain about? Such information has to be immediately accessible by your Customer Care Representatives, no matter if they initiate the contact with the customer or the customer calls them.

Finance and payment: Once you know the customer better, i.e. once he has built up a payment and credit history with you, you can endeavour to allow him deferred payments or loans. You also may consider to allow customers with a good risk profile, to pay by cheque, bank transfer or direct debit. So you need to extend your credit checking capabilities and your interfaces with financial institutions.

Infrastructure: In the beginning of your *e*Venture, many things may be improvised. Everybody in management and staff could serve as customer care representative – but after some growth the permanent phone calls are a distraction so you need to establish a special customer care group. They are in charge of answering the calls in a friendly way on 365 days per year and around the clock. You may have the opportunity to extend your POS presence, but still you have to stay consistent with your offerings on all sales channels. Your IT will permanently grow. Initially, you may have used the Website hosting of an Internet service provider. Order entry, logistics tracking, accounting and controlling, customer value management and data mining are some of the components requiring a more sophisticated approach at each step of growth. The monitoring of your business also will require the appropriate detailed analysis. Many of those functions can be handled inhouse once the *e*Business has grown larger.

Recommendations:

Your business processes and interactions with customers, suppliers and partners will require permanent tuning and reconfiguration. So you should put a team in charge of the ongoing optimization.

- Document your processes and interaction with your customers and partners throughout your organization: Research, Supplies, Production, Marketing and Sales, Distribution, Payment.

- Strive for ongoing improvements in your organizational efficiency and effectiveness.

7.3.3   Partnerships and networking

Customers prefer one stop shopping. This allows them to find their products more quickly and they can adapt to the sales integration with their provider. You may argue that this is not the case for the seekers of "best buys" – and you would be right in traditional business. On the web, though, even such buyers have their "one-stop" preferences. These are not the retailers any more, but the search engine providers, the online auctioneer, or the preferred price finding agent. Such companies run their little applications for huge numbers of people; they have created the new industry of Application Service Providers (ASPs). There's nothing they are dealing with except for some bits and bytes shuffled through the web. But these new companies are excellent in defining communities and they push the partnership models with their outsourcing partners (or suppliers) further and further. They have identified a narrow focus for their business and have complemented this core competency by a good (i.e. profit generating) treatment of customers and partners.

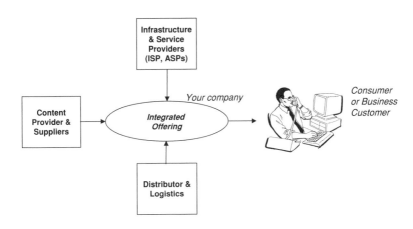

Figure 7-28: Networking – your new position as an intermediary

The most important thing to learn from them is outsourcing. In order to invest your energies into innovations of your core offerings, you need to release yourself of the burden of dealing with all the support activities that are not at the core of your business. You must outsource all such activities – at least for the launch. With that approach you win a tremendous amount of flexibility, e.g. when your business grows you can more easily extend the contract with your call centre provider or payment provider than adjust all those things in your internal organization.

You will find yourself engaged with many partners providing a good part of the environment your clients like (see Figure 7-28 above). In order to run your business effectively, you will soon have a broad network of ISP providers, telecom providers, ASPs for generating business (like search engines), sales partners, suppliers, banks, credit agencies, and ASPs for supporting your internal administration like ERP-hosting or accounting. In some areas or at some times you may compete with them, in others you cooperate. This is not unusual, even in traditional business, but in eBusiness it's also the case for smaller companies. And the cooperations will change more frequently than in traditional settings.

Such partnerships and networks are necessary to maintain an offering that beats the competition. As time-to-market is getting more and more important, you have to either invent and produce the ingredients for a leading offering yourself or you can integrate various ingredients to come up with a new blend of the ingredients that's unique and intriguing in the market. The capability to integrate and to market the blends will evolve to be a key competence in eBusiness, while the importance of traditional cornerstones like invention and engineering will diminish.

We've already discussed the impact of the changing roles of intermediaries in Chapter 4. Successful electronic businesses see themselves rather as a broker or intermediary balancing the customer requirements on one side with the offerings of their partner network on the other side. This is a complete redefinition of the traditional wholesaler or retailer roles! For this integration, you need to take care of managing the knowledge related to your offering across the boundaries of your partner network and of networking with other corporations related to your business. Your strategic task will be to monitor the quality of those partnerships. Initially, the focus will be on a high quality of customer services to gain market share, then you need to seek for operational effectiveness in order to increase your margin.

The evolution of the customer demand requires a regular review of your offerings – and a refinement of the distribution of work and of value generation (often going with revenue generation) between your company and partners.

Therefore, you as an entrepreneur should have a clear perspective on the activities you want to maintain as the core of your own business and any other activities partners can take over. Prepare for the evolution of those aspects of your undertaking from the beginning and throughout the life cycle of your endeavours. A good tool to keep the evolution of your offerings going are planned cycles for the release of new offerings, e.g. the commitment to launch a new offering every month. If it has taken longer in the past to develop such a new offering, you should have your teams work in parallel. If, for example, your standard lead time is three months, have three teams work in an overlapping manner to beat the speed of your competitors – and convince your partners of doing the same.

Recommendations:

- Outsource whatever's not your core business.
- Integrate closely with your partners in order to provide a seamless process across the companies boundaries from offering and ordering to delivery and servicing.

7.3.4   Architecture for customer interaction

Traditional business models were designed in times of demand exceeding supplies and are based on the assumption, that the customers are motivated enough to invest time, energy and money into finding the appropriate offerings and thus eventually fall over a company's product. Advanced *e*Businesses acknowledge the fact, that now the supplies exceed the demands (in the Western countries). Thus, each offering has to find its customers. The consumers and business customers get a broad choice listed when they run a search engine or bot inquiry. Therefore, you need to intensively interact with your customers make it as convenient and easy as possible for them to find your offerings, to like them and to decide to purchase them. The good news is, that you have quite a good support in doing so, if you deploy the right tools.

Let me outline now the emerging architecture to support his intensive interaction with the customers. Many *e*Ventures have adopted a system model as indicated in Figure 7-29 below.

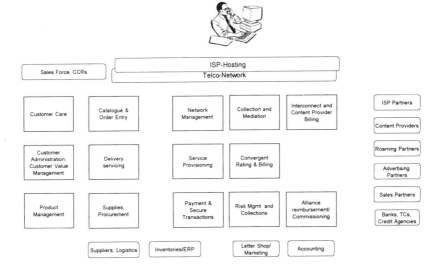

Figure 7-29: Emerging architecture for the IT environment

We will use this model as a framework to discuss the functional support by the various components, to identify vendors for each of them and to frame the project approach. Let me highlight here the most important components.

Customer Care is the front-end in larger organizations supporting the call centre with all the information necessary to serve the customer, e.g. the contractual agreements with the customer, the current status of his orders, the progress of problem reports.

Catalogue and Order Entry is the key interface between smaller *e*Ventures and their customers. All the offered products and services are presented to the customers and their orders are entered in self service and can be tracked online.

Finance with payment and secure transactions is obviously also necessary for each type of business.

Your **ISP** will make your offering as implemented on your website, accessible to the Internet public. We'll discuss details in the subsequent paragraph.

Those key components provide automatic support for each *e*Business. For the other components, software will only be necessary in specific business constellations, in particular for larger companies. In the following paragraphs we will focus on the services to be provided by your ISP and on the finance approaches. Later, in Chapter 11, we'll outline software configurations for different business scenarios and talk about concrete products and vendors.

Recommendation:

- Implement excellent software for the customer facing areas, in particular Catalogue and Order Entry as well as (for larger companies) Customer Care.

7.4   WEB ACCESS: ISP AND ASP SERVICES

7.4.1   Website-hosting

Now let's discuss the specific "*e*" of the *e*Venture. Most importantly, you need a place to put your website on. If you are a small venture, you should use an ISP. He will provide you with all the tools necessary to set up your web site, which is probably not overly complex in this case. Also, the ISPs take care of access and security and moreover you don't need to worry about the telco network. In the beginning of the year 2000, there have been more than 12,000 ISP globally. They interact with one another and are organized in tiers. The highest tier ISPs own large networks (communication networks, Internet web servers, content providers, consumers). They provide global access by partnering or "peering" with other tier one ISPs. The peering agreements lead to a mutual access to their respective networks without cost.

The lower tiers have smaller networks and have to pay the higher tiers for access to their resources, i.e. whenever their customers download information from the servers of the higher tiers. The lowest tier often have only one or two servers and provide access to a small group of subscribers, usually in a region.

The ISPs on the various tiers provide the following services:

Wholesale ISPs/Tier 1:

- Backbone transport of data
- Peering with their global partners
- Access
- Customers are retail ISPs and large corporations
- Examples of Tier 1 ISPs include: British Telecom, Deutsche Telekom, Cable&Wireless, Sprint, uunet.

Retail ISPs/Tier 2:

- Access for consumers and small professionals
- Often provide portals to bundle the contents and gain advertising and sponsoring revenues
- Subcontract with Tier 1 ISPs to organize global exchange of data. Examples of Tier 2 ISPs include: AOL, AT&T, plus thousands of small providers.

The web hosting services provided by the ISPs are not very expensive – you will get away with just a few Euro monthly (something like ten to twenty Euro). Once you've grown larger, you can host your own website on an own web server. In any case you should follow the hints below in order to create a good web presence.

Search engine entries: If you'll raise the awareness of your customers about your offerings by other means than the Internet, you may not need the references in search engines. But why would you let the opportunity to engage with additional customers pass? More than two thirds of the websites currently can only be found, if the user knows the website address, because the websites are not referenced in the popular search engines. Therefore, you have to make sure, that your website shows up in the big search engines in order to make it easy for your prospects to find your offering. There are some with a good coverage of all global websites such as Exite. Unfortunately, these are not the most popular search engines. On the other hand, you find the highly used engines such as Yahoo or Lycos. You can influence your chance to show up on the search engine and also to show up in an early position by a combination of things. First of all, you have to register with the search engines. This can either be done manually – most of the search engines provide an "add URL" feature by which you can register – or you can use a wizard from your ISP or an ASP service such as www.dsr1.com. Such services may costs something (like € 100 – € 200), but it's well invested money, because you can repeat the registration frequently and tune it. This tuning is based on a description of your offering on your homepage in a concise sentence plus a broader set of key words in order to "hit" all the relevant index words. Those key sentences and key words should also be embedded in the HTML meta tags for key words and contents, because some Search Engines prefer those meta tags over the actual text of the homepage contents. Additional criteria for the search engines may include how often the relevant index words show up on your website, how long the overall text is, and sometimes even how many links lead to your website. In addition to publishing this information on your website, you may be able to push your ISP to help you get on a favourable position on the search engine displays. Some of the ISPs, may allow you to link your offerings to the key portals relevant for your usership. Getting your offerings linked with as many other websites as possible and reasonable is a good idea anyway – each link increases the chance that you can win "walk-on" customers. Therefore, you should challenge your ISP even before you contract your web hosting with him to support your endeavours in getting good references in the search engines.

- Does he have special relationships with some search engine providers (like AOL with Lycos)?
- How do those search engines align or counteract with your business targets?
- What help can the ISP provide for a good search engine registration (e.g. registration wizards, HTML meta tag optimization, business pressure)
- Some of the search engine providers start now to create their own community portals – can you get a link from there and at what price?
- What's the reach you get in your target population?
- How can the link or portal provider make sure, that he's actually addressing your target groups?
- How can he prove that they've recognized your offering?
- Is the provider willing to guarantee you specific response rates?
- Can he run specific marketing campaigns for you?

They may ask you for advertising fees – decide upon such options similar to traditional marketing activities.

Design of websites: how fancy do you want your website to look like? On level one of the Maturity Model for *e*Business, it may be sufficient to just publish some standard HTML-information including some graphs and pictures. Or you may need to prepare a specific WML version for your mobile phone users. This can be best handled by your ISP or design partner. At later stages, starting with level two, you need to interface with your internal order entry, process controls and you need to give your customers access to some of your databases. Hence, it will be more appropriate, to keep your web hosting internally. At least, you have to have the full control over the software applications and interfaces – this means, that you possibly can have the hardware and operations outsourced, but you should keep the maintenance of the contents. For all those functions, the appropriate tools need to be in place; we'll discuss some available products in the implementation section.

Talking about *maintenance* and updates: remember Murphy's Law "whatever can go wrong, will go wrong"! Each change you apply to your website has to be thoroughly tested before you publish it on the web. Nothing is more annoying for the user than falling over empty references or links going to no longer existing websites. Therefore, you need to consider up front, how frequently you expect updates to your website. According to the frequency and content of the updates, you have to get your organization and systems support ready for it.

eMail/SMS: as the basic means for communication, *e*Mail has to be supported and for mobile phone customers also SMS. The good news is that all providers and most of the ISP hosting software does support it. If you want to extend the basic *e*Mail functions, then a closer look is necessary. You may want to allow your customers to fill in forms like orders, service requests, complaints and suggestions. Then you have to provide for these forms and for the back end services, i.e. the staff dealing with those kinds of customer interaction. You may want to inform your customers via SMS, so your ISP has to support sending and receiving *e*Mails via SMS.

Chatting: in particular, if you intend to establish customer communities, you have to allow them to exchange their ideas in chat rooms. The chat room needs to be provided technically.

Forum: The messages exchanged in the chat rooms may be recorded and assigned to various interest groups. Additionally, your community members may make direct contributions to a forum, i.e. a database where information on various topics is stored (like Cabana does with the various travel experience or like I do on my entrepreneur community website. The management of the forum needs to be covered both from an organizational (assignment and clean-up of the various contributions, knowledge management) and from the technical perspective (database storage, backup and recovery, indexing of contributions, deletions).

Interfaces: no matter if you keep your webhost in house or if you outsource it, all relevant interfaces need to be developed. First of all, you should check if your webhost supports all formats relevant for you (e.g. HTML, XML, WML) and if he has the good (i.e. low cost) agreements with credit card providers to support your payments. At level two of the Maturity Model, you'll need to interface with your order entry back end systems. This may include a check with the availability of certain products in your inventories and thus an additional interface. You may allow your customers to click on a button and be connected with a Customer Care Representative (CCR). This would require "Voice over Internet" capabilities, possibly a camera installed at the desk of the CCR – and you need to make sure, that during the normal opening times (e.g. 24 hours a day, 365 days a year), a CCR is available. So, CTI (Computer and Telephony Interfaces), and Call Centre support components have to be implemented. By the way, a lower cost alternative for the connection initiated by the customer is to implement a "call back" function. This means that the customer presses a button, an alert is given in the call center and a CSR calls quickly back.

Scalable hardware and software: In case you don't want to outsource your web hosting, you need to have the hardware in place where your website resides. Depending on the size of it and depending on the intensity of usage, the configuration must be so flexible, that you easily can add new servers once you observe bottlenecks in the responses. It's a major downside of small inhouse solutions, that the user requests (the hits on your website) at certain times may create overload situations on your server and thus lead to very long response times for your customers. A peak transaction time is always the early evening when people return from work. The performance requirements during that time drive your configuration: How many customers need to view your catalogue concurrently? How many shopping carts will be filled up at the same time by different surfers? How many payment authorizations need to be obtained simultaneously? How many customer care representatives will be engaged with customers on the phone at the same time? So, the performance has to be monitored and you need to act quickly once you observe peaks of traffic that can't be supported by the existing infrastructure.

7.4.2   Telecom and IP Network

In addition to an ISP you'll need a telecom provider. He has to provide you with the physical access to the Internet. Sometimes your ISP also can be your telecom provider, e.g. if you decide to use one of the large providers, in particular the ex-monopolist PTT that run in most countries now also their ISP services.

Your telecom operator takes care of all the underlying cabling and switching. In fixed wire (both for PC based and TV-Internet), it spans from the hook in the wall, the "last mile" between the business premise or household and the switch, then the switches and routers with all the connections to the location of the other party of a call (or data transmission). The connections are copper cables, fibreglass, terrestric radio transmission, satellite transmission to name some. For mobile communications, the "cells" for the radio transmission come instead of the "last mile" and a mobile phone with WAP display comes instead of the hook in the wall. For areas where a certain provider has no coverage, he needs to agree with partners: Interconnect partners for leasing their lines permanently or on a case by case basis and Roaming partners for using the mobile infrastructure.

In fixed wire and mobile communication, the end user is connected with the local switch. These switches keep track of all calls made and they provide the call details to the places where the bills are produced.

For the Internet, additionally routers and storages for the websites need to be provided. They are located both with the ISPs and with any content provider. At each time a certain website from a content provider is requested by the Internet user, the website is downloaded from the server of the content provider (or from the server of his ISP) and transferred to the user. In order to cut back transmission times, often cache or proxy servers are installed in between in order to keep a copy of frequently requested websites closer to the place of the users. But these are all the things you don't need to worry about as long as you outsource your website hosting to an ISP. Just make sure, that he (or your telecom provider) gives you a line with enough speed both to surf the web yourself with good response times and to quickly upload new information for your website from your systems to the ISP's web server.

7.4.3   Service levels

For the agreement with your ISP and webhost, you need to carefully check the service levels he's offering you and compare the various offers closely. First of all, what are service levels? These are guarantees given by the ISP, that his network will fulfill certain performance objectives. These should include:

- Access guarantees (e.g. 99 per cent availability for your consumers 24 hours per day and 365 days per year, 98 per cent availability for your website updates on all business days).
- Peak downloading performance (e.g. for videos with high motion)/maximum bandwidth.
- Standard downloading performance/bandwidth.
- Maximum number of communication abortion/dropped packet rates.
- Data transmission error rates.

The measurement of the quality also needs to be defined, e.g. if it's done by the ISP or webhost or by yourself. In case of a worse service than agreed, clear discount policies should be stated.

7.4.4   Security

The importance of security features is higher than reflected in most of the current implementations: three quarters of the websites can be changed by hackers! Consider, if the hacker changes the price of your offerings or the account where to send the money...

There's a simple, but very effective architecture to prevent hacker approaches – the firewall. The firewall has to be put between the Internet and your web server in order to allow only users with a proper authenticity to access your systems. Just make sure, that EVERYBODY has to pass the firewall before getting on your web server. If your marketing agency should have a direct access, a hacker could approach you via the agency's systems; if the laptops of your employees can be used for a direct access, any lost or stolen laptop would create the highest threat to your web security. So just don't allow accesses that circumvent the firewall!

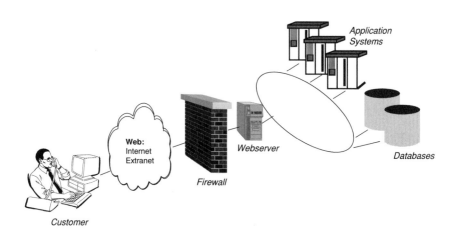

Figure 7-30: Firewall architecture protecting your data

In addition to the firewall, you need to protect the privacy of your own and your customers' data. This can be done by encryption and SET approaches when you exchange personalized data. The sophistication of the encryption is to relate to the sensitivity of the data: an order entry will require less sophisticated protection than the transfer of a credit limit or even an electronic payment.

7.4.5   An emerging type of company: ASPs

Second to ISPs, another type of business is starting, the Application Service Providers (ASPs). Their focus of business is to host certain software applications and generate their revenues either on a subscription basis or on a usage basis. For the subscription approach, often huge software applications are hosted by a third party (e.g. in case of SAP and mysap a multitude of authorized hosting partners of SAP "renting" the software). Customers of such ASPs are often small and medium enterprises.

For the usage based revenues, the software applications are often smaller and the target is the consumer market. The revenues may be either received from the consumers directly, e.g. for interactive research functions, or from marketing partners, e.g. in the case of banner advertising. We have been using examples of ASPs throughout the book, e.g. Search Engines and Bots are tiny applications as well – in this case even free to the consumer as they are funded by advertising revenues.

Recent analysis of industry experts indicates, that the trend will be to see more ASPs soon. This is due to the fact, that making software applications available on the web provides an easy-to-explain value to the customers and thus allows good margins. Another benefit is, that you can reduce the implementation overhead of your software at the customer site, so the customer doesn't need to worry about the operations. This reduction of overhead on both sides allows to more frequently update the functionality of the software and to concentrate the resources and know-how for maintenance, operations and support. The offerings become interesting also for customers that couldn't afford to run their own IT – like SAP who are now also targeting the smaller and medium enterprises.

Recommendations:

Select an ISP and webhost with

- a good standing to achieve a good entry of your offering with a search engine in order to raise a top awareness for your offerings;

- a commitment to support quick response times for your customers – that's more than just good bandwidth;

- flexibility to support your growth.

Use hacker-proof security approaches such as firewall and data encryption.

7.5   PAYMENT, FINANCE AND CONTROLLING

The considerations regarding the actual payments are similar for all types of eBusinesses and they are also similar to (but go beyond) those for a physical shop. The important extension of those considerations is the fact that the transactions take place remotely. So additional uncertainties and risks have to be reflected. Their coverage makes the implementation more complex than in a physical setting, where you always have the option to ask for real money in case you don't trust your customer enough to give him any credit. So let's look now at the options in a virtual shop.

Depending on your offering, you may only need one or two of the presented payment and risk management approaches, but you should be aware of all of them in order to use those most appropriate for your growing business. The same applies to the alliance reimbursement and commissioning.

We mentioned some aspects of controlling so far. Key point is to integrate the various perspectives of your business success into one concise planning and monitoring tool. The large enterprises show the way to approach it and the Enterprise Resource Planning (ERP) tools often are a good implementation of the best practice approaches.

7.5.1   Payment and Secure Electronic Transactions (SET)

For the different types of services specific forms of payment have evolved. It has become good practice on the web, that the provider indicates the payment vehicles he supports and the customer can pick one of them. Please remember our discussion of "clarity and transparency" in Chapter 3. Indicate the types of payments well before your customer stands at your cashier. You may highlight the credit card and digital cash options directly on your homepage – like the stickers on the doors of physical stores.

Credit cards are the preferred payment vehicle on the web. The reason is, that for credit cards, already well established routines exist, how the merchant will receive his money from a bank despite the fact, that there's only an indirect (or virtual) relationship between the two of them. On the web, the only thing to make sure is that the credit card number is safely transported from the customer via the web to the merchant and further to the credit card acquirer (in lieu of the classic physical presentation and paper sales slips). The data transmission has to be secured against interception – you don't want your customer's credit card details be abused by criminals and neither does the credit card acquirer want his retailer receiving an invalid payment authorization. This is supported by data encryption and encoding keys used by the banks and handled by data encryption and SET (Secure Electronic Transaction) protocols.

Figure 7-31 indicates the key steps of credit card transactions, namely: issuing the credit card from a bank to the consumer, presenting the card at the cashier upon purchasing by the consumer to the merchant, getting an authorization for the payment transaction and amount from the acquirer to the merchant, sending the cash from the consumers account via the acquirer to the merchant. We'll also use this figure to illustrate digital micro-payments a few paragraphs below.

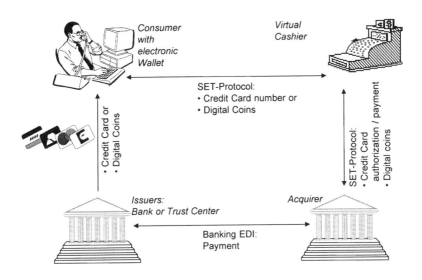

Figure 7-31: Credit card, digital coin and SET transactions

One word regarding the terminology and customer relationship at credit card companies: The credit card companies divide their business in the "issuing" and the "acquiring" part. Issuing deals with licensing the banks who are allowed to use the brand of the card, the physical fabrication of the card with the generation of PINs and the invoicing to the banks for the services provided from the credit card company to the banks. Acquiring deals with the merchants, who are running physical or virtual shops, to exchange their sales slips against money. The commission, i.e. the difference between the face value of the sales slip and the money given to the merchant is the major income for the credit card companies. This has to cover the handling costs, the incurred risk (e.g. payment defaults) and interests. The commission varies by credit card company, by country and by the volume of transactions you have with the credit card company. In general it's somewhere between approximately one per cent and ten per cent.

For you, the only disadvantage of credit cards is this very commission – which can be a terrible part of your margin! Your ISP may have a master agreement with a credit card acquirer, check with him if you can benefit from it.

An approach much cheaper than credit cards was developed by some European banks and coordinated by GZS (Gesellschaft fuer Zahlungssysteme) in Frankfurt, Germany: with a **ec-card** (eurocheque card), the client can make similar transactions as with a credit card, but the profile of the card is different. The credit line is only approximately € 200 per transaction, the transaction is immediately debited to the customer's account, so the risk for the bank is much smaller than for a credit card transaction. And for you the upside is, that due to the lowered risk of the ec-card, you are only asked for 0.2 per cent to 0.5 per cent fees per transaction! Actually, the higher per centage is applicable, when you want to have the bank's coverage for the risk, and the lower per centage applies for transactions, where you use the card just as a payment device without risk coverage by the bank. This approach works well in physical stores where the merchant sees the customer – he should be able to distinguish between a junkie buying some camera with a stolen ec-card just to resell the camera for some dope on one hand and a reliable customer on the other hand.

But does the low cost ec-card approach work in a virtual environment, either? Currently, the answer is yes, in particular for Europe: the Internet customers are still the early adopters, people with a higher education, openness to new ideas, bigger wealth, i.e. low risk customers that allow you to experiment with flexible payment approaches. Even the next wave of customers that the US market is now seeing, carries still reasonable risks, but you may want to cover yourself by some "insurance" premium paid to credit card providers.

Another alternative is, when the consumer entitles his provider to draw the money by a **direct debit** from his bank account, e.g. for recurring charges like the monthly subscription fee for a service. That sounds strange to American readers, but it's pretty common in Europe – and the customers see this as convenience, because they don't need to fill in money transfer forms or checks. The benefit for you is, that you won't have any charges for the financial transaction – unless it's returned because the account is overdrawn. So you need to consider that risk in your equation.

You can also allow **customer initiated payments**, such as bank transfers or cheques after the customer has received the goods. This type of credit requires that your customer has a low risk profile – it's the standard payment method for business-to-business transactions.

For some items or some customers you may insist on **pre-payments**, i.e. the customer has to transfer you the money up front as for many mobile telephone tariffs or you organize cash against delivery of your goods as long as your delivery partner can support that.

Smaller transactions such as certain database inquiries may be charged via micro-payments, i.e. a few cents to be collected from the customer and to be forwarded to the provider. A similar concept as for credit cards is used by the **digital cash**[13] providers. The bank customer converts his real money into digital coins to be loaded on his PC into his electronic wallet. Each digital coin carries its own certificate of validity. This certificate is issued by the trust centre cooperating with the customer's bank. At each exchange of a digital coin, the validity can be checked at the trust centre. This validity guarantees, that the coin can be exchanged against real money again. So you can get the digital cash from your customer together with his certificate and be sure to receive real money in the end.

Let's now summarize the advantages and disadvantages of the various approaches (Table 7-17).

Table 7-17: Payment approaches

Approach	Strengths	Weaknesses
Credit Card	Well proven approach Easy to implement You can get the guarantee of the acquirer to receive the payment	Often high charges (up to 10% of the payment amount) Some customers perceive security or confidentiality issues when transmitting their card number via the web
Direct Debit (including ec card)	If available, easy to implement Only little bank charges Convenient for customers	Only available in some countries No guarantee for payment, i.e. customer credit worthiness needs to be monitored by merchant Some customers perceive security or confidentiality issues when transmitting their account number via the web
Upfront payment	No risk, no bank charges	Handling overhead Customers will not like the perceived distrust
Cheque and customer initiated money transfer.	Little bank charges	Handling overhead No guarantee for payment, i.e. customer credit worthiness needs to be monitored by merchant
Cash upon delivery	No risk Easy to implement	High charges to be paid for logistics partner.
Digital money	Guaranteed payment Customer privacy is maintained	Standard approaches emerge only slowly.

---

[13] While the standards are evolving, also the terminology evolves. Digital coin, *eCash*, Cybercash, digital money are used as synonyms. They refer to trademarks of the various players in this field (see Glossary).

7.5.2 Risk management and collections

Depending on the credit worthiness of your customers you should allow only some of the mentioned payment methods. Starting with deferred payment and ending with a real loan to purchase your services and products, you may allow your customer to use credit lines. This is to be supported by an assessment of the customer's buying and payment behaviour and credit worthiness situation (wealth, income, regular expenses). For checking the credit worthiness, you can implement your own analysis models or you can use the services of banks and credit agencies: they earn their money by doing exactly such risk assessments. To take it to the extreme, you can sell all your accounts receivable to a factoring company, but again this eats into your margin.

In any case, you should closely monitor the payment behaviour of your customers in order to sound the alarms, if someone stops paying regularly. In case of such late payments you shouldn't only consider to stop extending new loans to the customer, but also to collect the outstanding payments before your customer goes broke. Best Practices indicate, that the sooner your alarms sound and the sooner you get in touch with your customer, the amount of collection increases. But be careful not to treat your best customers badly, only because they've defaulted once. Risk management and Collections need to be treated hand in hand with marketing and opportunity management.

The results of the risk assessment need to be fed back to the payment component. You may well continue business with a more risky customer, you just shouldn't allow him a credit, i.e. at the time of his next order, he only can select up front payment or payment on delivery.

7.5.3 Enterprise Resource Planning (ERP)

ERP software comprises of several components. Basically, all financial transactions are to be reflected, i.e. initially expenses paid and revenues received. That's the initial, so called "cameralistic" perspective on accounting. It shows how much cash you have on hand. You also need to consider the capital of the company, received loans, and the investments with their depreciation. Also accounts payable, i.e. invoices you've received but not paid yet, as well as accounts receivable, i.e. services and products delivered but with pending payments need to be reflected. The figures need to be viewed and analysed from various perspectives, e.g. by customer, by region, by products, by types of products, by types of customers, by sales channel, and during the evolution of time. They need to be compared against your budgets and plans; and the plans need to be updated regularly. Also, the day-to-day financial transactions need to be covered, i.e. payments to be triggered, standing orders to be maintained and direct debits to be executed, as well as tax declarations to be prepared at the tax due dates.

All this is handled by the financial components of an ERP system. Your other business aspects are to be reflected in the overall ERP system, too. A payrole component should take care of the paycheck calculation, the withholding tax of the employees, social security transfers, accruals for holidays and should also allow the planning of staff evolution and training. A risk sensitivity component should show the impact of certain risks on your plans and your financial performance and a balanced scorecard component has to track the discussed aspects such as customer satisfaction, employee performance and product innovation.

Recommendations:

- Use a credit card based approach for starting the eVenture – ideally your ISP should have a master agreement with reduced fees with a credit card acquirer, allow cheaper payment types for those customers you have a good risk profile of.

- For smaller transactions you may use the emerging micro-payment approaches.

- Reflect the balanced scorecard aspects in your ERP.

7.6   DISCUSSION POINTS

What of those emerging best practices is applicable to your situation? Let me highlight some key characteristics from the organization and the IT section for you to review.

- Which level of eBusiness maturity is your current target?
- How can you increase the speed of your eBusiness launch?
- How can you calculate the value each customer contributes to you?
- How can you segment your customers?
- Which software components will you need?

Recommendations:

- Maintain a clear customer focus.

- Build an organization with staff flexible for performing different tasks and close interactions between you, your customers and your partners.

8

Background: technological devices enabling the business paradigm shift

A smart integration of "dumb" technical systems has led to the new interaction tool with huge business potential. Use the appropriate strengths of each constituency for an intriguing web presence.

The technologies that currently allow the explosive growth of interactive communication with the consumers are all not too new, but the possibility to integrate a variety of technical tools into one easy-to-use device provides a new quality: the ubiquity of your service offerings. While we are already in the middle of an explosive growth with Internet offerings presented on Personal Computers, this growth will even accelerate with the roll-out of Internet to two additional consumer peripherals, namely TV and mobile telephones.

In the following, the constituencies of the new device are described. The characteristics for each of the constituencies are described in order to allow you to frame your web presence according to your targeted customers.

Additionally, the observation of the technology penetration of each of the components, teaches us an interesting lesson about the expected market acceptance of this new device, the "web" with all its peripherals: The speed of the business success is built upon initial offerings of "free" services. Everybody knows, that there's no free lunch, and the figures with expected revenues of more than € 1,000 billion within the next three years also indicate, that there is money out there. Many of those revenues, though, are not explicit and the consumers perceive many Internet offerings as "free".

Let us walk through each of the constituencies of the new device – they are both an example of how the innovation cycles decreased every time from the invention to an absorption by the market and underline the observation that the markets move once they get the products for free.

At the end of this chapter, we'll revisit the strengths and weaknesses of the various hardware options of approaching your customers.

8.1   TELEPHONE CONNECTIONS

Telephone connections are available for all interesting market segments

A century after the initial invention, telephone connections are now available for almost the whole industrial countries' population[14]. Initially, it was a luxury to get the equipment: cities had to be digged, telephone-poles had to be erected and transatlantic cables had to be deployed. For establishing a connection, the switchboard ladies had to work a while in order to route the call. Today, different technologies have emerged, such as copper cables, fibre optic cables, radio (mobile) or satellite connections – and the construction of such lines is just a commodity as is the dialling to get a connection. For the consumers, the telephone invoice is no reason for concerns. Communication and information is considered necessary for life, so the little money is just paid – and some providers even offer completely free services.

These telephone connections are now used for many other things than voice transportation: pictures, data and entertainment are now transmitted, too. The Internet is based on those telephone connections and you can easily outsource the handling of the telephone network to your network provider and IPSs. There are some service levels, though, you need to consider – and different service levels come at different prices:

- you probably want to exclude (or at least to minimize) dropped calls, i.e. abnormal terminations of the calls for example due to bad radio connections, lack of radio coverage (some regions have only spotty mobile phone cells) or when the subscribers drives in his car;
- you don't want to be in a situation where you don't get access to the telephone network, because your free provider just doesn't have enough equipment;
- you also probably prefer to get through to your ISP at any time – and you want to make sure, that your customers also get access to your website when they want;
- finally, the bandwidth of the lines he's using to exchange data with every possible customers is another important component for your customer satisfaction. If the loading times of your website takes too long or if he

---

[14] According to a study conducted by Ernst and Young, the figure for the US is 60 years of time to reach 50 per cent of the population.

has to wait long for a response to his requests, he may be embarassed and prefer the offerings of other providers.

So, you need to establish clear targets for the services to be provided by your ISP and clear agreements what discounts you get in case of lesser quality. In some cases, you may need to balance the cost for certain service levels with the "beauty" of your web presence: websites with photo images or even with films eat up a lot of disk space and require long times for downloading. I once tried to visit a virtual art gallery and possibly buy a nice picture – by the time it took to watch the website materialize I could have browsed through a thick printed catalogue. So I didn't continue to check the offering of that virtual gallery – and today they don't exist anymore on the web! They should have rather used images with a worse resolution and the dynamic loading possibility of the browsers.

We talked about bandwidth, i.e. the maximum of data exchange that can be handled for your customers by your ISP. When you define that, you shouldn't only think about averages, but also consider peak times. Those peak times are different depending on the countries; in the US for example people very often go to the web when they return from work. Just compare the response times of www.yahoo.com at six p.m. with other times! The cost of your web presence, though, isn't only based on those service levels, but also on the actual usage by your customers. While you want as many customers as possible visiting your website, be careful in swamping them with useless bulky files.

Recommendations:

- Avoid websites that eat up disk space unnecessarily – use photographs or films only when they provide a real value for your customers.

- Select your ISP carefully – based on provided bandwidth and other service levels (for a checklist, see Chapter 13).

8.2   TELEVISION (TV)

Television sets are available in almost all households of interesting target segments

The accessibility of TV by virtually all the industrial countries' population has taken only half a century[15]. Before PCs had a reasonable market penetration, early attempts were undertaken to link the telephones with the TV sets in order to quickly reach private households with commercial offerings. This approach was put at a halt, though, because the initial Internet wave was driven by a large enough PC usage. Assuming that the further penetration will be stalling after a while, the industry is now selling set-top boxes to use similar concepts as the

---

[15] According to the mentioned study of Ernst and Young, radio and TV took less than 40 years to reach 50 per cent of the US population.

technology of the late 1970s to link telephone connections, telephone and TV cable connections and Internet. The new set-top boxes will allow a big improvement of the current Internet presentations: much higher bandwidth is possible than for the current implementations. So it will be possible to run videos on demand and to use video sequences extensively – imagine a real estate broker or an architect allowing a virtual walk through the new building or a travel agency showing the beauty of the town to be visited. In the current Internet, the downloading of such video sequences would take a few minutes, then you run it and then the next sequence can be downloaded. With the new set-top boxes, a real time transmission will be possible. So, that's an opportunity for even newer business ideas.

You don't think of the next generation of business ideas, because you're still excited about the potential of the current Internet? Fine, but consider the fact, that by a web-connected TV not only 20 to 40 per cent of the population can be reached as is the fact with PCs hooked on the Internet, but almost 100 per cent of the target population! And the beauty and brilliance on the TV is also much better than on a small PC screen.

Let's briefly look back to why such approaches haven't been successful two decades ago. Well, it's easy: Interactive Videotext was killed by the cost situation. In order to link the TV set and the telephone, decoders were necessary – and they costed approximately € 300. Plus the PTTs at that time intended to make a margin immediately, so the offerings never really launched. You don't want to repeat that mistake? Very good! If you are really after the mass market, adopt the approach from freepc.com and the free ISPs – give away the set-top box for free and gain your revenues from advertising and sales commissions! This approach obviously wouldn't work for a "boutique" provider, but large corporations can quickly make money or save costs – like minitel in France, where the government-sponsored PTT gave away the minitel terminals for free, offered an online telephone directory and stopped printing the thick paper telephone directories. Quickly you found minitel terminals in many places.

So, I expect a large mail-order provider soon to become the sponsor for TV set-top boxes and use the same approach as the French government with minitel – or as the mobile phone operators when they subsidized the mobile phones hardware for their initial clients. With set-top box prices around € 200 now, the mail-order company would have a nice incentive for good customers by giving away the set-top boxes for the TV sets in order to show the fashion offering with nice films – and make the customers more loyal, also. They should start with the customer segments with the highest propensity to buy as a test segment and then expand the sales channel down to the level where they wouldn't make additional money. Who acts first, will be the winner! So, mail-order companies, hurry up. The catalogue printing business is old fashioned, and expensive, also!

The point to consider for start-up companies is, once the TV-Internet is further rolled out, how your website looks on a large TV screen. Do the colours blind the consumers, are the pictures sharp enough? Can you place the icon to dial up to the Internet and to place an order clearly on top of the TV spot? Or in case the TV set will become your preferred channel, think about how other customers without a large TV set perceive your offering – how will it look on a PC and what subset of information is advisable for a WAP telephone?

Recommendation:

- If you have a service offering that's much better to be shown on TV than on the PC, don't wait until your competition has developed the market – rather start rolling out set-top boxes to your most important customers.

8.3   PERSONAL COMPUTERS (PC)

PCs are currently the most important display for websites. After only a quarter century from their original invention, PCs have had their first waves of explosive market penetration. In western countries half of the households can access PCs – either at home, at work, or (at least for Internet surfing) on a case-by-case basis in Internet cafés.

There's a big choice of consumer sets on the market with basically the same technical ingredients, namely Intel (or Intel-like) processors and the de facto standard in the operating system and basic application with Microsoft Windows and Microsoft Office. For the Internet browsers, on the other hand, currently two major players persist: Microsoft with the Internet Explorer and Netscape with the Navigator.

In this industry, however, sustained success is not guaranteed. Hardware and software had a drastic cost decrease during the last 20 years and in the same way a drastic growth in the capabilities. Still the statement of the Intel chairman, Andy Grove, is true, that the cost/benefit ratio doubles every 12–18 months. With this trend, hardware and software are still improving drastically. So, in this aspect we cannot see that the technology is at an end of its evolution – and new providers may pop up any time.

This permanent development induces ongoing changes. The result is a persisting challenge for business people and consumers to balance the benefits of the technical evolution with the cost of adopting the next generation hardware and software.

The consumer needs to balance the always growing beauty of the presentations versus the cost for the equipment necessary to make the beauty visible and accessible. He or she is forced to purchase the most recent equipment almost year by year, if he or she wants to exploit the possibilities made available by the emerging generations of software and hardware. For example, many applications require Windows 95 at least and 300 MHz processor speed. Such software and hardware has been on the market only since 1996. The same is true for the Internet browsers: new releases or sub-releases are issued almost monthly. This challenge will still persist for quite a while.

The industry is pushing for even cheaper hardware costs (less than € 300) or even free PCs to allow the consumers a quicker replacement of the purchased equipment. So, maybe in a few years we will be used to throw-away computers that only are fit for a few months of usage, but offer reasonable quality – like the throw-away cameras that can be purchased with a film built-in.

For the service provider and *e*Venturer a similar balancing act is necessary. The customer segments he wants to access need to be assessed regarding the equipment they own or can use on one hand and the potential business, i.e. their earnings potential and sales channel costs, on the other hand. The entrepreneur has to consider which hardware, software and browsers to support with his services. If he supports "very old" (i.e. more than 2 or 3 year-old) versions, he won't be able to exploit the features of the newest PCs, i.e. has a less attractive offering. If he creates a fancy product benefiting from all the new features, he is restricting his market penetration to only the owners of the most recent PC generation.

The decision will be different depending on the type of services offered: games and multimedia presentations do need more computer power than standard business applications.

Recommendation:
- Test your website regularly with older as well as with the latest versions of the main browsers (currently Microsoft Internet Explorer and Netscape Navigator) in order to identify potential incompatibilities.

8.4   MOBILE PHONES/WAP

Surfing the web from mobile phones is the latest innovation. With WAP (wireless access protocol) servers, the ubiquity of access to service has become real – you don't even need the physical connection any more. The impact of not enough bandwidth gets another dimension on the mobile handset – even if the bandwidth is large enough, the display is still small. So the content of a website needs to be adapted to a format readable on the small screen. The first applications dedicated to this type of presentation have been launched now: As electronic banking requires no graphics, little text and just a few numbers, this is the ideal initial application. Other services will follow, so you may need to prepare a small band (i.e. small display) version of your web presence.

The interesting point about the mobile phones is, that we can assume the first users of Internet services to be primarily "big spender" consumers and business people. This is an interesting target group for you, so it may well be worth to adjust the contents of your web presence to the capability of your customers' devices. Some interesting considerations are to use the mobile phone characteristics, in particular the knowledge in which area (i.e. in which "cell") the customer currently travels, for dedicated offerings, e.g. hotel and restaurant recommendations (and ticket reservation), navigation aid, connecting train reservations or guide to entertainment and nightlife.

> **Recommendations:**
>
> - Observe the market penetration of mobile Internet usage in order to quickly react once your targeted market segments have gained enough penetration with mobile phones and WAP access.
>
> - Prepare a lean presentation using an information subset coded in WML for quick mobile interactions with your customer.

8.5   DISCUSSION POINTS

At the end of this chapter, let's review the key recommendations – please share your perspectives with your fellow co-entrepreneurs by using the discussion forum on my website www.success-at-e-business.com.

- How much graphic and video information have you found beneficial for what type of end-user sets?
- How do you experience the different buying behaviours in the respective customer segments?
- What's your experience in customer interactions for the different end-user front-ends such as PC, Mobile phone, TV set and others?
- With which browsers are you experiencing problems?
- What hints can you share regarding channel use and transparency of interactions?

> **Recommendation:**
>
> - Surf on the web yourself with the same device you anticipate your customers will use (e.g. PC, mobile phone, TV), in order to find the most appealing websites and to prepare your own website even better.

PART III
Implementation approaches and cost

Target of the implementation is to establish a flexible enterprise that's capable of efficiently generating the value proposition and effectively managing the relationships with its customers and suppliers.

The implementation discussion breaks down into the organizational evolution with the relevant business processes and a stepwise information technology deployment with the necessary integration of the systems of all partners. Based on the plan for the organization and information technology, the financial business plan has to be refined and the project activities can be identified and started.

CASE STUDIES AND BUSINESS SCENARIOS

In addition to the cases mentioned so far, we are going to drill into some different cases highlighting the implementation of the organization and IT. The recommendations in this part of the book are drawn from actual cases. In order to protect the competitive ideas and the business interests of the companies, the actual names cannot be provided. Instead, pseudonyms are used for each of the companies. Also some details of the cases are adjusted due to insights those companies gained in the meantime.

The cases are selected to show you a range of examples that are broad enough to view the implementation aspects from enough different perspectives. Thus we will answer the majority of your questions and concerns you are having while you are about to establish your business. The cases cover new launches, extensions to existing business, and a new approach at an existing service provider. The covered industries are Retail/Sales, ISP and ASP services in Europe and the USA. For an easier navigation in the upcoming chapters I summarize the characteristics in Table III-18 below.

Table III-18: Characteristics of case studies for the implementation section

Pseudonym	Business situation	Offering	Focus
TV-Sale, Europe	The company is established in marketing of household and entertainment goods via TV and handling the actual sale via telephone/ call centre A new retail sales channel via Internet as second pillar for mail-order is to be created Customers are the mass market	Special product promotions by TV or via Internet	Inventory reduction, logistics and electronic channels
Book-Publisher, UK	The company is established as a book publisher Now, the attraction of additional consumers is targeted together with the defence against electronic book shops Customers are professional readers and students	Virtual reading room providing the full text of the books with links to actual purchase possibilities	Marketing
ERP-ASP, USA	Additional coverage of ERP market by offering services on usage pricing instead of licensing Customers are Small and Medium Enterprises	Outsourced ERP system accessible via the Internet	Internet/Intranet as platform for the transport of application data; integration with customers' systems
Free-ISP, Benelux	Launch of services as Internet Service Provider free of ISP charges Consumers are the mass market; partners are a telecom provider and advertising partners	Full ISP offering	Strategic partnerships, billing for telco connection and advertising

We will now discuss the implementation details and highlight the lessons learned in the mentioned cases. Then, we will examine the business approach expressed by the procedures in the front office and back office operations and we'll go through the selection and implementation steps of the appropriate Information Technology solutions. This examination is based on a methodology gained from the emerging best practices framework for the processes and IT components. The methodology can be used by all *e*Ventures from small boutiques with only a few staff to medium sized companies with several hundred employees. To highlight the specific relevance of the various chapters depending on the size of your endeavour, let me summarize the key implementation characteristics.

I use three labels or categories to indicate those characteristics. First of all, the *boutique* category. If you have some product or service to sell and see the benefits from the web as a sales channel, but prefer to stay small instead of establishing a big empire, the boutique approach is right for you. With just a few employees and a small group of customers and partners, you have less dependencies, smaller budgets and less risks to manage than in larger settings. You have a hands-on approach and can make a hobby of yours, e.g. historic car races, model airplane flying, or water sports, your profession by offering the specialist supplies to your hobby-community. Don't expect, though, to work less than in a larger company. You'll work closely with your customers and in case of something going wrong in your "boutique", you'll often end up being the only one capable of fixing it.

The second category is a *small eBusiness*. If you have a new business idea enabled by the web, want to become a broadly known brand and get rich by an IPO, you should start with a larger setting. Your objective must then be to grow big fast! To achieve that, you have to prepare the flexible structures and systems to support that growth. Hence, you need to implement the infrastructure and partnerships ready for the next larger number of customers while at the same time pushing for new customers and hiring new employees. Your organization has to be broader and your investment needs will be bigger than for a boutique. And the examples you intend to follow will be *e*Ventures like Amazon, eBay, TISS or Yahoo. Your challenge will be the permanent re-balancing of growth of customers, organization, partners, IT and budgets. Regarding the software recommendations, I furthermore distinguish between "small" and "smaller" *e*Business to reflect that judgement need. Such components won't be needed initially (while you are "smaller"), but you should be ready to deploy them quickly when you grow.

The third label is a *medium size eBusiness*. That's how existing companies can leverage their traditional experience and transform it into a pro-active enterprise. The heritage of knowledge is usually scattered broadly in the existing organization and the cooperation with partners (sometime even a Joint Venture or a merger) is also handled by a multitude of people. Here, the focus will be on customer-centred streamlined processes based on insights of the buying behaviour of the existing customer base. Those processes will be implemented in close cooperation with suppliers and logistics partners. So, change management issues will be the top concern of the leaders of the *e*Venture project.

The list below can be your starting point for the "configuration" of your company, you then can adjust the indications according to your specific business situation.

For each of the categories, the initial focus areas are mentioned. On those you should put your emphasis when working through the next chapters. Moreover, I recommend to skim also through the other areas to be aware of possible solutions in case you grow faster than you were expecting or if you need a less costly fallback plan should you need to scale down.

It will be useful to browse the web for some of the mentioned software components while you work through the next chapters. Please refer to Chapter 14 for the websites of the software vendors and other service providers.

Table III-19: Implementation characteristics by *e*Venture size

Aspects	Boutique	Small *e*Business	Medium size *e*Business	Details
Customers	Small targeted group, e.g. regional market or small community	Complete coverage of a market niche	Complete coverage of one or several market segments, possibly multi-regional interactions	See Part I
Partners	ISP for Homepage, *e*Mail, Search Engine	Web design agency System Integrator for hardware and software ISP Suppliers Delivery logistics Venture Capitalist	System Integrator for hardware and software Suppliers Delivery logistics Marketing partner(s)	See Part I
Staff size	Less than 10*	10 to 100*	In the hundreds*	
Organization	Improvised	Dedicated teams of approximately 10 staff each	Dedicated teams of approximately 10 staff each, probably scattered over various locations	Chapter 9
Processes	Improvised	Documented processes, in particular for • Marketing and Sales • Customer Care • Back office and Supplies • Finance	Documented processes, in particular for • Community management • Marketing and Sales • Customer Care • Back office and Supplies • Finance • Quality Management	Chapter 10
Web hosting	ISP	ISP	On own web server	Chapter 11
Software	Microsoft Office Internet Catalogue, Order Entry, Payment	Internet Catalogue, Order Entry, Payment CTI, in particular mailing lists, *e*Mail and SMS generation Knowledge Management (e.g. Intranet or Lotus Notes)	Web personalization Order Entry, Payment DWH, Decision Support, CRM/CVM ERP, *E*procurement Database access to customer profiles and delivery status information + specific for business, e.g. Billing	Chapters 11 and 14
Hardware	Pentium PC for each user	Internal network/ LAN with clients and servers. Clients include desktops, laptops, printers. Servers include Webserver	Internal network/LAN and WAN. Webserver (e.g. Sun/ Oracle).	Check with vendor

Table III-19 (continued)

Aspects	Boutique	Small *e*Business	Medium size *e*Business	Details
Web presence	Do it yourself (with tools provided by ISP, Microsoft Frontpage or NetObjects Fusion)	Professionally designed by agency	Updated by internal professional staff	Chapter 13
Initial Costs *	(assuming 5 staff) Software: > € 7,000 Hardware: > € 5,000 Web-Design: € 10,000– 20,000 Integration with existing IT, e.g. database access: € 10,000– 30,000	(assuming 50 staff) > 200,000 €; the main cost driver being the integration with the back end systems, e.g. for real time inquiries of supply chain and delivery information A customized market survey should be performed based on the anticipated system configuration	International research, e.g. by Jupiter Communications and by Gartner Group indicates a range from € 150,000 or € 350,000 respectively and up to several million Euro. A customized market survey should be performed based on the anticipated system configuration	Refer to Chapter 12

* Approximate figures

9

Organizational evolution

Build a marketing minded organization with integrated processes and automation of high process volumes. Establish teams focusing on their respective tasks and ready to adjust their activities as needed by your business evolution. Lead and manage them with clear targets.

9.1   HOW TO BUILD YOUR TEAM

Many things can be copied or adopted, but nobody can copy your team. Therefore, the creation of a pro-active and high performant team is an entry barrier for your competition! Unfortunately, it's not so easy to build such teams. Many steps – and much time – are required until you have everything in place. Fortunately, though, *e*Ventures currently are very "sexy" for the staff and attract the best skilled and most motivated people. So you should have the choice from all backgrounds and ages. But do you really have this choice? Not really – because *e*Ventures are popping up like mushrooms.

So the first consideration for your team is similar to your customer marketing considerations: what makes you different and why should someone like to work with you? Likewise, you will later need to think of staff retention as you need to think of customer retention. We'll discuss now the ways to create a team, the phases of team building and the communication methods within the team.

9.1.1   Creating the team: start from scratch versus reshape?

In general, there are two different scenarios: either you can use the greenfield approach and design your organization from scratch or you inherit some organization and need to adjust it to the new activities.

If you design everything from scratch, your main activities and headaches will be:

- To hire staff with the appropriate skill sets.
- To clarify the roles and responsibilities of your staff.
- Being ready to be permanently understaffed.

Your primary focus should be on creative people with a dedication to get the job done. You should avoid hierarchical structures as far as possible, and rather use a task based and delivery oriented approach.

If you inherit some organization, your first objective will be, that your staff has to "un-learn" the old approaches and absorb the new setting. Don't accept any traditions – you are creating a new culture with new success stories, dreams, approaches. Old legacies are the worst enemy of success in this case. On the other hand, you have a big asset, namely the experience of your staff regarding your offering – and your experience with each of your colleagues. Therefore, your main activities will get some other gist:

- To assign the staff to the position each person is best suited for.
- To make them un-learn the old approach and absorb the new culture.
- Being aware of all traps due to unspoken "old" rules.

9.1.2   Team approach and team building

Different authors describe the team building activities with different words – but they all agree, that team building requires various stages. In the following, I only describe the major stages; gurus on that topic do refine that to some ten steps, but that goes too far for our purposes. And you probably won't have the time anyway to go through an explicit ten-step team building programme. You have to consider the basics, though:

Orientation: This is the stage where everybody has to find out what's expected from him and how he best should perform his task. To accelerate this orientation, it is very useful to share the conceptual considerations that you hopefully prepared using the checklists from Part I of this book with the team. Depending on your management style and on the amount of research you've invested already, this can be presented either as a given objective or as an idea to be refined by the team.

Trust building: To create a team spirit it's indispensable to have trust between all the individuals. Various little things help in achieving this. The easiest is to have joint meals while you work long hours anyway – this creates a more relaxed atmosphere, where people get closer to each other. Then, you might want to share your private situation with your team – this indicates that you trust them, therefore they are invited to trust you. Another exercise is to organize events, when the team gets together in a private or adventure setting – like hiking or rafting together or doing outward games. In the rush of everyday business, in particular at the time of business launches, this is often disregarded, because the entrepreneur and his team have so many other worries. You may decide not to spend some attention in trust building, but the consequence will be that your most important contributors will disappear after you've achieved the first joint successes, because they will be dis-interested in the common targets of the team – and they may be burned out anyway.

High performance: In order to have everybody understand his team-mate "blindly", it's required to come up with some rules and procedures. Depending on the size of your *e*Venture, the number of those rules and procedures may be different, but let me indicate the key areas you should agree upon:

- Commitment – how much is everybody willing to contribute: the team should agree on the details such as the objectives to be reached, responsiveness in case of urgencies, expected working time (daily, weekly, monthly, annually).
- Success indicators – what is it everybody is striving for: use the approach of the Balanced scorecard, i.e. span your monitoring from profitability, customer satisfaction, flexibility to team spirit.

Refreshment: From time to time, the team has to step back and rethink, if the approaches still fit. Therefore, the activities as described in the earlier stages have to be revisited and require updates. Also, individual refreshments are necessary to avoid extreme burn outs. Depending on your business requirements, you may decide to allow breaks like traditional holidays or apply sabbatical schemes like high performing US companies do. Such sabbatical schemes may be that every five years, the high performers in your company are entitled for a three-month paid break to recharge their batteries – by the way, you should fine tune such an approach in a way to prevent attrition. If you experience your staff being exposed to resignations after three years, allow them a break after four years, so the motivation to stay in should be supported.

This refreshment has also to include an increase of the joint capabilities of the team. In fact, many job profiles will change in order to follow the changing requirements of *e*Business. Forrester research estimates up to 40 per cent of IT employees getting new responsibilities and titles during the next five years.

9.1.3   Hierarchies versus flat organizations

Flat organizations work better than hierarchical structures. While traditional management approaches recommend a "span of control" of eight to ten people, the team and task force approach works effectively for up to 30 reports. In order to make it work, though, you need to establish a good environment. In particular, there must be an open communication with quick turnaround times and the leader of the team has to be approachable almost around the clock.

Technically, this means,

- that your team has to have a common working environment for cooperative work groups (like Lotus Notes) with access to the working materials of the whole team;
- that the team-mates need to communicate via eMail, mobile phones and voice mail;
- and that you implement issue escalation procedures that allow quick fixes of arising problems and risks.

Psychologically, it means to have "open door" policies with the leaders and managers being open to take the time in case bad news or new risks should arise – and of course also for new opportunities. They must personally be in charge of pushing issue resolution and risk mitigation in a constructive manner, i.e. by establishing the necessary task forces to fix the problems rather than the old paradigm to wait for the crisis, seek those responsible and punish the innocent.

Also, the objectives must be precisely clear and well communicated – once the team has agreed on the objectives, write them down on one page (or one chart) and pin them on the wall together with an assessment of the up-to-date progress towards this objective. Therefore, the leader of each of such task forces must have very good interpersonal skills – much more than traditional managers of a smaller unit. Less will be regulated than in a hierarchical structure, but more requires good ad hoc judgement.

Recommendations:

- Organize your eVenture team by going through the explicit phases Orientation – Trust Building – High Performance – Refreshment.
- Organize your teams around tasks, keep the organization lean and flat.

9.2   ORGANIZATION FOR THE LAUNCH

Let's recall the key functions we discussed in the Emerging Best Practices section. Depending on your business approach and also depending on your insourcing versus outsourcing decisions, those functions include:

Providing the service or product
Marketing and sales
Customer care
Order management and logistics
Payment and collections

In this chapter we discuss the configurations of the organization units in charge of those functions for the presented cases. The functions are further detailed in this chapter regarding Processes and Responsibilities. At this stage, let's work with some pre-understanding of those terms[16]. In addition to the different configurations of the above mentioned functions, you need to support some internal functions:

Human Resources: They are in charge of recruiting, supporting the line managers in monitoring the performance of staff, supporting the training needs and aligning the compensation packages with the market. In all these cases, the actual decisions should be taken by the line managers and entrepreneurs, but HR has to establish the appropriate "mechanics" to increase efficiency and effectiveness. This may include checklists for performance evaluations, sample training programmes, and salary comparisons. They also have to trigger the activities to make sure, that each employee gets a performance review in the agreed cycles (e.g. annually).

Finance and Controlling: As you need accurate figures about the performance of your overall company, the finance and controlling staff needs to take care of all your money related activities. This includes the payment of your invoices, salaries and taxes, the tracking of receivables and the preparation of your accounting records. In addition, you may add the monitoring of the other objectives as expressed in the Balanced Scorecard to the responsibility of that group.

The discussion of the organizational implementation starts with the smallest company and ends with the largest case.

9.2.1   TV-Sales Internet launch

Our first example deals with a company reselling physical goods. This company has already experience in selling their goods remotely by using TV as marketing vehicle and getting the phone calls from customers ordering the goods. Accordingly, this company has already implemented a good customer care and

---

[16]You may argue, that the topics organization, processes and IT should be discussed in another sequence. Theory suggests to first look at the processes abstractly, then configure the appropriate organization around it and finally look at a well integrated IT support. In my experience, though, the sequence used in this book is most easy to understand: start with the people, i.e. the organization, then discuss what those people are supposed to do, and finally look at the technical support they can get. In real life, you'll need to go through the various design decisions in iterations, anyway.

the agents talk all languages the company is dealing in. In addition, the whole logistical is already covered: receiving the orders for the goods from their customers, handling the delivery of the goods, getting additional goods from their suppliers, and tracking the payments (Figure 9-32).

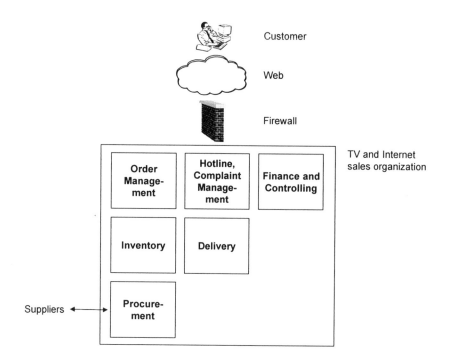

Figure 9-32: Organization of TV and Internet-based retailer

Order management includes the order entry and order execution. Order entry can be done by the customers via the Internet or it can be handled by Customer Care Representatives. For both those alternatives, it has to be made sure, that the order entry system has all products listed and that the prices are accurately reflected. Order execution covers the regular information to the customer of the order status (this can be done by eMail or by a call depending on the value of the good and the importance of the customer); it further includes the triggering and monitoring of this order in conjunction with the adjacent functions that are described below.

Inventory in this case is a separate function as next to receiving the orders, the most critical aspect is to fulfill the customer's requests. It deals with tracking of the goods that company has on stock. Main result of inventory keeping is the triggering of additional supplies once the inventory falls below certain thresholds. This sounds like relatively trivial, but consider cases where a product consists of more than just one component like a set of music CDs together with a CD rack. In those cases, each of the components must be separately monitored and the trigger for re-order must be set independently for each component.

Procurement includes all the activities necessary to get additional goods into the inventory (or immediately forwarded to the customer). Here, the price negotiations are to be reflected, the order quantities, the delivery commitments and the entitlement for specific people (or even systems) to exercise an order of specific supply volumes. Also, the concrete implementation of such re-orders (be they automatic or manual) is to be done. In a small setting, an approach using just some lists or spreadsheets should be sufficient. In larger organizations, you will probably need a full blown Enterprise Resource Planning system.

Procurement deals with the suppliers that have agreed to general ("master") rules and procedures with their customers. Those rules are used to empower the employees to directly order the goods without needing additional approvals. and it can be used for automatical implementations (see next chapter).

Hotline support/complaint management is a very important means to improve the company's perception by the customers. The hotline can fix most of the problems of everyday use of the products – so they avoid the customers getting angry. In fact, complaints often lead to a better understanding of the customer.

Delivery deals with all the details from the providers' shelves to the customers: Packaging the product including printing of address labels, attaching an invoice, providing the status of delivery in order to inform the customer and the actual delivery. Delivery is usually outsourced to a logistics provider such as the incumbant of the former monopolist like the state owned postal services or private providers like UPS, FedEx or DHL.

Finance and Controlling is implemented with a small ERP system.

Lessons learned from TV and Internet Sales retailer launch:

This implementation highlights the importance of integration:

- The customers are integrated with the offering by self service, e.g. to adjust their profiles
- The suppliers are integrated by *e*Procurement
- The delivery is integrated into the service concept.

9.2.2   Electronic marketing channel for Book Publisher

This company intends to open an additional marketing channel to the existing paper based marketing activities. Aggressive direct sales are not intended via this channel in order not to spoil the relationships with the existing sales partners, i.e. book stores and retail chains. Instead, an interesting feature is used: the company makes their books fully available for an online browsing. People can in theory read the complete book. There's a little trick, though: each page is stored separately, so that someone desiring to read or print the whole book would need to open up as many Internet pages as the book contains. The expectation therefore is that it soon will become boring to read through the whole book and that the surfers will follow a link to an online bookstore to obtain a paper copy of the book.

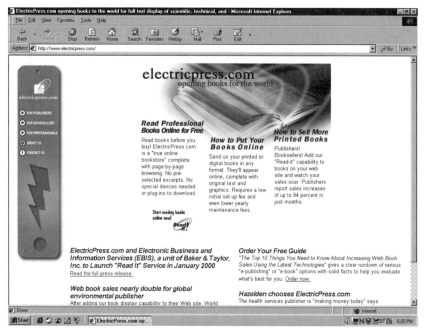

Figure 9-33: Electronic book marketing; electricpress.com

As the Book Publisher didn't implement a sales function, it's sufficient for him to provide a general support function in order to check incoming *e*Mails. They are treated like paper mail, i.e. they are forwarded to the person in charge, e.g. the publisher, marketing people or the direct sales partner. As the Internet is seen as a marketing channel and the number of users is still relatively small compared to the total population, a low cost approach had to be adopted. No specific organizational unit could be afforded, instead all the scanning of the text and providing it for the web surfers was outsourced. The partner covers the areas of website design and hosting as well as scanning the most recent books.

Lessons learned from Book Publisher's web approach:

- Use creative ways to attract the customers' attention.

- Outsource efforts for website preparations, if you need to follow a low cost regime.

9.2.3   Providing IT services via the Internet (ASP)

For the ASP extending his earlier software licence sales by the possibility to pay for the service on an "as used" bases, the key point is to have state of the art services, e.g. accounting or ERP software. In our case, this is provided by the existing business activities. The Internet is just an additional channel and needs to be profitable pretty soon. To make the software fit for the global Internet market, the company has to make it compliant with the local regulations of his customers in all countries he's serving and of the industry trends. Those local regulations include for example accounting rules, VAT calculation procedures, or keeping of auditable records. The industry trends in this case have been dominated in the last years by easy-to-understand management reporting as well as risk management considerations. Therefore, the organization is focused on the IT services; those are embraced by the necessary support functions (Figure 9-34).

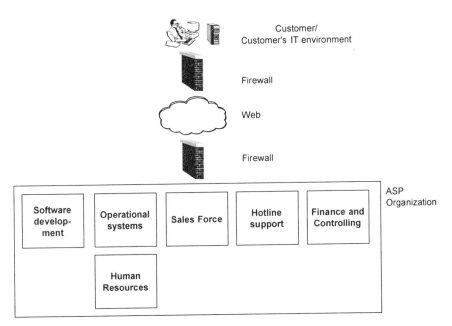

Figure 9-34: Organization of a web-based Application Service Provider (ASP)

Software development: Based on the mentioned industry trends, changes in the legal regulations and feedback from the customers, software updates are to be designed, developed, tested and transferred to the operational unit. A variety of releases need to be understood and require support. Usually three generations of software have to be handled by the development team: the one currently in production, the next generation which goes through the various release stages before it's taken over in production, and the next cycle where developments have started.

Operational systems: Those systems are the backbone for the business concept. They need to run smoothly and have to be operated according to the agreements with the customers, and data backups and archiving has to be performed. In addition, the performance needs to be closely monitored and hardware extensions or software tuning need to be deployed. Moreover, the functionality needs to be regularly updated based on new releases made available by the software development unit. Each of the hardware and software updates and extensions require tests, updates of the operational procedures and possibly informing the clients of new or changed features.

Sales force: As this company is dealing with business customers, a strong sales force is appropriate. This sales force has to generate leads, identify prospects and close service contracts according to the offering scheme of the company. Some of the sales activities can be done centrally supported by sales planning and sales controlling activities, but the majority of the sales activities will take place in close contact with the customers. Depending on the size of the sales force, a breakdown in various regions, industries or a distinction between cross-sales to the existing customers and new prospects applies.

Hotline support: The standard features of the software need to be explained on the phone in case of questions of the customers; this is handled as first-level support. In case that the hotline support unit cannot answer the customers' questions, they relay back to operations or development for second-level and third-level support. Moreover, the hotline support unit stays in contact with the operations and system development in order to summarize problem reports for them, e.g. handling issues that suggest re-designs of some functions, or desired additional functions.

Finance and controlling: Beyond the internal finance planning and controlling as already discussed, this unit also needs to take care of timely invoicing the customers for the services they use. Payment regimes may follow subscription approaches or usage based pricing, e.g. how long customers have been using the services, how many transactions have been processed, or how large the business value (financial amounts) of the produced reports has been.

Human resources: In addition of the standard responsibility for HR to perform recruitment and development of staff, a particular attention in this case is the training of staff according to the functional features provided by the software systems, the software development approach and operations requirements.

Lessons learned from ASP launch:

- If you have a strong reputation, benefit from it for your launch.

- Use a low cost approach for the technical implementation, but invest heavily in getting your brand known in the market, e.g. Internet references, paper media, advertising.

9.2.4   Launch of an Internet Service Provider (ISP)

The largest enterprise finalizes our discussions regarding the organizational implementation: an Internet Service Provider. The focal area in this case is the telecom and webhosting network. Not many readers of this book will intend to launch an ISP company, but almost everybody will have to deal with them – so I guess it's interesting for you to "look behind the curtain".

The units necessary in an ISP beyond those of the earlier discussed cases are in charge of the necessary activities for the network and around it:

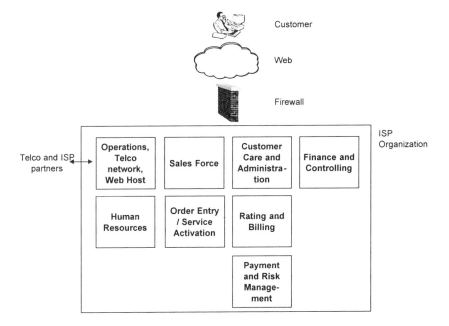

Figure 9-35: Organization of an Internet Service Provider (ISP)

Operations (telco network management), web hosting: Primarily, the operational systems include the telecom and internet networks. Those networks require a large IT environment which will be discussed in the IT section. However, this network needs permanent maintenance, performance monitoring and extensions. Therefore, the organization has to deal with operating the network 24 hours a day, every day in the year. Several hubs for the operational service need to be established and are to be supported by a three- or four-shift teamThe teams have to commit to certain service levels, e.g. minimum availability of the local hubs and fallback solutions in case of problems. The commitments are expressed in SLAs (Service Level Agreements). In order to fullfill those SLAs, the local organizations need to have field forces for upcoming repairs. In addition to quick reactions in case of problems, maintenance such as upgrade of software releases, extensions of hardware and software as well as the connection of new subscribers.

Human resources: A particular attention for the HR unit is the balancing of workload with the available staff in the various locations. Relocation policies need to be prepared and/or local hiring approaches need to be adopted. In such a decentralized organization, assimilation and training needs to be prepared in order to have the same service quality in all places. Regular exchange of skilled resources may be appropriate and additional quality assurance programmes will become appropriate.

Sales force: Many sales aspects can be covered by a central call centre as describe before, but additionally, local sales agents are in charge of dealing with key accounts and resellers.

Order entry/Service activation ("Provisioning"): At the closure of a contract with a customer, a quick activation of the agreed services is necessary. Two approaches have to be supported: an Internet based approach and a manual approach. The Internet based approach is that a new customer applies via Internet and immediately gets his confirmation with accounting details and access control such as password back. The manual approach can be used for customers or transactions with a higher risk profile, where a traditional identification of the customer is necessary. The latter can be used for customers where the company has doubts about their payment morale or for transactions that require additional security or that need to comply with specific regulations such as banking transactions.

Customer care and administration: The standard features of the services need to be explained on the phone in case of questions from the customers; also the customers need to be pro-actively informed about pricing and tariffs. The customer care unit "owns" the relationship with existing customers and needs to take care of marketing activities including customer retention. Another important aspect is, that the customer care needs to be in close contact with the networking units in order to report problems back to them (e.g. non-availability of certain switches or services) and to proactively inform the calling customers about the status of fixes of network problems.

Rating and Billing: The products, tariffs and discounts in the telecom and ISP area have become pretty complex and are subject to regular changes. Given the big number of transactions, but each of them amounting to only a few cents of payment, the processes need to be implemented very efficiently. While the support of those processes usually is handled by dedicated systems, the organizational responsibility can be handled in one unit, at least at the launch stage. The dedicated systems have been identified in the Emerging Best Practices section and will be further explained in the next chapter. They cover:

- Collection and Mediation of the call records as provided by the switches and the Internet hits.
- Convergent Rating and Billing of the transactions and of recurring charges such as annual or monthly fees.
- Interconnect and Content Provider Billing based on all the transactions received from each particular partner.
- Alliance Reimbursement and Commissioning such as advertising fees or sales commissions.

For the automatic processes to run properly, the rating and billing unit has to take care of setting up the products and tarrifs, of testing this set up, of checking applicable discount schemes and of course of performing permanent quality checks of the processed data in order to send quality invoices to the customers. With larger sizes of bills, separate print shops to produce the physical bills may become appropriate or electronic delivery of the bills; for private and business customers this delivery may be via the Internet, for business customers with large numbers of transactions CD-ROMs can be desired, either including an analytical framework to check the bills. Also, the agreements with the various partners such as interconnect partners, content providers, advertising allies or sales agents need to be reflected properly in the systems.

Payment and risk management: The different payment approaches need to be agreed with the payment providers, e.g. credit card issuer organizations such as Visa Card or Mastercard/Eurocard, Trust Centres for Secure transactions or with the banks in case of direct debits. Also, the monitoring of the customer performance is done in this group. In case of late payments, the customers have either to be reminded by letter, eMail or calls or appropriate steps need to be taken to make sure, that the customers don't default depending on their risk profile. Such steps may include preventing further use of the system in case of sustained payment delinquency.

Finance and controlling: Beyond the internal finance planning and controlling as already discussed, this group needs to consolidate the figures from Billing as well as Payment in order to come up with the full picture of the financial situation of the company.

> **Lesson learned from ISP launch:**
>
> A high degree of automation is required in order to deal with the big volume of data to be processed.

9.3   GROWTH PHASES

So far, we have described the structures for the launch of the companies. Each of the structures is designed in a way to support subsequent growth. Whichever of the models you intend to adopt – be ready to split any of the described units once your growth demands such a step – and also look for areas where it may be more appropriate to insource activities that were outsourced earlier or vice versa. Look for synergies between various groups once you have reached a certain size. For example, sales and customer care require similar information regarding the customer behaviour. In a larger enterprise, you can support both those units with customer care software including data warehouses, data mining and automatic workflow procedures.

9.4   LEADING AND MANAGING

In this section, I'm referring to the descriptions of leadership that Howard Gardner wrote with many great examples of well known leaders in politics and public life plus my own experience from the big number of projects I've executed myself or with my various colleagues. In general, the job of leaders and managers is to align the energies of the team members in order to maximize the outcome. The team has to share one objective in order to be most efficient and effective instead of wasting energies by working against each other.

9.4.1   Leaders and managers

Every undertaking requires a person equipped with an idea, able to create an image or vision about how beautiful the future will be when you go with him and how lousy you feel, if you fail to do so. This person has to be capable to influence significantly the thoughts, feelings, and behaviours of the individuals around him. In our business setting, these are both the individuals to make up the organization of the *e*Business company and the customers who are ready to experiment with a new sales and service experience. So, this person is what we call a leader. Major measurements of success for leaders are personal fulfillment and effectiveness of the team. And I assume that you are such a person, because you are couraged enough to endeavour the journey to an unknown continent. What makes a leader happy is to see how his idea materializes. His primary attribute is vision and an awareness of the industry and market trends. To stay in the picture of a journey – remember the saying:

> If you want to build a ship, don't teach how to build one, but describe how beautiful it is on the other side of the ocean.

Different attitudes and capabilities are required from a manager. They are in charge of execution – either the execution within an organization, then they usually manage a group of people or a department, or the execution within an organization, then they manage the task forces in charge of the activities. Their primary attributes are consistency and accuracy. Managers have to have each single process in the organization or each task in a project in mind, they must be aware of the dependencies, develop the skills and cooperation within their team and strive for excellence in the processes or tasks. The measurement of success for managers is to meet their objectives like

- Sales figures
- Process efficiency (e.g. number of calls handled per hour)
- Deliverables (e.g. a timely implementation of the components for your virtual shop).

In a small environment, often the leader has to be the manager, too. It's good to have both capabilities together in your person – actually you probably were managing a team before you started your *e*Venture, but I want to make you aware of the different attributes you have to cover. And you have to be clear, when you wear your manager hat, e.g. during project execution, and when to wear the leader hat, e.g. for pep talks.

Both types of people, leaders and managers, have a good part of characteristics in common, that's why the those two are often confused in discussions. Leaders and managers

Motivate other people to support them in achieving their targets. Different forms for that motivation do exist, but that's less a question of leaders versus managers, but of personal style and the concrete situation. The most advanced form of motivation is to have enough charisma that people just do what you like them to do. That's nothing you can learn or preserve, often you may find out that it works in one environment while in another environment, you need to complement your charisma with other capabilities in order to achieve what you want. Those other things can be to establish incentive systems be they of a financial nature like sales commissions, or non-financial like special events and joint fun at reaching certain milestones. In general, leaders and managers can show the benefits in joining the journey.

Communicate clearly and concisely with the people around them, e.g. employees, customers, partners, competitors and the public. With those, the communication is not only about benefits generated by your vision, but also about things you don't want them to do, e.g. when they violate your interests. Usually, the communication will be oral in meetings, written in *e*Mails and letters for official documents, e.g. formal proposals, complaints, issue escalations and in the form of presentations, e.g. for performance and risk reviews. In order to be understood clearly, leaders and managers can easily abstract from all the unnecessary details and adjust their arguments according to the recipient of the message. This means they keep it simple and tangible – more often than not disregarding academic relativity and sometimes even disregarding fairness.

Think in structures, i.e. they don't see only the surface of how the vision looks like, but also the "machinery" necessary to get there. This machinery is less a question of brick, mortar and physical engines, but of human interaction, mutual and individual interests, responsibilities, capabilities and processes. And leaders and managers are able to explain the machinery to provide the people around them with an appropriate frame.

Judge in a way optimizing the benefit for the company, the team and the customers. Usually, this means fair balancing acts – but dependent on the situation some decisions can be perceived with some frustration. Still, it shouldn't be allowed for the staff to challenge the judgement capabilities.

Are accepted authorities; authority is based on strengths, experience and achievements together with a high level of integrity and showing a good example. So, a project manager needs to deliver to his own standards of delivery; a group or department manager has to follow the procedures he has defined; and the leader of the company has to be as innovative and forward looking as he wants his company to behave.

Let me summarize with a practical remark: leadership characteristics and managerial capabilities can be found in many persons. In fact, the roles and responsibility within the organization prescribes to what extent every leader or manager has to apply the appropriate skills.

Recommendation:

- Be clear, when to wear your manager hat, e.g. during project execution, and when to wear the leader hat, e.g. for pep talks.

9.4.2   Setting and communicating targets

Defining targets is a top down and bottom up process. Step by step, the overall targets need to be refined and broken down into managable pieces, like sales figures, performance objectives or concrete deliverables. Each person in that chain has to add his own experience and judgement, his understanding of his own skills and the skills of the group he's managing. And he has to consider the values and beliefs of the group when setting the targets – in particular when new frontiers are to be encountered. Then you get the feedback from the people you want to commit to the plan – and they may have some valid points why specific targets cannot be achieved.

Your actual planning process depends on the number of organizational layers you have in your organization. Evidently, the less layers you have the quicker you can come up with committed targets (that's one of the many reasons for "flat" organizations). Also, it may be wise to set the targets initially slightly higher (e.g. by 20 per cent), than what you really need to achieve. Raising the bar often pushes the creativity of your top performers, so you may even achieve a better result than you originally thought. The first step in the regular planning and review process is to take the company vision, break it down into some high level measurable numbers (e.g. using the business plan and balanced scorecard approaches) per major operational unit. Then the managers of each unit have to review how they can achieve the targets; this is done again by subdividing the figures into the responsibilities of the various groups within their unit. The feedback each manager gets from his reports needs to be balanced, and the higher level responsibles need to discuss, compromise and approve the various plans.

This process indicates, that each target setting happens in iterations. It's now the leader's job to make sure, that there is an end in the iterations. It doesn't make sense to refine the plans for ever; instead clear timely deadlines have to be given until the targets are agreed and the organization commits to them.

When you follow this outline of the process and record the results (with their iterations), you have a sound base for communicating plans and actuals. I described an approach where you broadly share the planning considerations with your key contributors and thus achieve a high degree of buy-in. The resulting plans then need to be presented to those people not involved in the planning process.

This presentation should include the key figures (financial and non-financial achievements) and the considerations that lead to the figures. Also, the impact on the staff and on customer interactions should be highlighted. Use the target definition as a vehicle to align the activities and orientation in your team! Also, review the results regularly, share them with your team and invite for suggestions how to improve, in particular in areas where you recognize to fall back behind the plan. The presentation of the plan and the review of the achievements will be the base for you to increase your corporate performance, to celebrate the success with your staff and to deepen the team spirit.

If you want to implement the balanced scorecard approach as discussed in Chapter 7, the key question is how to measure the various figures. In fact, you should only use such attributes in your scorecard where you have an idea how to measure them. Let's walk through the various options.

Interviews or surveys are a great way to obtain informal data, but not for quantitative data: Once you ask people for rankings (or even yes/no) questions, you can't be sure that the answers really compare to what they answered the last time. So the main purpose of the scorecard, namely to monitor trends, is jeopardized. So, yes, perform interviews and surveys, but don't try to get too many measurable answers out of them – and don't do them too often because people get bored.

Manual tracking and statistics are another option, actually this is a pretty good possibility as long as the numbers you are working with in the various fields are statistically large enough while not too high. So if you work with a small number of business customers, it may be appropriate to implement a process to daily count the customer calls, complaints, proposals made and other possible interactions relevant for you, to enter them in a spreadsheet and to perform the monitoring with the spreadsheet. Actually, this even gives you nice charts at no extra cost and you get a real "visibility" in case of problems.

Automatic counting is the only choice whenever you have larger amounts of items to count. In particular that will be true for the financial aspects. But here's a danger: such activities are often outsourced, e.g. to your accountant. You can outsource it, but you need to make sure that you get the results in a format to reflect it in your scorecard spreadsheet.

Recommendations:

- Develop your company's plans jointly with your key staff.

- Manage not only financials, but also pride of employees and satisfaction of customers by using the balanced scorecard with the areas Customers, Staff, Innovation and Financials. These figures have to be recorded and be collected, e.g. in a spreadsheet and you should regularly check the trends.

9.5   MISTAKES TO AVOID

Above we have discussed the breakdown of the organization into units. Well, at least it could be understood that way. But I must tell you, that I don't like this connotation. The contrary should be achieved, namely a smooth cooperation across all units without consideration of the "borders" of the units. Each unit is just a cluster of specific skills and capabilities in order to support the overall interactions with the client. None of the units has a purpose in itself!

Mistakes to avoid:

- Make it clear to your staff, that units have to provide services and that they can change, i.e. they can get new responsibilities assigned, they can increase or decrease in size or they can be relocated or split.

- Don't assign names to your units that sound too fixed. Rather have an activity-oriented name.

- Your salary and incentive systems shouldn't relate to number of staff managed. Rather they should be synchronized with your targets as expressed in the balanced scorecard, i.e. you should demand certain service qualities and performance objectives.

9.6   CHECKLIST

The subsequent checklist is prepared in order to help you architect your organization properly.

Table 9-20: Checklist for organization

Item	To check	Recommendation	Self-assessment
Team building	*Orientation*	Highlight the targets of the team using the balanced scoredcard approach: • Clarity of financial targets • Measurable customer satisfaction • Measurable team performance • Speed of adaptability and innovations	
	Trust	Support trust building by social activities	
	High perfor-mance	Create a spirit of commitment Allow constructive criticism Encourage risk awareness	
	Refresh-ment	Implement regular reviews and innovation cycles	
Organization structure	*Flat structure*	Create a task force with commitment to targets – this should allow a span of control of approximately 30 staff instead of the traditional 8–10 staff	
Tools for perfor-mance moni-toring	*Balanced Scorecard*	Implement a measurement programme to regularly check key indicators from the areas • Market/Customers • Staff • Innovation capabilities • Money	
Project Organi-zation	*Leaders and Managers*	Assign key contributors that can share their enthusiasm with the team and motivate them for outstanding results Have an excellent project manager with *e*Business experience and interpersonal skills	
Launch Organi-zation	*Providing the Service*	Be aware of your core competency leading to the key pillar of revenues Establish clear Service Level Agreements (SLAs)	
	Customer Care	Focus on good electronic interactions with the profit generating customer segments Give your customers and their communities the impression of being understood and taken care of	
	Order Manage-ment	Allow quick turn around times from closure of a contract to starting the service	
	Procure-ment and delivery	Organize quick supplies (e.g. by electronic procurement) and quick delivery Keep your customer informed about the status of his order	

Table 9-20 (continued)

Item	To check	Recommendation	Self-assessment
	Finance and Payment	Monitor the cash flow, the performance of your offerings, and the payment behaviour of your customers	
		Get rid of bad performing offerings and customers	
Growth	*Readiness to adapt*	Prepare for ongoing changes, adjustments and improvements	

For a softcopy of this checklist please see my webiste.

9.7   DISCUSSION POINTS

Share your experience regarding different organizational structures with other readers of this book. If you contribute to the website, please indicate, what type of products and services you offer (e.g. Mail-order/Retail, Publishing, ASP, ISP, other).

10

Processes for a learning organization

Have your staff work "hand in hand" with your customers, suppliers and partners, and amongst themselves in the areas:

- *Marketing and Sales*
- *Customer Care*
- *Back office and Supplies*
- *Finance*

In this chapter, I want to tell you how you can create the spirit of everybody working together, in order to support your customer in a profitable way. Large organizations have made great experience in achieving such a common spirit by analysing, redesigning and documenting the business processes. The major benefit usually is, that people realize where waste did occur, e.g. delays due to waiting queues, or where checks and reviews were applied without added value. An example from the finance industry is, that loan applications in the old times required reviews and signatures of more than ten individuals! A substantial check, though, was only performed at two or maximally three places. All other steps were redundant. Guess what the cost for such a loan application was – and even worse how long the customer needed to wait for an approval. In the Internet time, such a process is cut back to a few minutes for standard cases which even can be automated.

So you need to streamline your processes according to the standard cases and deal with the exceptions separately – rather than organizing everything around the complex exceptions and make the normal activities suffer. Remember Pareto's 80 : 20 rule. With 20 per cent of the effort you can achieve 80 per cent of the results, while the remaining 20 per cent of the results costs you 80 per cent of the efforts.

10.1 ACTIVITIES AND THEIR CONTEXT

Each of the persons in your staff performs activities. The danger now is, that people only see their individual part. In order to support the cooperation and interaction, you should show how each of the activities is embedded in the overall context.

If you would follow the approach of big companies, you would come up with dozens of pages of process charts with lines and arrows going all over the place. That wouldn't help you much. Instead, it will be sufficient for you to define the key processes according to your situation. So what's the level of detail you should have for your process definitions? It is best, if everything fits on one page, maybe you would also accept two pages pasted together (i.e. the European A3 format).

I've prepared an illustrative generic example indicating the organizational units as discussed before and the integration of the processes. In Figure 10-36 I show you how such a process definition can look: it's a list of all the activities assigned to the organizational unit and the linkages between those activities:

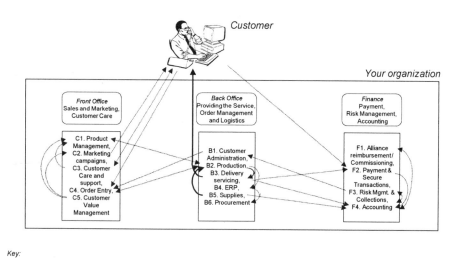

Figure 10-36: Illustrative example: processes and activities

To clarify the terminology: Each process comprises of several activities; the activities are listed in the boxes for each unit, e.g. Product Management,

Marketing campaigns, Customer Care and support, Order Entry, Customer Value Management for the Front Office. An activity can be part of various processes. The most important point about processes is to make it clear to the staff, that they don't work independently from each other, but that there's a chain of activities (i.e. a process) where everybody needs to contribute to the overall success. This chain of activities is indicated by the arrows. Let's walk through some process examples based on the picture above. This example is based on a mail-order enterprise assembling ("producing") the items to be sold, as here the activities are most easy to understand.

New offerings definition: Triggered by suggestions from customers or behaviour of the competition (C3. Customer Care and Support) and based on an understanding of the performance situation by customer and by product (C5. Customer Value Management) as well as the current production capabilities and the future product plans (B2. Production), new product ideas are framed (C1. Product Management).

Marketing execution: With an understanding of the client preferences (C3. Customer Care and Support) and the buying behaviours (C5. Customer Value Management), concrete marketing messages can be formulated for each customer and delivered, ideally to very small target groups (C2. Marketing Campaigns). For your Internet project, the concrete result will be a virtual catalogue you publish on the web with the product description and price, or you can decide to run *e*Mailings where you inform your customers about new offerings or special prices.

Closure of an order: The prospect or customer calls you, because some questions still remain after he saw your virtual catalogue or your *e*Mail. The questions are answered (C3. Customer Care and Support), the order is entered (C4. Order Entry) once the customer data are collected if you didn't have the data of this customer on record yet (B1. Customer Administration). This triggers the production of the good (B2. Production) or the supplies you need to get (B5. Supplies). Production or supplies in turn inform when the product can be expected to be ready.

Production (or assembly) and delivery of the item: Once the production request comes in from the order entry (C4), the necessary supplies need to be ordered (B6. Procurement) via the ERP system (B4). Then the supplies arrive (B5) and can be assembled (B2). Once the product is complete and ready, it can be shipped to the customer (B3). The steps relevant for the financial monitoring are indicated to the accounting system (F4): When the supplies arrive, the entry to accounts payable have to be made and upon delivery of your item to the customer, accounts receivable need to be debited. At the same time, the customer payment should be initiated (F2. Payment).

Payment: Now the customer pays after he received your items (F2) and you can balance his account (F4. Accounting). Depending on your agreements with your suppliers you need to pay them upon certain dates (F1. Alliance reimbursement) based on the deliveries they have made (B5. Supplies). In case your customer doesn't volunteer to pay, you need to push for the payment (F3. Collections). If he still defaults, you need to put him on a watch list and be careful with new orders (F3. Risk Management), therefore that information has to be fed back to the customer information (B1. Customer Administration).

Let me repeat the key point: it's not so important to have all the details of the processes and activities documented in meticulous detail, instead it's essential to make sure, that all cross-unit dependencies and interactions are understood by your staff.

10.2 RESPONSIBILITY CYCLES

Besides the clarity of the overall processes, dependencies and interactions, the next key objective is to help your people to improve permanently. All your processes have to be included in a feedback loop, i.e. they should be structured in a way that at the end of a transaction your staff and your organization has learned something for the next transaction. For this continuous improvement let's have a look at the various cycles of responsibility as they emerge for Sales and Marketing, Customer Care, Back Office Operations and Finance.

These cycles of responsibility are pretty close to the organizational units – in fact, the start-up companies should align their emerging business units with the process cycles discussed below. For traditional companies, where organizational changes require a lot of energy when trying to change reporting lines and career aspirations, it's often just easier and more pragmatic to overlay the existing static organization with the appropriate process cycles.

Let's discuss the activities within each of the responsibility cycles now. By the way, I'm using the term responsibility cycle here, because I think that other terms like knowledge centre or centre of excellence are inappropriate here. They are a very good label for pulling together know-how in geographically disperse enterprises, but in the cases of smaller companies I have in mind here, I assume that the staff still has a personal contact with all the other related staff and that a hands-on cooperation takes place. Everybody performs the processes frequently and each of the repetitions can be closely observed leading to ongoing improvements and possibly innovative ideas for your next generation of offerings. So the term responsibility cycle is more appropriate.

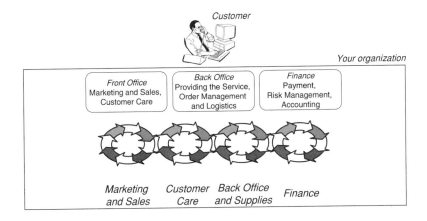

Figure 10-37: Emerging units of responsibility

10.2.1   Marketing and Sales

Marketing has to raise the awareness, inform prospects about the offerings and make them interested. Sales on the other hand has to identify those prospects who are ready to buy and to actually make them buy.

As the marketing campaigns eat up a lot of money – consider TV spots or paper mailings, the campaigns should be as concise as possible, i.e. as much focused to the target segments as possible. Subject of such campaigns may be to cross-sell additional services to your customers and to prevent them from stopping their purchases with you and shop with the competitor instead. It may be to push them for an additional usage of such of your offerings they've already been using or they should refer you to relatives and friends.

The campaigns have to be clearly defined:

- Targeted customers or prospects
- The messages to bring across
- The channels to use for the various targets (e.g. eMail, SMS, personalized web-site, mailing, call from sales force)
- Expected outcome.

In the figure below, you see an example of a flow of activities for a campaign with the target to make the customer sign a physical order, e.g. for the ongoing subscription of some services.

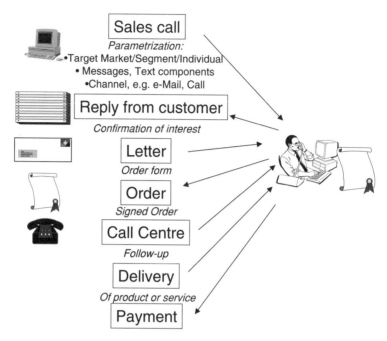

Figure 10-38: Campaign example

At each of the steps, the results should be closely monitored. You may find out that some of the customers accept the spoken order, but don't return the written contract. Check if they don't like the hassle of paper mail – then you may look for the electronical delivery of the order forms. Or did they just forget to return it, then a reminder might be the right approach. Moreover, you should monitor the responses of the customers to your different types of offerings and analyse the probabilities and segments of your customers. Once you can identify what characterizes a customer who is about to make a referral rather than buying again versus a customer who will never recommend you, but is loyal in buying more and more from you, you can save a lot of unnecessary mails and eMails.

To implement focused marketing campaigns, several steps are necessary. Let me highlight the key characteristics of each of those activities (see figure below):

Product Management: That's to "dress up" the products as they come from production, from assembly or directly from the suppliers. One important feature is the packaging and wrapping, simple things like using the right colours for a product consistent with the positioning of the product need to be considered. There's a famous case of Black & Decker: they suffered for a long time from unsatisfying sales of their DeWalt heavy duty product line. The machines were really better than those for do-it-yourself purposes, but the professionals disregarded them, because they didn't want to be perceived as do-it-yourself people. Then the DeWalt machines were painted yellow (like the construction site heavy machinery) instead of do-it-yourself blue. They were packed in heavy steel boxes to allow being pushed around when the professionals had to kick it out of their way. Not surprisingly, sales figures boosted.

Figure 10-39: Marketing and Sales cycle

For Internet business one difficult question to be resolved by Product Management is, what should be offered for "free" in order to attract certain quantities of customers – and which products to offer for certain prices. Some examples of the dynamics around "free" offers include:

- Free ISP service – but the consumer pays for the telecom connection time and the marketing partners pays for the banner ads
- Free set-top boxes for the TV set – but the consumer buys regularly from the mail-order provider configured as the portal on the TV set
- Free trial period for a rented software or ASP service – but if the consumer forgets to terminate the agreement, a long-term rental or subscription is starting.

But Product Management is doing more – actually, for new products, the market needs are discussed with the production people in order to come up with a product even better suited to the market needs. This requires careful decisions regarding the price for products, the cost of production, the quality attributes and appropriate compromises between the conflicting targets.

Segmentation: Having the packaged product ready, the right people need to be approached. If you plan a physical store, you need to decide if you open your shop in the middle of the town (e.g. when you want to sell books to professionals) or if you do that in the farmland (e.g. when you sell farm supplies). That's applied segmentation.

In our virtual world, you need to do a similar thing. You need to select the appropriate "neighbourhood". This neighbourhood is the websites you have links with, the people you invite to your chatroom, forums and communities, your subscribers of mailing lists, and the contents and language of your contact zones. You want to approach your prospective customers via different channels: traditional print media, TV, radio, paper mail and eMail. And each segment of customers needs to get the right marketing approach assigned. So you need to implement the behaviour analysis models and customer profiles discussed in Chapter 3.

Approach Management: I mentioned some examples in the two paragraphs above – for each segment of customers you need to decide how to approach them. What products should be offered, e.g. the low price version versus the full featured version? What are the right channels for marketing and for sales, e.g. TV plus telephone for the low price version and Wall Street Journal plus Internet for the full featured version? Which language levels or slang should be used for each segment? How do you create loyalty of your customers and the appropriate communities for your customers, e.g. football fan clubs for the low price version and historical car interest groups for the full featured version?

These considerations make up the design of your personalized websites and contact zones for each segment, as well as for larger campaigns. The personalization has to include that you show the "right" products and prices for the customer segment and that you show the respective sales messages and banner ads on the website seen by the particular customers. If you want to see how the consumers perceive the personalization, try the website from Amazon or Yahoo. Depending on your last search, you will subsequently see different advertisements. Have you been searching for business subjects? You'll get additional information regarding business success. Did you ask for leisure activities? Some travel offerings will be on the next display.

For a campaign, you also need to plan the financials and the expected response rate, and prepare the exact wording for each channel. Then the campaign should be tested and subsequently run. In contrast to traditional practitioners, I mean more by "running" a campaign than only sending out the mails or publishing the ad and then waiting. In my integrated philosophy, the campaign is not completed before the interested addressees closed the business with you. Don't fragment your campaigns! You need to see the process as a whole until closure of the deal (or the rejection, of course). Only then, you'll be able to really come up with results of the campaign useful to learn from the outcome.

Review of Results: We want to measure the results (e.g. the response rates), compare them against other results, e.g. the same campaign a year ago, or the same campaign in another segment, or (pay attention!) another campaign for a similar group (a test group). You can draw your conclusions from these comparisons and tune your campaigns permanently. What you need to adopt is an educated way of trial and error. With "educated" I mean, that you need to structure your campaigns in a way to learn something from them. You should have a certain hypothesis up front, e.g. how many of your existing customers are ready to accept a new offering, and then try out how you best can approach them, e.g. with different pricings, via different channels, by different sales messages. Don't try everything at once – because then you don't know which factor was the success factor. Test the reactions of the market systematically. In the beginning a monitoring of the response rates and of the closure rates with some spreadsheet program should do – but after some time you will need more complex algorithms to monitor buying patterns and identify now closure opportunities (please refer to Chapter 7.2). But you don't only tune your campaigns – you tune your whole process. Be aware that we are still all at an experimental stage with the business via Internet. Those will win who manage to learn the most quickly from mistakes – be it their own or those of their competitors – and who can transform this experience into better suited processes, services and products.

Decision Management: This is not a real process, but an underlying capability each of the activities need. It's a discipline using tools like paper, spreadsheet, or sophisticated statistical systems to record the results of your activities and to compare them against each other. In Marketing and Sales it's applied as discussed here for Segmentation of Customers (e.g. profitability comparisons), Approach Management (e.g. response assessment) and Analysis of Results.

In other areas it can be applied, too, as for your business planning, performance monitoring of your partners, or risk rankings of your customers.

Iterate and innovate: Walking through the cycle, we can start a new round now. In your business, you should revisit your assumptions based on the increased experience and "start the new round", i.e. repeat each step factoring in the experience from the cycle before – and of course also all earlier cycles. Condense the customer behaviour to some key characteristics and events and highlight outstanding results of what your customers are attracted by or what keeps them from buying.

A mobile telephone provider found out, that his customers liked the fact they could still be reached by their former number when they had ended the contract. He provided a gift to them: a pre-paid card with a small credit on it and their account was kept open. The result was overwhelming – a big number of the customers returned to the provider and paid the normal rates again.

An example of what keeps people from buying are overly long order forms to be entered on the web. According to my observations, the consumers are still pretty patient and allow some mistakes in the new medium, but wait until there will be more and more easy shopping buttons like Amazon is currently trying out with the "one click purchase".

Recommendation:

- Build your marketing and sales activities around personalized messages for the individual customer.

10.2.2   Customer Care

Customer Care is the second client facing area. It is handled separately from Marketing and Sales because at the majority of the companies I know, this is actually split into two units. There are some good reasons in favour of that split. The most convincing reason is, that those people who "hunt" new customers just have another mentality than those who have a deep understanding for his situation, care for his concerns, and give him advice. Also the interaction cycles with the market are different before and after closure of a transaction: before the closure, every activity is focused on getting the deal, i.e. the contact frequencies are increasing until closure while for post sales a regular frequency is appropriate, even if no particular events have happened. Thirdly, you can outsource customer care to a third party call centre that shouldn't design your marketing campaigns and that usually is unable to perform your mailing activities.

There are also many reasons against that split. Foremost, it's the trend to achieve customer loyalty. If you want your customer to be loyal and to contribute a high profitability, you just need to treat him nicely unless you want a competitor to pull him away. Therefore, forthcoming customer care, well organized support and anticipation of his needs will support that embracing of the customer. So, the customer care representatives are actually closing the deals with the customers in this scenario. Another reason in favour of joining the two units are synergies: the same information about the offerings and about the customers are needed in both groups, both units have to sell, and the tools they use to do their activities are the same.

Here's my advice: for those customers who purchase your products and services like a commodity a forceful sales approach is appropriate with massive marketing efforts and ongoing contacts initiated by you, while for the high value and loyal customers you have to maintain an emphatic understanding and an environment where they call you and you fully support them. You may need two separate brands and separated delivery channels, not to risk that a high value customer will be repelled by some of your sleazy salesmen...

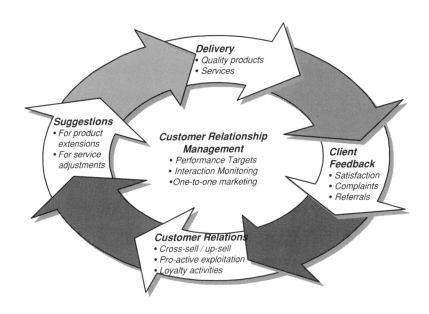

Figure 10-40: Customer Care cycle

Again we have a cycle to iteratively learn and improve the process. For Customer Care the overall process can be refined as follows.

Delivery: You may think that it's trivial that the customer has to get the products he has ordered, you owe it to him anyway, and eventually he should receive it. Well, that's not the attitude I'm pleading for. Instead you have to make it your top priority to enable your customer to exploit the benefits of your product or service. That starts before the actual delivery, the customer is curious about the feature he will get, he may want to get in touch with other customers (i.e. your community), he wants to know when he can enjoy what he has ordered, i.e. you have to keep him informed about the expected delivery date. Therefore, you had better organize a friendly delivery and show the same competency and customer orientation as with your products and services.

Client Feedback: We talked earlier about complaints being an important source of information that could be improved in your offerings. In addition of course, praise for your products is important: you can use it as references to convince other customers – and you can monitor if the praise increases over time or if it decreases. The feedback can (and should) be obtained pro-actively, i.e. the customer care representatives should occasionally (but regularly) ask how the customers perceive the quality of the products and services.

You also should support by all means the most important multiplier for sales – namely referrals from your customers to their friends. The standard approach is to give cash or some kind of a gift to your customer. That's not bad, but there are more effective means, if they fit into your company culture. One better example from the consumer world is to give out free shares of your company – that's binding your customer more to you than a take-away gift of the same face value. For the business market a good approach is to create a community of "active" customers: they get a preferred treatment like the first possibility to buy your new products and services or the option to earn some points which can be used for a reduction of the next bill due to you.

Customer Relationship: Yes, here's the interface with the Marketing and Sales area discussed before. Usually even in the organizations that have split Marketing and Sales from Customer Care, the execution of the sales calls, telephone marketing and other one-to-one marketing campaigns is handled by the customer care representatives. Also order entry can be handled by the customer care representatives unless the customer can do it in self service. Given the sometimes different characteristics that make cold calls a success or that lead existing customers to the next buy, you should assign the different activities to those of your staff most successful in the particular type of sales.

Suggestions: Based on all the sales successes and also on lost proposals, you customer care representatives get a rich impression of the customer demands. You should exploit those impressions by inviting them to share those impressions with the product management in order to tune the offering. This sharing can happen as a very formal process (e.g. written suggestions with or without official recognition for the submission or for the acceptance of the suggestion). Or it can be less formal or completely informal, e.g. regular events where the best ideas are distilled in a brainstorming group including product managers and customer care staff. If you organize such events as parties, you are improving your team spirit at the same time.

Customer Relations Management: So far, everything only costs you money – producing the product or providing the service, all the people being friendly to the customer, all the additional ideas people push you to transfer into your product or service. Here's the element that keeps it all together – the planned value for each customer relationship (or for particular customer or product segments). For each group relevant for you, you have to define performance targets (please refer to Chapter 12 below for a Business Plan). These targets are the orientation (either a recommendation or a commitment) of what the customer care representatives have to achieve. With a good mix of empowerment for your senior staff members to do what they experience is the right thing to do, plus some technical tools to actually get the performance reports, you will achieve the best success.

Iterate and innovate: Walking through the cycle, we can start a new round now. As for Marketing and Sales, the responsibility is with the product management to tune the products or services. At the same time, there may be improvements possible in the internal processes or in the interaction with the customers. Search for those improvements actively!

Beyond the performance of the customers and products, you also should check the performance of your processes. Above you have read about the Balanced Scorecard to monitor the effectiveness of processes. Here again I want to encourage you to compare your performance, e.g. to benchmark with other companies in your industry or to benchmark various departments, products, regions against each other. By this approach you can identify suspect areas for waste. You may find out that your inventories are higher than necessary, you may find out that activities could be centralized that currently are replicated in various places, or you may find out that you need peak staff for the support of some cyclical business.

What can you learn during each iteration? Here the focus is on producing the goods you are selling and on the actual delivery and support aspects. For example, you may find ways of how the product configuration can be facilitated, how the delivery processes can be better aligned with the customers needs or how you can come up with the right answers more quickly when the customer needs support. Such changes can be implemented without an interaction with the product management – you just improve the internal efficiency of the customer care group.

Outsourcing: If you consider outsourcing the customer care activities to a call centre, you should check, if he can provide all the necessary services, in particular:

- Customer community support
- Sales
- Order acceptance
- Complaint management
- Hotline.

You should check the qualifications of the call centre staff and how you can include your particular aspects in their training programme. Moreover, the software used and the possibility for interfaces with your back-end systems need to be checked.

Recommendation:

- Use the information of all existing customer interactions to serve your customer pro-actively.

10.2.3   Back office operations

In your back office you have your "factory". There are some key differences between *e*Businesses and traditional businesses. The brick and mortar piece of your factory is pretty small and often a large part of your factory will be outsourced to third parties. Instead, you have many things covered by information systems or by teams cooperating across organizational and regional boundaries and even working together across different companies – like Dell is rather managing its suppliers than running their own production. You should be permanently challenging the approaches and invite for ongoing improvements. Those improvements can be implemented within weeks or a few months (rather than taking years in the traditional brick and mortar heavy machinery business).

Most of the activities mentioned in Figure 10-41, have been discussed in general before as far as the topic of the book is concerned. Some specific implementations have been described in Chapter 9, so I trust you can map the figure above to your company situation. Let me give a few recommendations for your *e*Venture, though.

Order Management: Cut any redundant order entries back and push the order entry as far as possible in front of your customers. Ideally, the customer can enter the order himself via the web. Companies have experienced tremendous reductions in error rates by having the customers enter their orders themselves and by seemlessly integrating such orders into production and supplies instead of paper shuffling between various units in the organization and multiple data entries. Also keep your customer informed about the progress of his order by allowing him to track his orders. It should be easy for you, if you are in a mass market and just selling physical goods. But more and more companies (even in the business-to-business area) integrate their production (and I mean real brick and mortar production) so far with their order management system, that their customers can get real time updates regarding the day and hour of expected production completion. Urgent updates like unexpected delays have to be sent via *e*Mail, SMS or paper mail (you can allow your customer to configure his profile, e.g. how many days of delay he's tolerating without a specific information), while regular information can be provided on your database records for lookup by the customers.

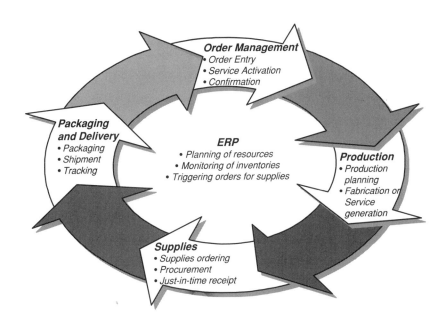

Figure 10-41: Back office = Supplies and Delivery integrated into Customer Care and ERP

Supplies: This is the wide field of electronic procurement. Global research and project execution indicates, that in large organizations one procurement transaction costs approximately € 400. Based on this figure tremendous cost-benefit estimates have been made. For big enterprises in fact a lot of potential savings can be exploited there, but for small and medium enterprises I wouldn't focus on that aspect, at least not in the beginning and not for your interaction with suppliers. What may be very interesting though, is the electronic procurement your customers implement. If you observe your customers implementing such approaches, integrate your systems with them, i.e. provide the information regarding your products in their procurement catalogues and malls.

Packaging and Delivery: Here, the comment regarding integration with your customers' systems is valid as well. Don't do it only for the sake of neat interfaces, though, but only whenever you can identify business benefits for your customer or for yourself.

ERP[17]: Your ERP system should cover:

- Finance and Accounting including profitability per product and customer and also including planning and monitoring of current status with a deviation analysis.
- Production, inventory and supply management including planning and monitoring of current status.
- Human resources including payroll (with all your local tax and social security regulations reflected).

So far, it's straightforward. In addition you need two more things. We have been talking about the Balanced Scorecard – it has to be supported by your ERP approach. And your ERP has to support the speed of your business. Ideally, you should get at least weekly trend reports plus monthly full analysis of your performance.

Iterate and innovate: Again, we have the iteration and innovation. In this area it means primarily searching for operational efficiency and for cost savings.

Recommendation:
- Outsource all activities where you won't become excellent and integrate those outsourced activities neatly into your service offering.

10.2.4   Finance

Before you start a new business, you should dig into that topic by reading the appropriate literature regarding accounting and taxation rules in your country and you should get professional advice from accountants. Let me make a few comments how those aspects differ in an *e*Venture from traditional businesses.

Budgets and accounting: On top of planning the financials, you have to monitor the achievement of your balanced scorecard targets. Make sure that these can be reflected in your system and are monitored regularly. Also make sure that trends can be easily and flexibly shown. Unfortunately, even some expensive ERP tools as well as outsourcing service providers for accounting activities, often don't have built in analysis functions for budget versus actuals or comparisons with the months before – not to talk of nice graphical representations. If you don't have this in the standard functionality, you need

---
[17] I'm using the abbreviation ERP in its original meaning, i.e. a tool for planning and controlling your company. This doesn't necessarily mean a full blown "ERP" system, basically paper and pencil could be used in the very beginning. A spreadsheet can cover the planning and monitoring aspects later for a small company or an outsourced ERP solution for medium sized companies. As far as accounting and payroll are concerned, in the beginning or for small companies it can be outsourced, e.g. to an accountant, and later or for larger companies, it should be run in house.

to re-enter the results from the ERP system into a spreadsheet to come up with the trend analysis.

Payables: We discussed it, but I want to emphasize it here. In your *e*Venture you will have more business partners than in normal business. And you may be allowed to offset payables with receivables when you have relationships with mutual business exchanges. Make sure to cover all relationships with your payment approaches.

Receivables: The main peculiarity is the possibility to obtain money electronically. We discussed the possible approaches – and you should avoid creating hurdles for your customers by not providing the "right" payment method. Credit card payment via SET is the most common form of payment, but the consumers don't support it in all countries (due to perceived security issues), so at least for those cases other payment possibilities need to be foreseen.

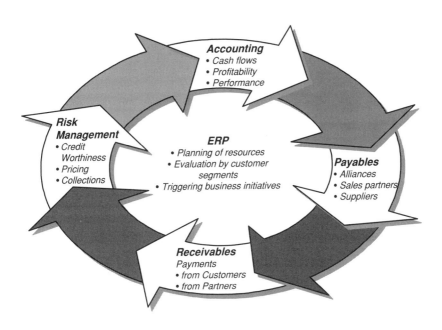

Figure 10-42: Finance = provide the measures to manage the customer value

Risk management: If everybody paid by credit card and you always requested an authorization from the credit card processor, then no additional risk management would be necessary. Usually, though, you offer also other payment means, because either your customers don't like it or because you want to save the commissions for the credit card transactions. Therefore you need to check, who of your customers is good for deferred payments and you need to enforce the collection of all receivables that weren't paid on time.

Practically, the people responsible for the risk management, will also deal with the credit card authorizations and the definition of credit policies, i.e. who can get goods on a credit base.

Iterate and innovate: In this case, the iterations will happen less in the Finance group itself, but in the overall organization based on the figures Finance has pulled together. The ongoing monitoring of the company's success will trigger the permanent alignment of the business strategy and organization. Additionally, there may be some tactical issues (like payment delays or critical non-achievement of targets) to be quickly discussed with the company's leaders and managers. Such activities should lead to quick fixes in the processes and policies.

Recommendation:

- Include the balanced scorecard aspects in your planning and monitoring.

10.3   OWNERSHIP

Each process must have a clear owner for the execution from the beginning to the end. In your customer focused organization, this should be somebody close to the customer, e.g. a customer care representative. This person has to monitor that the activities are performed within the committed time frames and with the appropriate quality. In case of priority conflicts, the front office person should have the biggest power to adjust priorities of the back office. In very pro-active companies, the front office is even allowed to subcontract certain activities to another company, if their own back office isn't capable of delivering the necessary results with the appropriate quality. Moreover, this person is in charge of compiling suggestions for improving the processes.

Additionally, you may assign specific competencies to individuals executing an activity, e.g. the competency to negotiate prices with the customer or the competency to assign certain priorities for handling the customer's order.

Recommendation:

- Empower the customer care representatives to deliver results to the customer.

10.4   CHECKLIST

Consider now the generic processes as presented in this chapter and map them to your anticipated organization.

Table 10-21: Checklist for your processes

Area	To check	Recommendation	Self-assessment
Marketing and Sales	*Are all activities covered in your anticipated organization?*	To cover: • Product Management • Segmentation • Approach Management • Results Review • Decision Management	
Customer Care	*Are all activities covered in your anticipated organization?*	To cover: • Delivery • Client Feedback • Customer Relationship • Suggestions • Customer Relationship Management	
Back Office	*Are all activities covered in your anticipated organization?*	To cover: • Order Management • Production • Supplies • Packaging and Delivery	
Finance	*Are all activities covered in your anticipated organization?*	To cover: • Budgets and Accounting • Payables • Receivables • Risk Management • ERP	

For a softcopy please visit my website.

10.5   DISCUSSION POINTS

Publish your experience with specific processes on my website. Each contributor will get free access to updates of the materials of the entrepreneur community. When you contribute to the website, please indicate, what type of products and services you offer (e.g. Mail-order/Retail, Publishing, ASP, ISP, other).

> **Recommendations:**
>
> • Be pragmatic – start with a small number of process descriptions and refine them while your organization grows.
> • Implement feedback and learning in your organization.

11

Information technology implementation

Automate those business areas where a high number of interactions is to be expected. Start with customer facing processes:

- *Customer interactions for mail-order type transactions and communication between customers, yourself and suppliers.*
- *Service provider interactions for configuration of services.*
- *Payment and risk management.*

Pragmatism is needed for the IT (information technology) implementation. Start small, not to throw away money for a huge IT environment. But start big enough not to disappoint your customers by a deterioration of your service quality when more and more new customers use your services. How many transactions do you expect, how many customers will use your services? In the beginning, you only have your business plan, but your actual figures might be off by a factor of ten or even more. Be ready to deploy additional features regularly and have your IT staff dedicated to overtime work whenever your systems are stretched.

This requires a flexible IT architecture combined with flexible agreements with your hardware and software suppliers. For the IT architecture this means, that you only should include client server systems (e.g. Unix based) with software components that can easily scale with your growth. For the software, larger providers have the advantage of offering a richer functionality but smaller providers are more ready to negotiate special flexibilities like options to upgrade quickly or even to allow an early termination of the contract. In such a dilemma – go for the flexibility! Additionally, you should plan for a major review of your IT approach after one year in business at the latest – and you should prepare your contracts with the suppliers accordingly. The option to change to a larger environment has to be included which is relatively easy to agree with the suppliers. Also the option to down size has to be covered; that may be more difficult to negotiate, but you should encourage your partners to share the upside potential and the downside with you.

The system architecture we started to discuss in Chapter 7 is structured in a way allowing you to flexibly "plug in" additional components as your business grows:

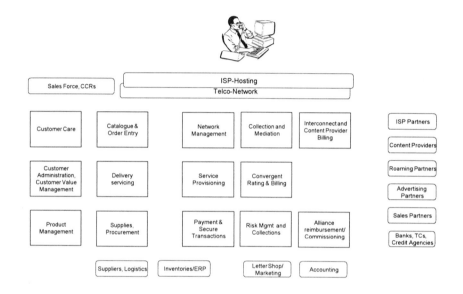

Figure 11-43: Emerging architecture for the IT environment

Please be aware, that the discussion below follows the functional structure of the architecture chart and not a sequence of importance. The checklist at the end of the chapter, though, is sorted by importance allowing you to efficiently obtain vendor information in more detail.

11.1 MARKET SURVEY FOR THE COMPONENTS

The survey is organized by the different types of overall business leaning on the business scenarios as discussed in the case studies of the last chapter. Initially, we'll discuss front office components for mail-order types of eVentures, then we will discuss components for ASPs and ISPs, and finally we will cover back office components for all types of companies. If you want to go quickly through the following pages, check at the beginning of each paragraph, if it's relevant for you; I've indicated at each component for which types of business it's applicable.

Let me highlight the most important insight from the market survey: many of the providers of the components are in start-up mode – like you! This means, that you cannot expect overly well established support from either of them despite the fact that support is exactly what you need. As a general recommendation, you should select a partner with support engineers near you. Then at least the travel overhead is smaller if you need someone in your premises and you don't need to struggle with different time zones. And whoever you are considering to provide you with the software – ask their other customers how satisfied they are.

The market survey is a snapshot as of January 2000[18]. In order to come up with a description useful for all readers, I don't look into specific regional vendors. Instead, I use offerings from companies doing multi-national business. Those offerings usually have the most comprehensive coverage of functionality. Regional packages, on the other hand, can be better suited for your specific local situation (including language preferences on screens and reports and legal or taxation requirements). In any case, you can use the discussed packages as a functional benchmark when you check regional offerings.

With the information provided below, you can select the components best suited for your initial business requirements; then you should check the web for the current features and prices of the components from the primary providers. In order to support you in this activity, I've included the web pages of the discussed vendors at the end of the book.

11.2   CUSTOMER INTERACTION

The components particularly relevant for *e*Businesses are depicted in the two leftmost columns of the architecture (see Figure 11-44 below). They include Customer Care, Customer Administration, Product Management, Catalogue / Order Entry, Delivery Servicing and Supplies / Procurement. Those components will be appropriate for most *e*Ventures, for the number one Internet business approach, namely "mail" order, they need the most sophistication.

The primary components, Customer Care and Catalogue / Order Entry will be used by:

Your customers: Most of the transactions, in particular orders and inquiries, should be handled directly by your customers. Exceptions are changes of data critical for your business such as price information or risk data. You should encourage your customers as much as possible to do their

---

[18] The information and prices provided are quoted from sources I believe are reliable; they may be overtaken by changes at the time of reading this book.

transactions in self service, because that saves you lots of effort and cuts back error rates. Also, you can make more attractive offerings due to these cost reductions. In online banking for example, the fees are further discounted than if the customers use the call centre. Specifically priced products may only be offered for orders in self service and self configuration as Dell is doing.

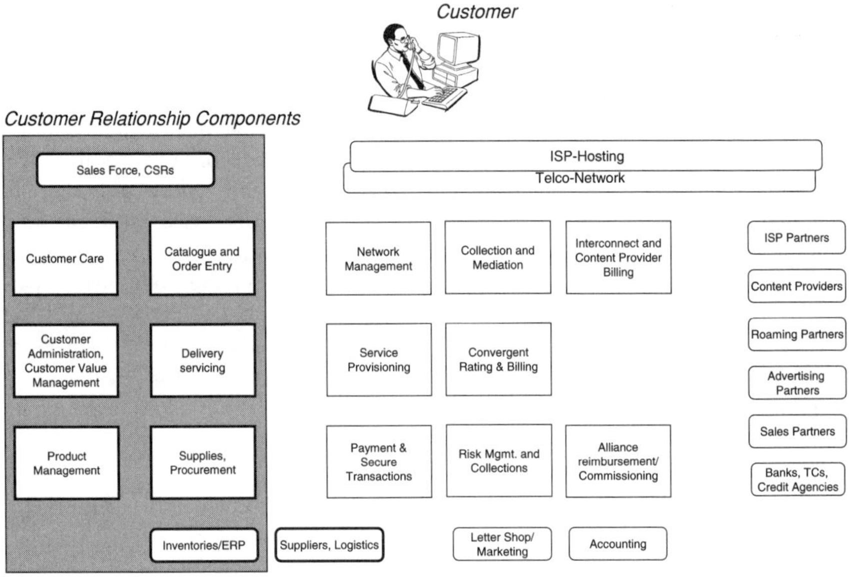

Customer

Customer Relationship Components

Sales Force, CSRs		ISP-Hosting
		Telco-Network

Customer Care	Catalogue and Order Entry	Network Management	Collection and Mediation	Interconnect and Content Provider Billing	ISP Partners
					Content Providers
Customer Administration, Customer Value Management	Delivery servicing	Service Provisioning	Convergent Rating & Billing		Roaming Partners
					Advertising Partners
Product Management	Supplies, Procurement	Payment & Secure Transactions	Risk Mgmt. and Collections	Alliance reimbursement/ Commissioning	Sales Partners
					Banks, TCs, Credit Agencies
	Inventories/ERP	Suppliers, Logistics	Letter Shop/ Marketing	Accounting	

Figure 11-44: IT components for customer interaction

Customer Care Representatives (CCRs): usually your CCRs are located in one or several call centres. You may also have them working from home provided each of them has access to complete, accurate and timely information about your customer. Depending on the size of your operation you may decide to distinguish between inbound call centres handling orders and complaints and outbound call centres running particular marketing campaigns.

Your sales agents: usually the sales agents are in charge of key accounts, i.e. your business customers. If you engage other partners as a distribution channel, they need to have access to the same information.

Your field force for maintenance and repair: usually they have a different objective (namely to perform maintenance or fix the problem), but they should have access to the same information as the sales force and CCRs – and what about the idea to incent them, if they manage to sell another of your products and services to the customer?

11.2.1   Customer Care

This functionality is relevant for all types of companies in particular for the call centre support. Boutiques can handle it manually, small and medium businesses should use a software component for it.

The functional objectives of the Customer Care component are:

Selling – you guessed that anyway, but I wanted to include it here because this is the most important task your software and your Sales Force and Customer Care has to perform. Your staff needs concise information, e.g. marketing messages personalized to the consumer, hints that can be shared with the customer and the up-to-date agreements with and transactions performed by the customer.

One-to-one marketing – the distinction between selling and marketing will diminish over time, but I still use it here for clarity. The traditional connotation with selling is that a sales person makes a very unique offering to a customer either in a shop or in the customer's premises and convinces him of closing the deal. The connotation with traditional marketing is that you broadcast your messages to a large audience. In contrast to that, one-to-one marketing doesn't use shot-gun approaches, but triggers an activity, e.g. a mailing or a special offer, at specific customer events and personalized to the more concrete situation in order to get to an immediate closure. The preferred channel for each customer is to be used: e.g. *e*Mails, short messages (SMS) to his mobile phone, a personalized greeting page on the web indicating the special offers for this particular customer, or a phone call from the call centre.

Support – in case of problems the CCR can help out. Such problems may be regarding a product just received by the customer, questions regarding the offering or complaints to settle.

The software component to support those activities is the bridgehead for your marketing interactions with the customer. It needs to have all information bundled at one place and available "on a fingertip". While the CCR is talking with the customer he has to be able to pull up the screen with the appropriate information on it. Technically, this component has to provide a complete picture of the customer relationship. Between the various areas of information an easy navigation has to be supported in order to allow the user quick answers to the customers' requests. The complete picture should cover:

- The *contractual agreements* between the customer and your company, e.g. subscribed services, tariffs, discounts, service levels.
- The *last interactions* with the customer such as pending orders, the last deliveries, pending and resolved complaints, the payment status.

216 INFORMATION TECHNOLOGY IMPLEMENTATION

- The *profile* of your customer. Usually for easier use by the Sales and Customer Support, you translate the complex analysis as performed with the value based approach into simple labels like Platin customer, Gold Club, Preferred Service or similar. Each of those labels has specific handling approaches.
- *Marketing information* such as special offerings.
- *Current campaign* and sales message for the customer segment with the respective marketing message for the particular customer has to be indicated and if he is subscriber of specific information (e.g. mailing lists).
- *Procedures* for handling the marketing and sales activities. Depending on the particular request (e.g. placing an order, raising a complaint, running a marketing campaign) and on the customer profile, a script will be pulled up. The CCR can read it off his monitor and take the steps following the customers reactions, e.g. he can pull up an order entry form, or a complaint form, or trigger sending the customer specific information.

Table 11-22: Customer Care packages

Provider	Product name	Characteristics
Clarify	EfrontOffice CommCentre	EfrontOffice: Integrated application for medium size businesses. CommCentre dedicated to telecom providers, e.g. sales force support, trouble ticketing of network elements
		Recently broadening of Clarify's offerings by eFront office, after acquisition by Nortel new focus on eCommerce
Genesys		CTI and Mail generator: paper mail, eMail, SMS, Unified Messaging
Siebel	Ebusiness:	Complete coverage for front office
	Esales, Emarketing, Eservice, Echannel	Targetted to middle and large enterprises
		Proprietary data structures and workflow
	Enterprise:	Integration with back office systems necessary, but
	Sales, Service, Call Centre, Field Service, Marketing	interfaces require conformity with Siebel standards instead of open industry standards, therefore expensive to integrate with other applications
Vantive	Enterprise:	Large scale solution
	Sales Support, FieldService, HelpDesk	Development driven by US market demands

The prices for the components start well above € 50,000. For websites and additional vendors, see Section 14.4.2

Table 11-22 above indicates the major global players for dedicated customer care packages that are best suited for larger numbers of customers. Alternatively, catalogue and order entry software can handle the requirements for smaller numbers of customers. In larger enterprises, the Customer Care functionality needs to be integrated with other aspects:

CTI (Computer and Telephone Interface): If you don't want your customer to go through a time consuming dialogue with the CCR to identify himself, to get his records and then only to start with the business, you may implement systems recognizing the customer. Recognition can be based upon the telephone number he's calling from, he might identify himself by entering his customer number and a PIN, modern voice recognition system could identify him by his voice, or if he's in an Internet session and pressed a Help button on your website, your systems can transfer his identity directly. You also might lead your customer by telephone through a brief menu regarding his desires. Then your CCR is better prepared from the start.

Navigation: Depending on the conversation, the CCR must be able to pull up the relevant information (e.g. last order, last invoice, delivery status) – or even better it should be there proactively based on automatically derived assumptions as described above. The CCR must be able to trigger activities with the appropriate forms (e.g. for order entry, complaint, address change). Those electronic forms should be integrated with the back end processes, e.g. it has to be checked if an ordered good is in stock or when it's about to be delivered. In case of a complaint, the CCR has to be informed how long it's going to take to fix the problem, and the address change has to be performed right away.

Workflow: Activities like marketing campaigns or complaints require a workflow to be followed. The progress of this workflow has to be automatically monitored – and if delays happen, the CCR should have the opportunity to inform the customer. Maybe you don't want to do this with every customer, for any delay and for any problem, but you better have the tools in place for your most profitable customer segments.

Response times: Having identified the customer, the information relevant for the call should be on the monitor of the CCR as soon as he starts his conversation with the customer, based upon the data from the CTI in combination with the customer profile information and the most recent transactions. If the customer ordered something three days ago, you promised to deliver within 24 hours, but your delivery monitoring indicates that it hasnt been delivered, then the customer is probably about to complain – and if he's a Platin customer your CCR better be nice to him.

Recommendations:

- For smaller numbers of customers, customer care should be handled manually or can be covered by Catalogue and Order Entry software.

- Once your customer base has grown larger, you should use a dedicated customer care component integrated with an automatic decisioning tool and allow self care on the web.

11.2.2 Customer Administration and Customer Value Management

Customer Administration and Customer Value Management is relevant for all types of companies. Boutiques and smaller eBusinesses can use standard low cost software packages, larger eBusinesses need a dedicated software integrated with their other applications.

Customer Administration covers the aspects necessary to execute the transactions. Usually, the catalogue and order entry system offers sufficient functionality. If you run an own system instead, like an ASP back end system, custom extensions need to be implemented.

The Customer Administration should be used by your customer care representatives as far as security critical or business critical data and processes (e.g. credit worthiness checking) are concerned. All other areas should be used as much as possible by your customers. For example, imagine a mail-order company. They may save huge amounts for printing and sending their big catalogues, if they allow their customers to maintain their preference profile, i.e. select those topics they want to be informed about: Gardening, Furniture, Cosmetics, Fashion for example could be unbundled and the customer can receive the specific brochure. If you allow your customers to maintain their non-critical data such as mailing address or preferred treatment regarding marketing activities, your customers will enjoy the convenience and control of their data plus you save effort on such data maintenance.

To make it more advanced, you can map the profile as indicated by your customer with the actual transactions he's performing with you – you'll probably find some mismatches over time. Those mismatches create an opportunity to engage with your customer and ask him or her, if he or she is dissatisfied about your products and what you can do to improve them.

For the Customer Value Management, i.e. the personalization of the marketing and sales messages based on the customer behaviour and customer profitability, the solution highly depends on the size of your business. Below, some of the available tools for the various numbers of customers are mentioned. Be aware that each tool requires customization; the more complex it is the more you need to configurate it to make it really meaningful.

For a small number of customers (i.e. ranging up to approximately 10,000), you can develop a low cost custom solution to monitor the customers' performance with database and spreadsheet tools such as Microsoft dbase and Excel. In this case, you should record behaviour data like last orders (items, amount), interactions (returns, complaints, hotline usage) and credit worthiness information (payment history, credit rating). This information together with the socio-demographic data you obtained like age of the customer, children, neighbourhood, employer, can be used to identify basic buying behaviours (e.g. which types of your offerings are bought by what type of customers, how often, which price segments) in order to support your cross-selling activities as described in Chapter 3. You also should store those identified buying preferences to trigger specific marketing campaigns for the respective market segments.

The transactions of intermediary numbers of customers (i.e. from several thousand to some hundred thousand) can be analysed with statistical tools such as SAS or SPSS. If you have a very big number of customers (i.e. in the millions) first of all, you need to collect the data in one physical place, the data warehouse. Then you can analyse your customer behaviour, and you should support the Value Management with automatic decisioning tools. Such decisioning tools have to automatically assign the treatment strategy according to the customer profiles; this means that your Customer Care Representatives get the appropriate scripts for the customer treatment when the customer calls, that the marketing activities are personalized accordingly – and that also the responses in Internet dialogues are triggered by those profiles. In order to define the appropriate segments and profiles, you need to perform data mining in your data warehouse. An example of a large enterprise is Amazon.com, where you have probably recognized, that the banner advertisements are personalized according to the type of books or music you have selected before.

Table 11-23: Customer Value Management tools

Provider	Product name	Category	Characteristics
AMS	Strata	For large customer base	Focus on Risk Management
Broad vision	One-to-one commerce	For large customer base	Customer Relationship
	One-to-one relationship		Personalized Net Access
Fair, Isaac		For large customer base	Focus on Marketing (predictive modelling of buying behaviour) and risk management
Microsoft	Office (Excel, dbase, Word)	For small customer base	Flexibility
			Manual integration with operational systems
NCR	Terradata	Hardware for high performing data warehouse	
SAP	CRM	For medium to large customer base	Integration with financial information (R/3)
		Campaign Management	Little support for front end (to be integrated with one of the other tools)
		Workflow	
SAS	EDA (Exploratory Data Analysis)	For medium size customer base	Integrated view on
	OLAP (online analytical processing)		• Statistical analysis • Balanced Scorecard • Data Warehouse
Seagate	Crystal reports	Scalable reporting	Some products are offered for free
	Info, Analysis		
SPSS		For intermediary customer base	Statistical analysis
			Mainframe background

For websites and additional vendors, see Section 14.8

> **Recommendations:**
>
> - Customer Value Management is important for each company and should reflect profits and costs from the service and the product part of the activities.
>
> - Smaller companies should implement low cost approaches.
>
> - Larger companies should develop custom IT solutions.

11.2.3   Product management

Product management is relevant for all types of companies, an automation is advisable just for medium and large eBusinesses.

Product management needs to be neatly integrated with your operations. You should have your performance figures per product segments and customer segments at hand in order to tune your existing services and products. Your product managers should leverage the fact, that your enterprise is much better integrated and customer focused than traditional enterprises. You can use the additional information, e.g. from your customers' communities, to frame new offerings and to have easily demarcable test markets in order to try the acceptance and performance of your new offerings.

Some companies have developed statistical simulation models to perform the appropriate sensitivity analysis and forecasts. Such simulations include forecasting of the market behaviour in case of anticipated changes in your product offerings, e.g. price cuts, split of offerings or combined offerings. Also, such simulations may be appropriate in order to get some reasonable estimates of the market behaviour when you launch a new company.

Table 11-24: Customer behaviour modelling

Provider	Category	Characteristics
Janus Enterprise International	For large customer base	Focus on product performance analysis and market sensitivity models
Fair, Isaac	For large customer base	Focus on Marketing (predictive modelling of buying behaviour) and risk management

For websites and additional vendors, see Section 14.8

> **Recommendations:**
>
> - In smaller companies, product management should be done based on the judgment of their leaders.
>
> - Large companies should perform simulations of new products based on statistical models.

11.2.4 Online Catalogue and Order Entry – the key *e*Business software

This component is relevant for all types of companies. With a good software here that covers most of the customer care requirements, boutiques and smaller eBusinesses don't need additional customer relationship components.

Without your offerings published on the web, you won't be able to do any electronic business. You need an online catalogue to store and present your offering descriptions and prices. On top of that, some can include a picture of the product, a film about the service, or delivery information. Catalogues can address different types of customers and support different internal users (e.g. for maintaining the product information updating prices or the availability).

Table 11-25: Ownership of electronic catalogues

	Maintained by	Controlled by	Viewed by
Mail-order	Staff (product manager) of mail-order company	Mail-order company	Consumer (via Internet) and by CCRs
Electronic procurement	Suppliers (following electronic formats defined by purchaser), e.g. via Internet	Purchaser	Staff of purchaser

In the consumer market (e.g. mail-order), the catalogue is defined and maintained by the mail-order company and viewed by the consumers. In the business-to-business market, the larger institution, i.e. the purchaser who is pursuing an *e*Procurement approach, controls the format and owns the catalogue, while the suppliers feed their information into that catalogue – see Table 11-15 above.

The Order Entry system, now, must collect and record the customers' orders, in particular the ordered items, the quantity, the price you quoted at that time, the customer identity, the delivery address and payment agreements. Let's be clear, that "order" is meant here in a broad context. In extension to an order for a physical product (like a book), it may be (to name some):

- the subscription to your ASP service, e.g. an electronic newsletter,
- the initiation of an ad hoc service like a request in a search engine (e.g. Find all websites with the words "Internet", "business", "success"),
- a bid in an electronic auction,
- the expressed desire for a financial transaction, e.g. an insurance policy application or a loan application.

The Order Entry has to interface with your inventories and with the procurement and supply systems. Visit for example amazon.com's website and you'll see a good catalogue implementation with pictures of the book, prices, reviews, text excerpts and delivery information like "This book is usually shipped within 24 hours" or "Unfortunately this book is sold out, we will try to find you another copy. Please allow 2–3 weeks for delivery".

In detail, the functional requirements for the Online Catalogue and Order Entry are:

Presentation of your Offering: Two options exist: either you enter your product and service descriptions directly on the website or you store them in your database and make them available to your customers via an interface to the web. The approach to enter them directly on the website is advisable, when you have a relatively small number of offerings which don't change too frequently. Once you have a larger number of items to sell or the availability changes often, you should keep your offerings in a database which you can easily update and which can be accessed by your customers via the web.

Interactive Search: Allow your customers to enter specific demands to save them the time to surf through a series of websites. Such a search function requires a database in the background and an understanding of how your customers may call certain items. Ideally, you should have multiple ways implemented in your search function to get to the specific items, as for books a search by title, by author, by publisher, by year of publishing.

Shopping Cart: Provide your customer with the transparency of what he's considering to buy so far. Make sure, that items can be taken out of the shopping cart if the customer changes his mind. Allow him to change the numbers for a given item. Also the current total cost of the goods in the cart should be shown. Good applications additionally include the possibility to park the shopping cart for some time and to pick it up at a later visit – thus the customer doesn't need to go through the selection process again once he returns after he has thought about his purchase or after he has checked other sources.

Payment: The more payment options you can provide the better. The Internet "classic", credit cards, are a must. In addition it's good if you can provide debit cards and electronic cash, because you save significantly on commissions and direct debits are even less costly provided your customers have a sound risk profile.

Information about expected delivery: Your customers want to know when they can get the items they have offered. You may want to allow them to choose between different speeds and forms of delivery – and pay according to the different quality levels of service. This has to be integrated with the delivery system in order for you to be able to commit to the service levels. This integration also has to allow for the customer to track the status of his order and delivery.

Monitoring of customer behaviour: Your system should be able to measure and monitor the interactions of the web-surfers with your website. Analysis conducted by Shop.org and Boston Consulting in the US in 1998 have shown, that only five per cent of the visitors started purchasing and only less than two per cent actually made it through the cashier![19] To help improve that performance you need to implement tools that highlight the constellations when customers actually buy and also when they interrupt the buying process. This can be supported by click stream analysis conducted by some of the online shop packages.

Marketing support and personalization: The system should allow you to define specific customer segments and to handle specific marketing messages for each segment. For a larger number of customers, special offers to dedicated customers should be configurable.

Additionally, here's a list of technical requirements, that needs to be checked depending on the other IT components you are planning:

Flexibility: Your catalogue and order entry application is the primary interface visible for your customers. Therefore, it must support them very well and under different circumstances. You should start with a small implementation and then add components when your customer base and the number of transactions grow. Also, the hardware architecture should be easily scalable, i.e. by adding additional servers you should get the respective performance increase. When you engage with a provider for your catalogue and order entry application, make him commit to specific performance figures, e.g. the number of concurrent users at peak times, the response time of the system (e.g. average and maximum in seconds) for given numbers of users (according to the ranges indicated by your various business growth scenarios), the number of overall transactions to be processed (e.g. per day, per peak hour).

Stability: The service has to have a very high availability; it's too frustrating for a customer to get a message like "server not responding" or "connection time out". Also the implementation must be thoroughly tested and abnormal terminations must be kept almost to zero. Also it should run without operator intervention to avoid costs in operating and support.

Interfaces: The online catalogue and order entry has to be integrated with the delivery service. This integration has to cover the end-to-end processes from order entry to the delivery at the client site. When the customer selects an item in the catalogue he should be able to immediately order it (by just one or a few mouse clicks). Once he has ordered it, the item has to be either taken from the catalogue (if it was only available once) or it has to be re-ordered. If you currently don't have other systems in place, the front-end

---

[19] Source: www.shop.org/nr/98/111898.html

should be ready to interface with back-end applications at a later stage, e.g. with a delivery tracking system or the ERP. In this case, the interfaces must be "open", i.e. adaptable to different formats of data records, and they must support real time single transaction handling, i.e. not only bulk transfers of batches of transactions at certain times of the day, but also immediate processing of incoming transactions and immediate forwarding to the next component in a processing chain. If you have back-end systems already in place, stable interfaces to them must be provided as well.

Extendability: Most applications for online shops provide a good basic functionality. You need to have the possibility, though, to extend them by specific features dedicated to your offering. Usually, those extensions will be done in Java in order to make them executable on your customers' browsers. If you plan to have special audio or video presentations, you should check, how effectively the provided tools support such features.

Security: The software and the technical implementation has to support the key security features. Between your catalogue and the Internet users a firewall needs to be erected (see Figure 7-30) to protect your application and data (e.g. price information or order details) against hackers. Your staff and marketing partners also have to go through the firewall when maintaining the catalogue design or contents. Data transmissions (in particular order and payment information) have to be encrypted by SSL to make sure that the transmitted data cannot be intercepted and changed. And authentication of the customers has to be implemented (e.g. by cookies placed on the customer's PC), by Smartcard/SIM-card, or by passwords in order to prevent fraud commited by the consumers.

In organizations with existing back end systems, Order Entry has to be separated from those existing applications in the back end – this allows flexible changes in either system and you will be able to exchange your back end system without the customers recognizing it. The price you pay for that flexibility with the high integration effort is well invested, because the only alternative would lead to security risks and operational issues. This alternative would be to add the order entry as a customer friendly interface to your normal back end system. Here, you could more easily give the clients information regarding the actual operational processes (e.g. goods in stock), but hackers could more easily enter your back end systems. Furthermore, the different operational patterns would require everyday synchronization leading to difficulties in backup and recovery, e.g. due to 24-hour availability of the order entry system versus some possible batch windows in your normal operations.

Like for the Customer Administration, the Order Entry front end can be used by the customers in self service or by the Customer Service Representatives. Likewise, you should target for as many customer self service possibilities as is reasonable.

Table 11-26: Available tools for Catalogue and Order Entry

Provider	Product name	Characteristics
Ariba	Shopping Mall	For electronic procurement: catalogue to be maintained by the suppliers of a company
Blaze Software (former: Neuron Data)	Advisor	Wizard to guide through online shops Learning system refining the interactions based on past communication Complex setup of business rules Costs: > € 300,000*
Cat@log	Online shop	Award winning application for catalogues to be presented to consumers
Clarify	ClearSales ClearSupport	Front end handling the interactions of Customer Care Representatives of medium to large size businesses with their customers
IBM	Net.Commerce	Integrated Shopping package with Catalogue, Order Entry, Payment, Database, IBM hardware for medium size businesses Costs: > € 5,000*
ICat	ICat	Order Entry and tracking with good integration concept to back end systems
Intershop	Enfinity	Web enabled Catalogue and Order Entry for small businesses; currently prepare a version to also support WAP Costs: > € 5,000*
Oracle	Portal-to-go	Application to make contents of databases accessible from the Web, e.g. via HTML, WML and SMS
Smart Order		Flexible order entry for sales representatives of medium sized businesses Costs per user: a few hundred €*

* Approximate costs for software (excluding hardware and installation efforts)
For websites and additional vendors, see Section 14.4.1

Table 11-26 above lists several of the products available on the market. Many providers, in particular the regional ones (which are not listed in the table), offer their packages at pretty low costs, e.g. for a few hundred or a few thousand Euros. Often the ISPs provide another low cost alternative. For specific customer segments (e.g. frequent travellers or discount seekers) or special offers you should additionally register your offering with bots (see Chapter 5 for a list) and provide the information via mailing lists.

If you want to exploit additional buying potential, you should dynamically reorganize the presentation of the contents of your catalogue in order to highlight such offerings that your individual customer may buy on top of his or her initial desires. This can be achieved by web personalization tools. They have to be linked with the profiles identified in the customer value management and they should use the respective marketing messages as part of the overall marketing campaign. The international market leader for one-to-one marketing for large enterprises is Broadvision. Another provider is Vignette. Please see Sections 14.7 and 14.8 for additional providers.

Recommendations:

- Order Entry should be handled ideally in self service by your customers on the web. The next best option is by the customer care representatives in your call centre or during a sales trip.

- Select your Catalogue and Order Entry software carefully. This component can include at little cost many of the requirements of the other components discussed so far, in particular for boutiques and small eBusinesses.

11.2.5　Delivery servicing

This component is relevant if you deliver physical goods. By service providers, a display of the service quality should be made available.

The components needed for getting to the customer what he wants are now described. Once the goods are available, they need to be delivered.

Delivery servicing covers two major approaches: one is for physical goods, the other one for virtual "goods" and services. For physical goods, the process to take it from the storehouse's shelf, to package it, to label it, to produce the delivery note and invoice, and to transport the goods to the customer is to be covered. This requires a monitoring of the workflows: the actual sequence and duration of activities has to be compared against the anticipated (or desired) sequence and in case of exceptions or delays alarms have to be raised. Such monitoring is handled by workflow software or messaging software. The whole chain from Order Entry to Inventory checking, to Supplies and Procurement and finally the physical tracking of each parcel on its way to the client has to be watched. You can decide then, at which of the stages you want to share that information with your customer. At those stages you can implement "push" messages, i.e. sending out mails or eMails or you can have your customer "pull" the information, i.e. give your customer access to your status tracking database. Your customer may wish to be notified by eMail once the parcel is shipped, so he can expect the delivery one or two days later. And you need to be informed about any delays. This requires an integration with the systems of your partners responsible for the delivery. And they in turn need to have their tracking systems in place: in their distribution centres, in the delivery van, up to the door of the customers.

For virtual goods (e.g. for the electronic newsletter mentioned, or for the search results), you should be able to immediately deliver, i.e. you can send a confirmation of the agreement back, you can show the customer the data he requested or you can activate the new services. Service activation is an important area for providers of telecom and Internet services as well as for ASPs. Whenever no immediate delivery is possible, the delivery process has to be made transparent to the customer and he has to get some physical evidence of the agreed transaction, e.g. confirmation of the deal by Internet, or paper document for the insurance or loan.

The status information of the delivery progress also needs to be fed back to the customer care representative in order to keep him informed about the status of each order, and eventually of the location of each parcel.

Let's walk through the whole delivery process chain:

- Once your Order Entry system has stored the order, your order tracking system has to reflect that accordingly. In fact, the Order Entry system may be extended to cover the aspects of the order progress. If you want to give your clients access to this database, you should rather create a database separate from the Order Entry system to make hacker approaches impossible. Moreover, the uncoupling of the time critical application Order Entry from the less critical application of monitoring the order status allows the front end to be kept up and running with very high service quality.

- Now you need to check your inventories if the ordered items are available. If the goods are in store, you can announce to your customer that it will be packed and shipped immediately (I recommend, that this packing and shipping doesn't need longer, but really means immediately, e.g. the same day or even the same hour).

- For items you need to order from your suppliers, you still should have some information available about how long you expect the order to take. Do you see how the same approach (order entry, inventory checking and possibly checking with their suppliers) applies for your interaction with your suppliers? You should be able to automatically include the information obtained from your suppliers into your own order tracking database. And you should let your customer know it.

- Next, you'll have the item ready for packing and shipment. When the item leaves your premises, you may want to inform the customer again so he can double check, if he receives it shortly after. You should also have your internal rules, when to do a shipment of partial orders and when you wait for all items to be complete. Actually, you also should invite your customer to decide that for himself. For example, if you are a fashion mail-order company, your customers may prefer to wait until the suit is complete, while for books it's okay to receive them one by one. On the other hand, each delivery triggers costs, so you may want to keep the number of partial deliveries low.

- Additionally, in business-to-business constellations, it may be appropriate to track each parcel on its way. Big logistic organizations like DHL, FedEx or UPS, have their own satellite supported parcel tracking systems – and they allow their key customers to check the status of each of their shipments. If you want to relay this information onto your customers you may do so, at least for critical orders and key customers.

- If you realize that the delivery takes longer than the customer may have expected (or even longer than he has requested), you have to let your customer know, maybe by an information channel separate from the usual channels. For example, if you can't stick to an expressed request from a customer, because your supplier ran out of stock, send a very friendly apology to the customer, explain the reasons for the delay, and try to talk him out of the option to cancel the order.

Depending on how well all your applications are integrated, you can decide not to send the status information at each of the stages to the customer. Instead, you can wait until you can write something meaningful, such as "Thank you for your order. Unfortunately, we don't have the item you ordered in stock. Instead, we have checked with our suppliers and they promise to deliver within seven days. So, you can expect our shipment afterwards".

Such delivery status updates are a great way to mentally relate your customer back to his last order – and to the company serving him so nicely. So, it's a good (and low cost) way to strengthen the relationship with your customer and to increase customer retention. Amazon.com has implemented these features in a well balanced way; check their homepage and submit an order just to see how they keep you in the loop.

I've described the functions with a leading edge model in mind – and I'm sorry to tell you, that you don't get it supported with an off-the-shelf solution. You can get approximations from various angles. The basic feature applicable also by small *e*Businesses is a generator of *e*Mails. You can use it to send out pre-defined texts at the different stages of your order progress. To trigger the *e*Mail messages, you can expand your Order Entry system and set flags whenever the next stage of an order is achieved. If you want to invest in a further integration with your suppliers and your delivery contractor, you may use a workflow tool: then you can flexibly configure service levels, time limitations, you can trigger alternative activities and launch escalation procedures.

Now let's look at some of the available packages. For the additionally mentioned *e*Mail generator, check with your ISP; he should be able to offer you some standard functionality.

Table 11-27: Tool instances for delivery servicing

Provider	Product name	Characteristics
ERP systems e.g. from • Baan • JDEdwards • Peoplesoft • SAP		Inventory tracking as one component of ERP Support for large enterprises; SAP also offering an easier-to-use version for small and medium enterprises usable as outsourced service
FileNet	DMS Panagon/Visual Workflo	Document Management System: Imaging of paper mail and *e*Mail, automated handling of documents according to indexes. Workflow to integrate the process steps and to trigger alarms in case of delays

Table 11-27 (continued)

Provider	Product name	Characteristics
ICat	Order entry and delivery tracking	
Lucent	Netcare	Monitoring the performance of the network and pursuing fixes by the field force
		For medium and large network providers
Microsoft	Excel Spreadsheet	Low cost approach for small companies
		Flexible tool that can be set up for inventory tracking; needs to be customized in order to be useful
		Manual interface with Order Entry and Supplier system necessary
Smart Order	Online catalogue with integration to delivery service	

For websites and additional vendors see Section 14.4

Recommendations:

- Keep your customers informed about the progress of their orders, in particular when they can expect your delivery.

- Have the actual delivery carried out by an outsourcing partner.

- Integrate the ongoing information from your delivery partner into your information stream provided to your customer.

11.2.6   Supplies and procurement

This component is relevant if you need to purchase supplies regularly; in particular if those supplies are the key items of your day-to-day deliveries.

Supply Chain Management can be implemented by boutiques and smaller Businesses based on manual processes supported by spreadsheets. For example, when the inventory spreadsheet indicates that a certain item falls below a pre-defined threshold, the employee in charge can send an earlier agreed type of *e*Mail to the supplier or he can directly enter it into the supplier's order entry system. As the payment terms have been agreed in the contractual framework, the employee in charge doesn't have to worry about this area. Of course, the different agreements with the various vendors need to be clear, i.e. if there are specific minimum orders or if there are price advantages if you order larger quantities.

In larger enterprises, the same can be handled by an automatic procurement system. And the procurement system can automatically optimize the order quantities, the timing of the deliveries and their costs. Such optimization should consider: the cost per item that can be smaller, if you order large quantities; the cost for shipment that can be smaller, if you allow for more time in the delivery process. This means, that you may need to have several thresholds in your ordering and procurement systems: a higher level threshold where you can re-order a large quantity by slow transportation and a lower level alarm threshold, where you need to re-order quickly, but only as many goods as you need to fulfill the short-term customer demand.

The functions of a procurement system include:

- Purchasing including contract and vendor handling, order entry and checking/approval.
- Reception handling including service and quality level tracking, external receipts and internal communication regarding reception.
- Pricing optimizations, e.g. discount schemes, delivery sizes and costs.
- Finance including budgeting, controlling, payments.

A few more comments regarding the implementation. Consider your interaction with your suppliers. They use the same eBusiness approach you are using with your business customers. In good relationships between the provider (or supplier) and the customer, you will find a seemless integration of the process activities inside the provider (or supplier) organization and the customer organization. In fact, you can agree on where the limitation of the two organizations have to be: In our example with the suppliers you might allow your supplier to look (electronically) into your stocks and to send automatically additional supplies once your stock has fallen below the thresholds you defined (in your profile maintained on your suppliers' IT systems).

Table 11-28: Procurement systems vendors

Provider	Product name	Category	Characteristics
AMS	Procurement desktop	Software framework	Approach for large organizations Not feasible for SMEs
Ariba	Operations Resource Management System ORMS	Catalogue ("Mall") to publish offerings of all suppliers to the recipients	Integrated solution In US, many suppliers have their standard offerings ready for ORMS users
Commerce One		Purchasing and procurement	
Intelisys	i-Procurement: IEC-Enterprise	Procurement and SCM	

For websites and additional vendors see Section 14.9

To help you to plan the thresholds mentioned above, to balance your supply ordering with your financial performance and to keep track of the various resources such as physical goods, money, human resources, Enterprise Resource Planning (ERP) systems are on the market. In any case, you'll need the business considerations reflecting the Enterprise Resource Planning aspects; it depends on your size, if you need a full ERP system or if a spreadsheet approach is sufficient.

Are you dizzy from all those inversions of provider/supplier/customer? About suppliers checking their customer's inventory in their customer's systems? From lower level employees being empowered to order goods on your behalf – or even systems doing that automatically directly with the suppliers' systems? That's why I was talking about a new business paradigm earlier in the book.

Recommendations:

- As a smaller company, you have to be ready to submit your offerings information into the procurement mall of your business customers.

- As a large company, you should implement a procurement system and ask your suppliers to enter their offerings into it.

11.3   ISP HOSTING AND TELCO NETWORK

The selection of your telco and ISP partner will be crucial for your start. You will be interfacing directly with the telco network. The quality of the services provided by your web hosting partner will be very visible by your customers.

11.3.1   ISP Hosting

Access to the public Internet is a prerequisite for every eBusiness.

We've discussed the focus of the different tiers of ISPs in Chapter 7. In order for you to select the right partner, I recommend to start talking to the big players, i.e. the tier 1 and tier 2 ISPs in your region. This is often the ex-monopolist in a country and thus also the telco provider (e.g. British Telecom, Deutsche Telekom, AT&T) or their primary competitor (e.g. Mannesmann Arcor, Sprint, Qwest). The discussion with those providers and the materials you obtain from them will give you a head start into the details of your country's telco choices, regulations, and pricing schemes. You will see several different telephone lines offered, e.g. ISDN, DSL, Leased line transmission types, and you will get the service package for ISP offerings with a choice of quality levels.

All decisions depend highly on your specific situation. For the telco environment of a start-up in Europe, for example, with only a few staff that use Internet services simultaneously, I would recommend ISDN with one or several lines depending on the number of staff, because this has achieved a high quality here. In the US, DSL is rather the candidate of choice, because this is wider spread. For larger companies, a leased line to the ISP may be appropriate. Here, the situation is different country by country, or even town by town. In some big towns, fibre-optic cables have been installed by private network operators, e.g. COLT, but you may not be able to access them from the suburb nearby.

The ISP offering is also to be selected based on your initial needs. The larger providers offer the full service for complex projects (like Qwest in the US) and others offer entry packages for small and medium enterprises (like Deutsche Telekom, Sprint, uunet or IBM to name some) that include already catalogue and payment solutions. An advantage of those preconfigured packages is, that you don't need to worry about all the details and that you can obtain the professional help to set the systems up for your sales situation. So it's good for a start. The disadvantage is that some of your flexibility may be restricted.

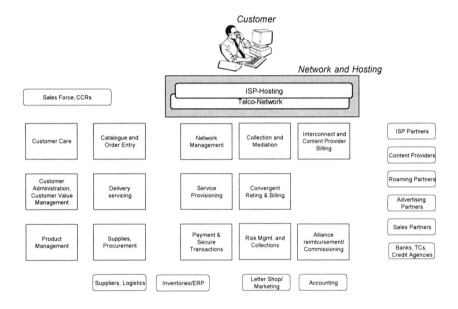

Figure 11-45: Network and Hosting

Once you have gained the initial overview of the general network and ISP offerings from the information provided by the large players, you can check the local offerings regarding some specialised providers. You get this information from the usual sources, in particular local press with rankings of the various providers. With the higher ranking providers you then can compare the service offering and pricing against the offer from the large players.

Here's a brief checklist for your selection of an ISP; first of all the necessary ISP core capabilities are listed and secondly "nice to have" additional services.

Domain: Can you get your own domain (e.g. mycompany.com) or will it be a sub-domain of the provider (e.g. provider.mycompany.com)?

Security: What types of secure transmission does the ISP provide, e.g. encryption of *e*Mail attachments and other data transmissions like order entries, what's the length of the encryption key (the longer the better)? Where are the firewalls and how often are they re-tested, how is the system protected against viruses?

eMail: How many separate eMail addresses can be maintained (e.g. one per website, one per your departments, or even one for each of your staff)? How are mailing lists supported, e.g. can you define mailing lists for marketing activities, can customers subscribe and un-subscribe from mailing lists?

Statistics: Do you get hit statistics for your website? Do the hit statistics include the link from where the customer came before he surfed on your website?

Support times: Does the ISP support you whenever needed, i.e. 24 hours a day and 365 days a year? Is there also support available for your customers?

Service levels: How is the commitment for sufficiently high bandwidth to support quick downloads to your customers? Which points of presence at the places relevant for you and your customers allow you and your customers quick and cost effective dial up to your ISP? How's the availability guaranteed, i.e. what's the promised maximum down time per month and what compensation will you get in case that promise can't be kept? What are the plans to improve the network and the services?

Flexibility: How quickly can you get more server space, higher bandwidth and different contractual agreements (including early termination of the contract)?

Value added services: Does the ISP support your website implementation, does he provide web design tools, and eBusiness software (in particular catalogue and order entry?

Payment: What payment features at which payment partners can be offered via the ISP, e.g. credit card acquiring at discount fees, digital cash?

Interfaces and compatibility: Can your databases be interfaced with the ISP's network using the standard protocols provided by your existing systems? Are the tools supported you intend to use, e.g. CGI, Java?

Marketing support: Can you approach people by different channels (eMail, SMS, personalized website) and does the ISP help you to create market awareness, e.g. introducing you to other providers for links and search engine entries?

Own server: What are the possibilities for you to connect your own server and your own name server to the ISP once you've grown larger?

Cost: How are the price packages structured – in particular which of the components mentioned above are included in a package and what comes on top? How much cost for accessing the network is to be expected, in particular for dialling up to the points of presence of your provider, or for leased lines if you need to connect your servers directly with the provider.

The more your provider can offer, the easier for your implementation. Let me give you a little advice here: even if the selection of your web host is one of your most visible decisions, you shouldn't invest overly much time in finding the partner with the absolute lowest price for your particular configuration. It might easily happen, that your configuration has to change soon and then your selected partner suddenly has only expensive offerings, or it might be, that your partner is the subject of a merger and acquisition so his business policy changes. So, it's preferable to follow a safe approach and stick to some of the bigger players, provided they offer you the service quality and flexibility we discussed in Chapter 7. You may change those decisions anyway later, in order to achieve better pricing or better performance. And in fact when you grow you should insource the webhosting into your own company. For this stage of your evolution, please refer also to the subsequent paragraphs.

11.3.2   Network access

This component is relevant for every eBusiness.

The physical telephone environment (switches, routers, cables) and the Internet network (servers to host the websites) are needed. A small content provider can outsource its network fully to their ISP, while the ISP or a larger company should use its own Internet server. For the necessary network components please see the following paragraphs.

11.4   ISP AND ASP SERVICES

The creation of the ASP market is a recent development; thus only few best practices are available as yet. Many of the ASP requirements are close to the ISP requirements, though. Therefore, we are now going to discuss the components with an ISP setting in mind. If you intend to launch ASP services, you can use the specific ISP components still as a reference. But even if you neither want to launch an ISP nor an ASP, you are probably interested in sneaking behind the curtain of a very important partner. The ISP components are the five boxes at the right upper side in the Architecture Diagram in Figure 11-46, namely Network Management, Service Provisioning, Collection and Mediation, Convergent Rating and Billing, Interconnect and Content Billing.

11.4.1   Network elements and management

This component is relevant when you host your website yourself and for ISPs and ASPs.

First of all, the physical networks for telephone (switches, routers, cables) and the Internet (servers to host the websites) are needed. The size of the environment needs to be planned after a performance simulation. Once the components are implemented, they need to be operated and managed.

The network management needs to cover for the service quality of the telecommunication environment as described above. This includes availability and operations of the switches, the routers for the calls to find the appropriate and least cost lines for the call, the agreements with Interconnect, Roaming and Backbone partners to use their lines in case their own network can't handle additional calls, the bridges between various environments (e.g. WAP servers to make Internet information readable on the display of mobile handsets). Additionally, trouble tickets need to be created (some manually and some automatically) when network elements have problems and require repair or maintenance. Those trouble tickets need to be sent to the field service and the trouble resolution has to be monitored.

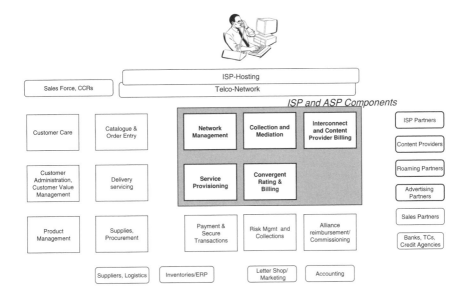

Figure 11-46: Components for ISPs and ASPs

The functional requirements of the Network Management include:

- Planning and monitoring of network performance
- Implementation and extensions of the network
- Operations, Maintenance and Repair of the network
- Service levels to be maintained.

This is to be supported by the appropriate performance monitoring tools in order to highlight problem areas and to give early warnings regarding bottleneck situations or to switch over to fallback lines in case of problems. It may also be supported by tools for the field service, e.g. planning for new implementation or repair, recording of problems and monitoring of the progress of problem fixes. Some of the vendors in that field are listed in Table 11-27 below:

Table 11-29: Network component vendors

Provider	Core activity	Comments
Cisco	Hardware, e.g. routers	The routers handle the communication aspects between your web-server and the public Internet. Has to have the firewall implemented
		Cisco has a great website highlighting the eBusiness approach: online orders, online self service, active communities
Lucent	Full network solutions: hardware, operations, services for third parties (as for ISPs)	Subsidiaries of Lucent provide additional software, e.g. for telco billing
NCR	Hardware, e.g. financial peripherals	
	Software, e.g. performance tools	
Sun	Hardware, e.g. Internet servers	On the Internet server, your website is physically stored. Each hit, i.e. request to see your website, triggers that the appropriate frame is downloaded to the surfer via the routers and the communication connection

For websites and additional vendors see Sections 14.8 to 14.10

Recommendations:

- Smaller companies should outsource their webhosting to an ISP.

- All other eVentures should run their own web servers.

11.4.2   Service Provisioning and Configuration

This component is relevant if you provide ISP or ASP services as well as for telco operators.

Provisioning is necessary whenever a change of the activated services needs to be applied. Consider in normal telecommunication a new customer: the provider needs to indicate his telephone number to the switches, he has to configure the service as if the customer is entitled to have call forwarding or mailbox services, and the switches need to activate the recording of the usage according to the payment scheme you have set up with the customer. Once the customer cancels a certain service (or the provider wants to stop him from using some of the services), the switches need to know as well. This provisioning is pretty complex for mobile telecommunications, because you need to make sure, that at any place where a customer can initiate a call, the authorization is properly reflected and the call details are properly transferred back to the billing. In fact, this becomes even more complex with roaming partners: whenever the subscriber switches his mobile on in another country, the system of the provider must exchange the appropriate information with the system of his roaming partner.

For ISPs similar areas have to be covered: the subscriber service has to be configured according to the contractual agreement, e.g. set-up of eMail, web-hosting with functions like website editing, quality and bandwidth of lines, security features. For ASPs provisioning means to set up the appropriate configuration. In case of an ERP system provided via the web, for example, it means establishing the appropriate chart of accounts for the customer, define his payment preferences and store the data of his budget.

The areas to be covered by Provisioning are:

- Automated flow-through service activation with configuration of the service via the web
- Full range of services, from simple to complex
- Interfaces to network media and network technologies (for ISPs)
- Interface to back-end application (for ASPs)
- Flexibility to cope with heterogeneous network and IT equipment.

For the provisioning, two major steps need to be taken. You need to initiate billing for the usage of your services (i.e. an interface from provisioning to your payment component; we will discuss the payment aspects in Section 11.5). Additionally, the activation of the specific service is necessary. For Internet and telco services it can be handled by specific tools, which are indicated below.

Table 11-30: Service Provisioning packages

Provider	Product name	Coverage
Architel	ASAP	Telco activation
	InterGate	Interconnect requests
Comptel	MDS	Telco activation
XaCCT Technologies	XaCCTusage	Internet service activation and billing

For websites and additional vendors see Section 14.9

The activation of services in the operational systems from an ASP still require some specific manual tasks, for example configuring new areas in the database, setting up the appropriate parameters such as accounting structures, or preparing the reporting schemes. As this is to be done in close conjunction with your operational application, no standard tools are available – I still want to recommend you to strive for an easy configuration of your operational systems in order to support the activation of larger number of customers.

Recommendation:

- Check references provided by the vendors, if they are applicable for your business situation before you decide for any of the tools.

11.4.3   Collection and Mediation

This component is relevant for usage based pricing, e.g. for telco and Internet providers and ASPs.

Collection and Mediation is necessary to record the usage of services (e.g. telephone services like making phone calls or transferring data, or Internet services like the display of certain contents). It will also be relevant for ASPs that want to bill their customers based on the number of data records they have submitted for processing.

In order to understand the general approach to billing, let me explain the historical evolution of telephone billing. This is still the conceptual base for Internet billing. The telephone systems issue little impulses whenever one unit according to the tariff was passed during a call. The impulses were counted at the switch close to the subscriber, every once in a month recorded (e.g. by making a photograph of all the counters in the switch) and then used to produce a bill – simply by multiplying the units with the current price per unit. Since the deregulation of the telecom markets and the invention of many new tariffs, this doesn't work any more. Instead, the exact details of each call are now stored electronically in the switch, and so called Call Data Records (CDRs) are transferred to the central place where the billing takes place. The CDRs formats from various vendors of the switches differ. Therefore, a component is needed

- to translate all the various formats into a common format;
- to check duplicated records (due to transmission errors from the switches);
- to collate different physical records into one logical record – for example, some switches produce two separate CDRs, if a call begins before midnight, and ends after midnight; also if you use your mobile phone while driving in your car, there may be several CDRs for it, because on your way, you will be passed from cell to cell and each of them has a fraction of your actual call.

That's what Collection and Mediation is for. In addition, data integrity checks need to be performed according to a variety of rules. After those steps, the standardized CDRs contain data such as caller, called number, start and end time of call. Subsequently the actual billing takes place (see next section).

So far, I've described the functions by using normal telecommunication examples. The same approach has been adopted for content billing, but now the type of information is different. While for the normal CDRs you store information such as who did call who from where at which time, for ISP content billing you need information such as which website was called by who, what content was displayed, where the mouse was clicked, which advertising banners were shown, which data volumes were transferred. This information is not provided by the switches, but you have to collect it from the web hosts and store it in Transaction Data Records (TDRs). The further processing of the TDRs works then as for CDRs, i.e. a clean-up and standardization of the records is performed.

For ASPs, you can collect the usage data like the Internet TDRs. A different approach is possible as well. If the back end software of the ASP is capable of counting the transactions, those can be used as the basis for the bill, either.

Table 11-31: Collection and Mediation packages

Provider	Product name	Coverage
ATG	Dynamo	Web personalization
Comptel	MDS	Telecom Call Data Record (CDR) mediation
XaCCT Technologies	XaCCTusage	Internet transaction billing

For websites and additional vendors see Section 14.9

Recommendation:

- Check references provided by the vendors, if they are applicable for your business situation before you decide for any of the tools.

11.4.4   Convergent Rating and Billing

This component is relevant if you run your own telco or Internet network or if you charge for your IT systems based on actual usage, e.g. as an ASP.

The billing activities require a whole chain of action due to the large numbers of data that need to be processed. We've already talked about collection of the call data. The collection and mediation component provides the uniformly formatted event records, e.g. Call Data Records (CDRs) or Internet Transaction Data Records (TDRs). CDRs and TDRs can be from switched networks as a result of dial-up calls for voice or data transmission or they can be triggered by the actual view of the web contents. Other events can be based on recurring charges for leased lines or subscription fees triggered by a calendar date, or they can be the usage of specific data services (e.g. payable data downloads). In case of an ASP, the events have to be derived from the transactions that are processed by the operational system. Once the events (e.g. CDRs or TDRs) are provided and the data quality is checked, the rating can start: you need to apply the appropriate price tag to each of the events. The price tag needs to be identified by the system based on the tariff as agreed with the customer, the time of day, the duration, the region of the call such as local/national/international, and discounts. This is handled by the rating machinery using the underlying product and tariff data as well as customer groupings. So you get a "raw" price for each of the calls. This can contain something like the line you see on your itemized phone bill. Then, the actual bill needs to be produced. At certain dates of the month, at the end of the "billing cycle", all the itemized calls are taken, added up and printed on the bill. From all the itemized raw prices, the final price is calculated including additional factors like sales tax, overall discounts, or corrections from earlier periods. At this time the entries in the accounting system need to be made as well, i.e. debiting the customer accounts and crediting the income accounts.

At the time of printing the bill, the ISP may want to include some marketing material with the mail. In this case or for huge print volumes, the ISP takes a letter shop to produce this mailing. Or he allows his customers to see the bill on the web – then he has to publish it via the web. Some of the business customers may want to use the billing information for their internal accounting and controlling – so they can be sent on a CD-ROM or as a file via the Internet.

Billing either takes place at predefined days within a month or the customer can request "hot billing", i.e. the preparation of a bill on the spot. Additionally, for pre-paid services, the system must permanently monitor how much money is left on the calling card and switch the connection off once the card has no more money on it. A service required more and more by the customers, is to be able to inquire the status of their "account" permanently: when the customer ends his call, he expects to see the costs of the call a few seconds later on the Internet.

That's about it – except for the word convergent. This indicates, that many customers (in particular business customers) don't like to receive a lot of different invoices for their different services used. They prefer to have everything in one place: the telephone bill, conference calls and video conference costs, the monthly charges for the usage of the Internet services, and the charges for the web hosting. That's what the word convergent stands for: have everything on one bill. Well, not every customer wants that, so the billing system better be flexible again to support different bill formats, different levels of aggregation (e.g. with all the branches of a business customer or for each branch individually).

If you have to support all those features, you need a very well designed rating and billing engine plus a neat integration with the network management system. For example, we talked about stopping the call once the client runs out of money. In order to do this, your rating and billing must realize the situation and report it back to the network within a few seconds. More recent developments have made the networks more "intelligent", so some of those functions can already be covered by the network itself – but then you need to set up your network components in a more sophisticated way.

Table 11-32: Rating and Billing solutions

Provider	Product name	Area of scope
AMS	Tapestry INAdvance	Telco and Internet billing, Prepaid billing. For large and very large providers (up to more than > 20 million subscribers)
Intec	InterconnecT	Interconnect billing
Kenan	Arbor	Telco and Internet billing. For large providers.
Portal	Infranet	Internet customer care and billing; scalable to more than a million subscriptions.
Solect	IAF Horizon	Internet billing

For websites and additional vendors see Section 14.9

For usage based billing of ASPs, a different approach is possible as well, as mentioned already in the section above. If the back end software is capable of counting the transactions, those can be used as the basis for the bill, also. If your customer wants to have those charges printed together with his other billing items, you should integrate them as well into your billing system.

Recommendations:

• Check if the provided tools meet your performance needs and implement a scalable solution supporting your growth scenarios.

• As an ASP, look for the most effective way of payment; often a subscription will be easier to implement than a usage based price.

11.4.5   Partner Billing

With the various partners for interconnect, roaming, and backbone support, telco providers, ISPs and ASPs have payments to send and payments to receive. They owe each other money for their customers who used the other ISP's infrastructure. These amounts due in the two directions need to be balanced and reconciled in regular intervals, and the differential payment is to be made. This balancing and reconciliation applies of course to all the companies the telco provider or ISP is partnering with. This includes national and international partners in fix wire and mobile and partner ISPs on the various tiers.

Content provider billing has to take place in a similar way. First of all, the content providers owe their web host or ISP the appropriate charges. On the other hand, their ISP may receive micro-payments from those people who have viewed a chargeable website. Now, the ISP where the content provider has his website hosted, can be different from the one of the consumer downloading that site. Therefore, those micro-payments require a regular balancing and clearing between the various engaged parties.

Interconnect Billing

This component is relevant if you run your own telco network.

Interconnect and Content Provider Billing is based on similar events as the Convergent Rating and Billing. In an ideal world, you should expect that you only need one billing system taking care of the various types of billing. Unfortunately, this is only true for very large platform systems. Off-the-shelf packages are usually focused on a particular target group: the Rating and Billing system takes care of the subscriber and user fees, Interconnect Billing handles the charges between various telco providers and Content Provider Billing calculates and passes the fees for the particular web contents.

Before implementing such a system, you should assess if you get a reasonable cost benefit ratio. If you have a small number of interconnect partners and the agreements with each of them are not overly complex, you still might use your normal billing system in order to keep track of the call and routing details. Then, you can feed this information into a spreadsheet in order to calculate the fees to be cleared between you and each interconnect partner. As a matter of fact, audits of several interconnect implementations have shown, that the expensive package software often was not configured right, so the calculated charges were wrong. The reason for the mistake is easy to understand: in contrast to billing the subscribers, the number of bills is small, so constellations can be different every time and it takes long until everything is tested and runs properly. Guess, how the audits of such packages are performed – yes, spreadsheets are used! So, my argument is simple: don't invest much time in getting a complex system right, better implement an easier, more flexible and less costly approach.

Content Provider Billing

This component is relevant if you are an ISP and get significant revenues from your content providers

The common ground for content billing is that the Internet user has obtained some information or data for which he has to pay a fee to the provider of the information or data. This information, for example, can be the research result from a database or a dictionary, it can be news like weather, politics or stock prices. The ISP may get a fraction of the payment, provided that he's helping the content provider collect his money. Currently the business models for content billing haven't matured yet. Therefore, the package support for this area is still little. Let's have a look at the different business models as they currently emerge and their respective IT coverage.

Subscription: This is the approach used currently by most of the content providers. The Internet user can subscribe to their offering, e.g. journals. He pays the subscription fee, either as an electronic transaction by entering his credit card number, or with traditional means, i.e. invoice and/or direct debit. Then he obtains a password from the content provider and can access the information for the agreed period. As the payment is handled directly between the content provider and the subscriber, the only way to generate revenues for the ISP is to monitor the value generated for the content provider and charge for the transportation of the information underpinning that value.

Micropayments: They are charged to the subscriber or user together with the telephone and Internet usage bill, but the final recipient of the payment is not the telephone operator or Internet provider, instead it's the provider of the content. The content provider has to indicate how expensive the website or specific data on it are, before the Internet user actually opens the information. Then this price tag has to be used to be charged to the user's telephone/Internet bill and the telephone/Internet provider has to take care of payment and collections. Once the telephone/Internet provider has received the payment, he can forward it to the content provider. For these services, the telephone/Internet provider can get a commission from the content provider. This type of payment in theory is covered in modern subscriber billing systems (including pre-payment functions), but I haven't seen such systems in production in this area. Several providers claim, that such functions are covered by the design and that the system would be scalable enough to support the additional volume of transactions. But as you probably don't want to invest two digit million Euro amounts into this area, I don't include the platforms at this early stage of development in my list below. Despite the conceptual clarity of the micropayment approach, the question is, if it will succeed in the long run, because the difficulty will be to agree on the payment standards between all the various players (content providers, ISPs, subscribers).

Digital coins: I expect, that this approach will be the most commonly used in the next few years. Here, the traditional banking approaches can be re-used. The digital coins are issued by banks, the coins can be traded between merchants and customers and they are collected again (and guaranteed for their value!) by the banks. The practical benefit of digital coins is, that the payment approaches don't need to be re-invented; only the billing systems must be capable of carrying the digital coins along. The open business question remains, how the payment centres and ISPs can make money with digital coins. I expect, that the digital coins as such can be obtained by the consumers at face value (at least in the long run), so the whole process of issuing certificates for each coin will only generate costs for the payment centres. The banks may generate some margin from the consumers, if they provide the coins as a loan (resulting in interest income), or they can ask for some handling fees to transfer the digital coins back to real money. The ISPs may ask for some handling fees as well. But the value for the banks and ISPs should be rather in the overall service for each of those customer groups than in fees from payment activities. Regarding IT support, the digital coins are still in their early stages; no proven technologies exist yet (refer also to the next section). In my list at the end of the book (see Section

14.6), I indicate the providers that currently prepare digital payment solutions; you may check with their offerings once you implement such payments.

Recommendations:

- Check if the provided tools meet your performance needs.

- Implement a scalable solution supporting your growth scenarios.

11.5   FINANCE AND PAYMENT COMPONENTS

All eVentures need back office functions for payment and risk management. In addition to the eVenture specific components discussed below, namely Payment/ SET, Risk Management and Collections, and Alliance Reimbursement, standard accounting or ERP tools will be necessary. Depending on the size of the company, they can be outsourced or run inhouse. Some global ERP vendors are indicated in Section 14.4.

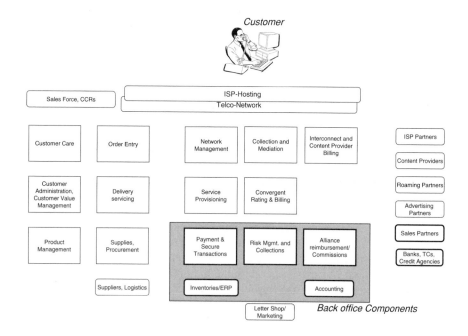

Figure 11-47: Finance and payment components

11.5.1   Payment and Secure Transactions

This component is relevant for all types of companies.

We've discussed the pro's and con's of the different approaches in Chapter 7. Now let's look at the implementation.

Card based payment: The easiest way to implement a payment system is to just interface with a credit card company (actually with the acquiring network of a credit card company) or with the ec card clearing. That's what each merchant is doing: he installs a little magnetic card reader that automatically dials up to the credit card acquirer, receives an authorization (i.e. the approval for the transaction) and compiles all transactions in order to claim the money from the acquirer.

On the web, the card information usually is to be entered when a certain transaction (i.e. purchasing) takes place or when the customer masterfile information is initially entered. At the time of a purchase, the card details are transferred to the credit card acquirer, they check it against the files of the credit card issuer, and once an approval is made to the merchant, the customer can proceed with his purchase.

The files with the card details need to be transmitted in the formats defined by the acquirers. They will support you in setting up the environment. For the transmission of the numbers, interception needs to be prevented by encryption software.

Other traditional payment methods: If you allow the customers to initiate the payment by themselves, e.g. by money transfer or cheque, you need to match your accounts receivable with the incoming payments. This can be handled manually in smaller companies or with your accounting and ERP systems in larger enterprises.

In the countries where direct debits are possible, you need to check with the local clearing centre for the file formats they require. Then you can set the interfaces up.

Digital money: Legal, technical and business standards emerge and implementations are now underway. For example, credit card institutions and the IT industry have agreed ECML (Electronic Commerce Markup Language). This allows the consumer to pre-define his standard payment profile in an electronic wallet on his PC or on his Smartcard. This information is transferred in an encrypted way to the service provider. He should follow the customer's preferred payment method and gets his money from the bank or credit card provider accordingly.

Still the implementation in your *e*Venture may currently be cumbersome, as only little standard software is available yet to transfer the data as provided by the consumer automatically into the IT processes at your side. Only for specific areas prototype approaches exist; we discussed the example of Adobe that allows to open transferred files only after the customer has performed his payment. Therefore, as of today, you need to do the integration by some customized code. But for the near future standard tools can be expected to fulfill that function, so you should hold off until some proven approaches are rolled out in the market.

Payment providers: Given the different payment environment in each country, the market is fragmented, again. There are no strong global players in the system market, except for the large credit card corporations. My recommendation is to get in touch with them – often they can supply you with the appropriate solution to link between your equipment and their payment authorization and clearing.

Table 11-33: Payment providers

Provider	Core business
Adobe	Document publishing
American Express	Credit Card
Brokat	SET
GZS/Euro-cheque	Debit Card
MasterCard International/Eurocard	Credit Card
Visa Card International	Credit card

For websites and additional providers see Section 14.6

Recommendations:

- As a minimum, interface with banks and credit card companies.

- Larger enterprises should handle key areas of payment and risk management inhouse where cost advantages can be exploited, e.g. by reducing credit card transactions in favour of debit card transactions or digital cash.

11.5.2   Risk Management and Collections

This component is relevant for all types of companies that want to step away from credit card commissions.

The alternative to paying the discussed premiums to credit card providers, banks and trust centres, is the implementation of an inhouse risk management system. The risk management system has to answer questions like: Who are the clients who usually pay (from a historic perspective and regarding their expected behaviour for the future)? How can you identify the "customers" that try to cheat you? With your risk management system answering such questions, e.g. by statistical data analysis, you can use different payment approaches for the different customer segments. Customers with low risk profiles can enjoy deferred payments, can get loans with low interest rates from you, and can continue ordering with a high payment amount outstanding. On the other hand, a customer with a high risk profile may be requested to do a pre-payment for the services, or pay higher prices to cover for their default risk which you in turn can use to apply more expensive payment means like credit cards or factoring approaches.

The first step of an implementation is to get a credit worthiness rating. For business customers (at least for those traded at stock exchanges), you can obtain ratings from various agencies, e.g. Moody's or Standard & Poors. For other customers you can get some restricted credit profiles and payment behaviours. The level of detail of this information is different country by country, but at least you get the records of past bankruptcies. Additionally, for consumers you can implement some easy formulas based on regular income and liquid assets minus regular expenses, in order to assign your customer to the various credit worthiness rankings. And of course, after some time you have your own records of payment behaviour of the various customers.

As a next step, you should define your credit policy for the various rankings. To give you some examples: the best ranked customers might get a credit of receiving your transactions up to their regular monthly income, the worst ranked customers need to pre-pay for the use of your services.

But all those rankings are just based on rear-view analysis – nobody can predict the individual future payment behaviour of your customers. Therefore, you will be confronted with some defaults. In order to realize the most of your accounts receivables, the choice is yours between different options. Either you can sell the accounts to factoring companies from which you'll receive some 80 per cent to 95 per cent of their face value, depending on the risk profile of the accounts. Or you can implement focused collection approaches with early reminders to the defaulting customers, agreements on down-payments of the owed amounts and a default-triggered change in the payment agreements for new transactions, i.e. pre-payments. As a third alternative, you can write off smaller amounts, if this is cheaper than the other options. The best recipe is to cover for the costs of risks that you incur with either of the discussed options by higher prices for worse risk customers. In some areas, you can only do that indirectly, e.g. by special price offerings that are only contracted with the appropriate customers.

Table 11-34: Risk Management and Collections providers

Provider	Characteristics
AMS	CACS: Software package with integrated workflow for collections
Dun & Bradstreet	Credit Worthiness Assessment and Information, Dunning and Collections
Moody's	Credit Worthiness Rating and Economic Research
Standard & Poors	Credit Worthiness Rating

For websites see Section 14.6.4

> **Recommendations:**
> - Smaller companies have to rely on information such as risk ratings and calculated default probabilities from outsourcing partners.
> - Larger companies can use custom IT solutions.

11.5.3   Alliance Reimbursement and Commissioning

This function is relevant for all types of companies; a manual implementation will be sufficient in the most cases.

Usually, your accounting or ERP system (even if it's spreadsheet based) should suffice for the payment handling with your alliances and sales partners. You should set up agreements with lump sum payments to be performed at certain times in order not to have a too complex monitoring and implementation.

Some business scenarios, though, need special support for such reimbursement, e.g. when you process large amounts of small transactions. We mentioned banner ads and links where a close tracking of the web hits is appropriate. Providers of free Internet services live to a good extent from placing such banner ads. The fees depend upon the number of hits generated by their subscribers and views (i.e. the number of times the subscribers have clicked on the banner) which need to be exactly monitored.

With your sales partners, e.g. resellers of your services or link partners that may get a commission for customers acquired, you also need to establish clear invoicing schemes. For small number of customers it can be done manually, for larger numbers an easy implementation is still to store the identity of the sales partner who acquired the customer in your master file information in order to generate a report with the newly acquired customers from time to time.

For a technical solution, first of all you need to track the single events that trigger the respective payments. Going back to the examples listed above:

- You have to count each time an advertisement (e.g. a banner) of one of your advertising partners was shown on the screen of one of your Internet users. This can be achieved by hit statistics based on the Collection and Mediation components as described above.
- You need to scan your contract files for the sales partner who closed the deal to come up with the overall quantity of closures for a periodic commission payment.
- You can extract the detailed transactions from your supplies, delivery and payment databases for calculating the respective handling charges or for checking, if your partners calculated their fees correctly.

Off-the-shelf solutions for all the aspects from event counting to invoice generation and payment don't exist. For some areas, you can get dedicated IT systems. I give you an overview of the platforms below – you probably don't need to implement any of the larger systems at your business launch, but maybe you'll find some of them appropriate at later growth stages. The low cost approach, again, is to use the counters for the various events as they are implemented in your different other billing systems and then feed them into a spreadsheet.

Table 11-35: Software platforms for billing allies and partners

Provider	Product name	Characteristics
AMS	Provis	Commissioning for sales partners
	Tapestry	Rating and billing, e.g. for Interconnect and micro-billing
ATG	Dynamo	Monitoring of Internet click streams and link usage
Intec	InterconnecT	Telecom interconnect billing for inter-operator billing
ERP systems		Financial status of the transactions can be monitored; invoices can be generated
• Baan		
• JDEdwards		Statistics can be generated in order to cross–check invoices from partners
• Peoplesoft		
• SAP		

For websites see Sections 14.4.3 and 14.9

Recommendations for partner billing:

- Smaller companies should monitor the transactions with their partners and use a spreadsheet to calculate the fees and commissions.

- Larger companies should use custom IT solutions.

11.6   CHECKLISTS

The checklists summarize the components relevant for the different eVentures; the providers are listed above and in Chapter 14. The components below are listed in the sequence of the discussions you should have with your prospective vendors. For boutiques and smaller companies the first items on the list should cover the requirements reasonably. Larger eBusinesses will need dedicated systems for the various functions in order to have the appropriate performance for the growing user base.

Table 11-36: Checklist for customer relationship components

	Recommendation	IT use	Your decision
Website	Static and dynamic **website**	Smaller eBus.: **ISP** hosting	
	To include eMail support and mailing lists	Large eBus:Internal	

Table 11-36 (continued)

	Recommendation	IT use	Your decision
Cata-logue	To be used **for all items to be sold or purchased** via the web With a good functionaliy of the Catalogue software, most of the subsequent components should be redundant	**Absolute must** for electronic sales and electronic procurement	
Payment and Secure Trans-actions	Depending on the profit margins, the payment channel costs (e.g. credit card fees), and the risk profile of your customers, you may **outsource** it, e.g. your ISP might have a standard agreement with a payment provider	Absolute must[*] Initially preference for easy implemen-tation, e.g. credit cards	
Order Entry	Target is **customer self service** to enter their orders themselves Should be integrated with Catalogue	Strongly recommended	
Customer Admini-stration and Customer Value Manage-ment	**Customer administration** to be supported automatically in conjunction with operational application(s) Target is maintenance of master data and preference profiles in **customer self service** Information regarding customer has to be in one place (e.g. **Data Warehouse**): contracts, transactions, prices, customer profile Analyse the past profitability of your customers and estimate their potential in order to assign them to **value categories**	Strongly recommended[*] Strongly recommended[*] Strongly recommended[*] Strongly recommended (low cost approach if possible)	
Customer Care	If Catalogue and Order Entry isn't sophisticated enough and the customer care unit is large while personal knowledge of customer interactions decreases, **Sales and Service** are to be supported by IT	Strongly recommended when larger call centres are planned	
Supplies	**Integrate** your supplies and procurement with your orders	Strongly recommended if you deal with goods	
Delivery Servicing	Keep your customers informed about the status of their orders; can be handled by manual *e*Mails or mailing lists in the beginning	Recommended for companies that physically deliver goods	
Product Manage-ment	**Simulations** can be performed, if you have large enough data volumes usable for statistical extrapolations	Recommended for large enterprises	

[*] Unless included in other component

To get a softcopy of this checklist please visit my website.

Table 11-37: Checklist for Internet service components

Component	Recommendation	IT use	Your decision
Network Components and Management	You need it, if you run telco or Internet **networks**	Telco operators and ISPs can't do without it If you run your own web server, you'll need the appropriate hardware	
Service Provisioning	You need **Provisioning**, if you are a telco operator or an ISP As an ASP, you should get a better efficiency, if you automate provisioning instead of setting up each customer manually	Telco operators and ISPs can't do without it Good for ASPs via the Internet	
Collection and Mediation	You need **Collection and Mediation**, if you have usage based pricing, e.g. as a telco operator, ISP or ASP *	Telco operators and ISPs can't do without it	
Convergent Rating and Billing	You need **Rating and Billing**, if you are a telco operator or ISP*	Telco operators and ISPs can't do without it	
Payment and Secure Transactions	As an ISP, you should provide a general service to your customers (you may even get some commission for the payment handling from them)	Should be implemented in cooperation with a bank or credit card acquirer	
Interconnect and Content Provider Billing	If you are a telco operator or an ISP and you have large numbers of partners or transactions to be monitored, you should consider an automated solution	Recommended for Telco operators and ISPs	

* Good for ASPs for usage based pricing unless back-end system monitors usage

To obtain a softcopy of this checklist please see my website.

Table 11-38: Checklist for back office components

Component	Recommendation	IT use	Your decision
Accounting/ ERP	To monitor the performance, accounting, planning and controlling tools need to be implemented	Low cost approach recommended	
Alliance Reimbursement and Commissioning	In a first step, a spreadsheet with manual feeds should be sufficient. If you have large numbers of allies or sales agents, you may automate it; in second step	Considerable for second step	

Table 11-38 (continued)

Component	Recommendation	IT use	Your decision
Risk Management and Collections	Publicly available data should be obtained and recorded in the customer masterfile Customers should report their income and expense situation before you offer them credit features Statistical analysis and pro-active collections should be performed, once the number of data is sufficient and payment defaults start to hurt	Recording of available information strongly recommended Statistical analysis considerable for second step	

* As a boutique, you can outsource it, e.g. to your accountant. After some growth you can use ASP-services from the ERP providers. And larger *e*Businesses can have an inhouse solution

To get a softcopy of this checklist please see my website.

11.7 DISCUSSION POINTS

Publish your experience with specific software vendors, i.e. their product and their service on my website. Each contributor will get free access to updates of the materials of the entrepreneur community.

12

Solid financials

Decide upon the investment for your eVenture after a proper calculation of the return on investment.

Once you have documented the business idea as described in Part I of this book, your organization is outlined and your IT is planned following the approach as shown in the preceding chapters, you should be able to quantify the benefits and the costs. The areas to consider are listed in the business plan section below. The target of the business plan is to identify the date when your investment will pay back. This return on your investment should be pretty quickly, ideally within twelve months. But pay attention; the business plan is just a paper recording your targets. To avoid unrealistically high flying dreams, we then discuss risks and possible mitigation approaches. Once you've also identified the risks for your undertaking, you should review your business plan – and possibly prepare two or three distinct plans: an optimistic, a pessimistic and an intermediary plan.

After your decision to go ahead, those plans can be used for the discussions with investors and they are the baseline for monitoring your actual performance against. Such an evaluation of the actual performance versus your plans has to be done usually monthly. At specific milestones, e.g. quarter yearly, you should additionally have an overall business review with an update of the risks and a full view of the balanced scorecard aspects. At these dates you can decide upon the release of additional investments for your growth, about cost streamlining or additional marketing activities. If you find out at one of those milesone reviews, that your sales develop according to the pessimistic scenario, but the costs according to the optimistic scenario, you probably face serious financial problems and you better tune your approaches – or maybe even stop your eVenture. I hope, that you'll be in another situation, namely to recognize that your revenues are above your plans and therefore you can push for extending your infrastructure and services.

12.1   BUSINESS PLAN

The "no cost" Internet start doesn't work. It's true that the hardware and software for an initial web presence isn't very expensive. In fact you could even start with a "free PC" and your only expenses would be the cost for the connection time. But that's no business. If you want to live from your eVenture you need to set it up right, invest money into your presentation and have sufficient support staff for the customer care. It's still possible to have a low cost approach; we'll discuss that in the following.

You have to organize a real project with sound financials – even as a start-up. The figures below are to be understood as an illustrative example for a three-year planning period. They are based on current market figures[20], but you should use your own research to come up with concrete figures for your situation. Your figures may be significantly different, depending on the size of your project, the environment in your country and region, and your staffing and marketing plans. What you should carry away from the examples, though, are the key messages:

- The biggest cost can be in another area than you were expecting. Usually, the biggest cost is for your marketing and staff but not for technology. You have to plan and monitor those biggest cost very closely and react quickly in case of deviations.
- You have to push for a quick return on investment – otherwise you may end up spending money for a long time without the appropriate revenues.
- The only way to win is growth – if you don't intend to grow, you better don't even start your eVenture.

One additional consideration: market research agencies assume, that you can only start profitable electronic sales activities once more than 20 per cent of your target population do have Internet access. This is so far only the case in a few target segments and in a few countries – please refer to the statistics in the first chapter, but it will change quickly with the web accessibility by mobile phone and TV. So you may need some patience before your sales are successful. Reflect those waiting times in your business plan!

12.1.1   Cost estimate

Before we start our exercise of a sample business plan for a small consumer business start-up company, let's also look at the big figures for business-to-business. That's a different kind of animal than our illustrative example – I just want to underline my statement that you shouldn't underestimate the operational costs. Moreover, one observation from large companies is completely consistent

---

[20] For external support, I've used an average cost of € 700 per day. Internal support is assumed at € 300 per day. For simplification purposes I assume that these costs stay the same during the three years. The effort estimates are illustrative; and the web hosting costs are based on the current offerings of ISPs.

with small start-ups: the cost for hardware and software is approximately only 20 to 25 per cent of your start-up costs and it reduces further to only approximately ten per cent when your business is running! Much higher costs are for your staff and for marketing expenses. Please see the figures below from some research agencies. Similar cost categories will be applicable also in smaller companies:

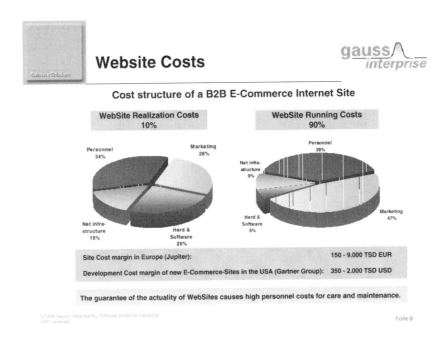

Figure 12-48: Cost categories for launch and operations[21]

It's the biggest risk for your success, if you run out of money to do the ongoing marketing and provide sufficient support for your web presence!

The cost estimate for our start-up boutique now breaks down in the two areas of initial investment and annual operational costs for the first three years. The cost items are[22]:

Hosting: That's the cost for having your website on the server of your hosting partner (e.g. your ISP). The benefit of outsourcing is, that you can use the

---

[21] Sources: Jupiter Research, Gartner Group, Gauss interprise.

[22] For a further detailed description of the tasks of your project, please refer to the next chapter.

most recent tools for the set-up of your website, that the servers are available and serviced around the clock, i.e. you don't need to organize the appropriate internal support, and that the servers are larger than you can usually afford initially. The hosting fee in our business plan includes the installation fee or the annual operational fee, respectively, with the underlying assumption of growth over the years. The estimates below are very conservative; you should actually be able to achieve lower costs. The significant growth in cost for the hosting is due to the fact, that the network traffic with the clients is expected to quickly grow – and the pricing models of most ISPs have attractive entry prices, but increase their prices more than proportionally with your growing data exchange. Some ISPs offer free hosting – they are interested in attracting good content providers in order to get traffic on their servers that can be exploited for their marketing partners.

Design of website: This includes the initial internal costs to define the contents for the website (for a small web presentation and offering), then the external costs for a design agency are reflected to implement the website (assuming a small complexity and "no frills"). For your ongoing operations, I assume that you do the maintenance and updates yourself, so the costs for the inhouse activities are estimated.

Interfaces with databases: In order to allow the initial sales activities, I assume that you want to show the catalogue of your products by directly accessing your product database. Should you not desire to do so, then you need to put all your sellable items on the static website – and update them each time when you change a price, a product description, or the availability information. Still, for the estimate, only a small interface with basic data transfers is assumed (e.g. product name, price, description, availability, estimated delivery time). I assume, that the initial implementation is possible without extensions to your existing database – just the interfaces to the web front end have to be developed. Please check carefully if this assumption is true in your case. For the ongoing operations and maintenance you also need to set some budget aside to support the maintenance.

Customer care: This doesn't cost you anything for getting started, as the basic eMail functions and the entry forms for the orders are included in the price for the web hosting, but it will be the largest block of costs during the operations. In the example I assume, that in the first year one person will be sufficient to support the ordering process – in the beginning this might be you; in the second year two people are needed and in the third year you'll need three. The good news regarding that cost is, that you can manage it – only assign the additional staff to the customer care if your additional Internet sales support it. But be ready once the sales pick up!

Hardware / Software: This is a conservative estimate. You may have the hardware already available, but for a full cost calculation you should cover for all the related costs (up to three PCs, file server, printer, connectivity with the web, software for the PCs). During your operations, you'll need some money for the maintenance of the hardware.

Rent: With the small number of staff, i.e. starting alone and then growing to three staff within the three years, we only need little office space, and desks. Still there's some cost related to that.

Training and Business Process Refinement: Your staff for customer care will need to acquaint with your business approach and the ongoing changes. Therefore, you need to set some time aside for the initial assimilation and training. In the ongoing business, you will have to adjust your business processes regularly to keep up with the changing demands of your customers, and you need to re-train your staff.

Your Salary: I agree, the anticipated figure is not too generous to yourself, but in the beginning it's better to be conservative – once your company is successful, you can decide to take the profits out, but in the beginning it's your turn to invest.

Marketing costs: As mentioned above, the most important aspect is to maintain the awareness in the market about your existence, your strengths and your offerings. As this company is too small to have the customers automatically remember you, you need to remind them again and again. The budget we've set aside here is pretty small for that purpose, but with our targeted market, we can do it, e.g. with going into specialized journals addressed to our small market segment, and with direct marketing activities via eMail and other media. Whatever happens – don't reduce that budget; on the contrary, you should put any additional funds you can get into the marketing in order to grow faster!

Cost Estimate for Launch of Internet Sales

All figures in Euro

		Initial Investment	Operations Year 1	Operations Year 2	Operations Year 2	
1	Web Hosting	3.000	1.000	3.000	15.000	
2	Website Design / Updates	17.000	6.000	6.000	6.000	=(8)*(15)+(9)*(16)
3	Interfaces with Database	17.000	6.000	6.000	6.000	=(10)*(15)+(11)*(16)
4	Customer Care	0	60.000	120.000	180.000	=(12)*(16)
5	Hardware/Software	5.000	5.000	5.000	5.000	
6	Rent	450	3.750	6.900	10.050	=((9)+(11)+(12)+(14))*((17)/200)
7	Training / Business Process Refinement	0	10.000	10.000	10.000	=(13)*(15)+(14)*(16)
	Entrepreneur's salary		50.000	50.000	50.000	
	Marketing (including travel, advertising)	10.000	30.000	40.000	50.000	=(13)*(15)+(14)*(16)
	Total	52.450	171.750	246.900	332.050	
	Accrued cost	52.450	224.200	471.100	803.150	

	Assumptions				
8	Website Design: External efforts (days)	20	0	0	0
9	Website Design / Updates: Internal efforts (days)	10	20	20	20
10	Interfaces with Database: External efforts (days)	20	0	0	0
11	Interfaces with Database: Internal efforts (days)	10	20	20	20
12	Customer Care (days)	0	200	400	600
13	Training / Business Process Refinement: External efforts (days)	0	10	10	10
14	Training / Business Process Refinement: Internal efforts (days)	10	10	20	30
15	External costs / professional support per day (Euro)	700			
16	Internal costs per day (Euro)	300			
17	Rent for office space and furniture (per staff per year)	3000			

Figure 12-49: Cost estimates for launch of Internet Sales

12.1.2   Benefit estimate

The benefits in this case are the sales generated by web transactions. This is straightforward and in my example I assume only one type of item to be sold by web transactions. In your actual situation, you can expect a whole list of items; for each of them you need to do the appropriate estimate – possibly supported by market research or indicated by similar industry examples. The benefit estimate breaks down in the following items:

Number of items sold by Internet transactions: This number includes only the sales closed on the web, possible separate sales via traditional sales channels are not included here.

Price per item: We assume, that we can structure more aggressive prices over time with the price going down from € 100 to € 80, because at the same time we have cost decreases and efficiency improvements. In the example, the improvements are shared with the customers in order to challenge possible entrants to the market as well as the existing competitors.

Supply/production cost per item: In our example, the cost for the company decreases, too, in a similar way as we cut back on our sales price. This may be influenced by economies of scale due to the larger quantities we order by then or by increases in efficiency in the suppliers' organizations (like eBusiness projects successfully implemented).

Packaging and delivery: Again, we have economies of scale and therefore can expect cost reductions. Moreover, the logistics providers are in a fierce competition and more aggressive costs from them can be anticipated.

Margin per item: Well, that's just the mathematics of your revenues per item minus all the costs per item (excluding the cost of sales as this is already covered in our Internet project cost calculation above).

Contribution: The annual contribution is calculated based on the annual sales multiplied by the margin per item.

Benefit Estimate for Launch of Internet Sales

All figures in Euro

		Benefit Year 1	Benefit Year 2	Benefit Year 2	
1	Number of items sold by Internet transactions	2.000	5.000	15.000	
2	Price per item	100	90	80	
3	Supply / production cost per item	40	36	34	
4	Packaging and delivery	14	12	10	
5	Margin per item	46	42	36	=(2)-(3)-(4)
6					
7	Contribution	92.000	210.000	540.000	=(1)*(5)
	Accrued benefit	92.000	302.000	842.000	

Figure 12-50: Benefit estimate for launch of Internet Sales

Of course, we could come up with a much more detailed plan, like monthly breakdown of all the figures – but unless we have to expect significant changes in the middle of the years nobody would need that right now. As a base for our decision to go ahead, this level of timely granularity is sufficient for a project of that size. Each of the products has to be considered in the case of a real company – so your spreadsheet will be much larger anyway. Once you ask an investor for capital or a banker for a loan, he may ask you for a monthly liquidity plan – but for our first goal now, namely to decide, if it makes sense to spend our good money on the project, don't get carried away with number crunching, but focus on the essentials.

Recommendations:

- Plan carefully your non-IT costs, in particular marketing and customer care, which are the majority of your operational costs.

- Focus on completeness for your financial estimates – rather than on level of detail.

- Prepare alternative scenarios in order to enable you to switch between the different plans depending on your business success.

12.2   EVALUATION OF RETURN ON INVESTMENT (ROI): GO OR NOGO?

In your actual business plan, you should prepare different scenarios. A sound business plan reaches break even within two years or even earlier. Unfortunatley, this is not the case here. With an ROI after only three years, too many things can happen in the meantime which might jeopardize our plans; for example, the market dynamics can change, like competitors cutting the prices way further than we anticipated. So we need to tune our plan; in particular in our example it should be carefully assessed, how the customer care can be further optimized. But we can't just tweak the numbers; we already assume, that during the first year, ten items can be sold during one day of a customer care representative while in the third year this number grows to 25 items per day. That's an efficiency increase by 150 per cent in 24 months. Can we really do better? We should, actually! Our infrastructure should support much more business than only the 15,000 items we intend to sell per year. Maybe we should start with a broader set of products.

Moreover, if we believe in our offering, if we can afford the investment and our investor has enough patience, or in the case of larger company, if we plan to grow our sales activities anyway, then we can go for the project. In fact, the Internet project should be cheaper than any other additional sales channel, like opening a new physical shop or dealing with a partner reseller who will ask for a significant share of our margin.

Recommendation:

• Target for a break even ideally after one and possibly after two years.

12.3   RISK MITIGATION

But the decision, if we want to launch the project or not, is even more complex. It's a really serious step, nothing we can just do in parallel to our day-to-day business. Several project risks have to be considered and quantified. In fact it's like starting any other type of company – all execution risks, legal constraints, taxation details, and staffing issues need to be prepared for.

For your Internet project, where you don't have in all cases a first-hand "physical" experience with your customers and with your sales environment, a number of risks comes on top of the usual risks. In the following I summarize the risks with a direct financial impact and recommend some mitigation strategies that have proven to be succesful.

Legal framework, warranty and liabilities: Even in your "home" market this can be tricky. In a physical shop, some legal issues are settled by traditional definitions, e.g. what the constituencies of a contract are, what is to be considered fraud, which prices are valid, and who to turn to in case of complaints or warranties. In a virtual setting, all those prerequisites are not automatically given.
Mitigation: You should make all the legal environment explicit in your contract closure with a customer. This doesn't mean, that you have to walk him through all contractual agreements, but you have to have your contractual understanding available on the website. Minimum requirements are:

• Who are the contractors
• Which law applies
• What are the payment regulations
• Which warranties are agreed
• What limitations of liabilities are applicable
• Where can the customer turn to in case of problems
• Where would legal disputes be handled.

Payment costs: We've discussed the different approaches with their pro's and con's before. At this stage, you should quantify the cost impact of your payment approach, i.e. either the cost for defaults or the cost for your risk coverage such as credit card processing charges.

Outsourcing partners, e.g. delivery and logistics: Your partners can fail (or stop) to support you. Today, this is often due to the fact that the companies merge and suddenly realize that some activity is no longer their core business. Or they consider you as a competitor who shouldn't be supported any longer.
Mitigation: Where possible you should have more than one partner ready to perform certain services or deliver specific supplies.

Existing partnerships: If you have already an ongoing business and are engaged in long-term partnerships, e.g. with retail channels like sales chains, you need to check if you are allowed to launch your own distribution channel. If you want to start your *e*Business, these partners might not like it – in fact you may have contractual obligations to get their agreement before you start competing against them in their markets or regions. I once developed a homebanking solution for a bank that realized after the first successful software tests, that they weren't allowed to run their own homebanking activities due to a merger they had undertaken before!
Mitigation: If you have such engagements with your partners, you need to discuss a change of the competition exclusion with your partners or possibly pay yourself out of such clauses.

Customer preferences: It may happen that existing customers of traditional sales channels are irritated when you offer your products also on the web. Usually, this should not be the case, but for products you offered traditionally bundled with a high consultancy service, you may be forced to make significant price concessions for Internet sales – take the companies for example that shift from software licensing to software renting. If this should lead to an erosion of your other prices or to a deterioration of the perceived quality of your brand, it can take you long to recover.
Mitigation: Two mitigation strategies are possible. Large enterprises often create new brands for dealing with Internet sales. You may do so, too, but brand creation is a long-term process and requires huge funding for marketing and communication campaigns. Alternatively, as a cheaper approach, you can test your Internet offering by showing it to your existing customers and ask them for their impressions. This can be done by professional market research or by your existing sales staff asking your customers during their normal customer care activities. In fact, a target of your Internet presence should be to increase the quality perception of your company and of your products. So, check if this increase does happen and keep tuning your web presence until you get the desired feedback from the market.

And if you want to do business outside of your home country: You will be confronted with many more risks.
Mitigation: Remember, that you're in unknown territory. Only one way helps, namely to work together with locals in your new target country. The

minimum is to have your web presence checked by local sales experts and by test customers of your target country. A better approach is to seek a cooperation with local partner companies. In fact, this would cover you against risks you may not be aware of. For example: for sales to French customers you have to have a physical presence in that country. Or: for sales to countries outside of the Cocom states, you cannot expect that the data encryption protocols you use in your application are allowed. Or: your domain or brand could be an embarrassment in your new target country. Or: you may run into double taxation issues, if you handle cross border business without having a legal entity in the country of your customers. All these issues can be addressed with a local partner. And with a local partner you have the support for your customers knowing the client language and mentality.

Last but not least: don't get frustrated about all those things to consider. I just don't want you to run into problems you could have avoided. In any case, I advise to plan for a stepwise approach. For example, you should not approach too many new areas at a time. If you want to address new countries, do so, but country by country. If you want to change your product offerings, do so, but product line by product line. If you want to use a different approach with your suppliers, try it out with one supplier.

Moreover, the business benefits and project costs should be aligned in a way to reduce the amount of net investment (i.e. investment minus accrued pay-back). Major milestones have to be used to check the results and decide, if you can pursue the anticipated next step, or if you want to tune the results achieved so far.

In particular for my European readers, I want to encourage you to exploit the opportunities in the whole European Union. With the unique currency and the emerging legal and security environment, you have the opportunity to approach all countries with the same offering. If you don't do the step, others will occupy the cross-border business that's now emerging and you'll never catch up. The strategic arguments in favour of a quick start of activities in another European country include:

- Customer mentalities are relatively similar – you can re-use your existing approaches and experience you've gained in your home country.
- Payment features are similar and the various banks and payment service providers have close cooperation.
- Internet connectivity is good between the various countries.
- We all live in the same time zone (plus / minus one hour).
- Contractual rules are not worlds apart and the EU has agreed on the online sales regulations.
- Taxation issues can be dealt with from your home country, e.g. VAT deduction and income taxation.

The upside potential is immense and the risks can be managed.

Recommendations:

- Establish a pro-active attitude to recognizing risks, e.g. by regular risk reviews, in order to mitigate the risks early.
- Reflect the risk mitigation costs in your financial plans.

12.4   MONEY SOURCES

At the different stages of your launch and growth, various sources of money are to be recommended. Of course for your start, the best money is your own money. It would be a pity should you lose it during your eVenture, but at least you won't have any debts challenging your next chance for success.

The worst money for your start is a long-term bank loan. No matter how your business performs, you need to pay interest and you need to pay the loan back, so you have regular instalments to pay that may be a drain on your liquidity at certain times. Actually, you still should talk to a banker to get some overdraft lines on your current account for short-term liquidity needs, but do this in a second step, after you have all the money together for your start-up investment.

There may be one more choice, namely public subsidies or subsidized loans. For the subsidies, it may be difficult to get them, but it's worth a try, as long as it just means filling out some forms. Regarding the subsidized loans, the same considerations apply as for the normal bank loans. The interest rates may be lower, but you still need to pay the loan back; so I would hesitate in going through the hassle of applying for such loans.

There's one more source of money, and actually a good choice, namely money from Venture Capital (VC) companies. The VC companies use the money the same way you use and risk your own capital. If your business performs great, you all can get your profits out (or you probably decide to re-invest), but if it shouldn't perform it's no bad heritage for the future, the money would just be gone. You don't need to provide any collaterals or securities to the venture capitalist as you would need for a bank, but you give him some shares of the company, instead. So he has some influence on major decisions, e.g. the employment of key staff or major investments (usually, his participation is a significant minority share). On the other hand, the VC company expects a higher return on the investment than a bank, usually at least 20 per cent annually. As discussed, this return is not to be paid by regular instalments, but the VC company plans to sell their share after a specific time, e.g. after three to five years. Usually, this is the time when your eVenture can be expected to go public. This is actually another benefit of the VC companies: they have the experience and will support you when you may take the step to materialize your profits by placing your company at the stock exchange.

You will easily find VCs – either on the web or by talking to Business Angels, but before you contact them you need to have your story straight.

- Who will be your customers and how do you plan your marketing?
- What's your great idea – and what are your qualifications to transform that idea into a business?
- Why do you believe it will be successful against your competitors?
- What can you do to get a next version of the offering ready soon?
- What are the major risks and dependencies, e.g. from a particular client, supplier or employee?
- What's the business plan?
- What's the concept for the company's operations, in particular customer support and supply chain, and how will you recruit your employees?
- What major milestones exist for a decision if a continuation makes sense?

Once you have documented your considerations in the checklists provided in this book and on my website, you have the major part of the preparation for your investor discussions. You also should remember the alternatives you considered with their pro's and con's – if there are some major alternatives where your decision is still pending, you may even ask the VC for his input. Additionally, you should prepare a little presentation of your product or offering idea, e.g. some screenshots of a prototype for your web presence, and you should be ready to answer questions about your personal profile as entrepreneur. Those questions will probably include your readiness to regularly work sixty-hour weeks, disregard holidays, your health and fitness, your resistance to stress, your practical experience, your knowledge of accounting/controlling/regulations, your sales contacts and experience.

On the other hand, also you should check your investor. For the selection of your VC you should be very thorough and invest enough time. In a way, he will be like a boss for the next years. Let's go through a list of criteria you should use when selecting the right VC company.

Focus area: How familiar is the VC with business around your core competency? It's a great advantage for you, if the VC is experienced in your business area. He may be able to provide you with some contacts to customers, business partners, and staff. He has observed mistakes other start-ups in that area have made and can prevent you from making the same mistakes.

Support: What can the VC provide on top of his money? All VCs will examine your business concept and plan, but they also should support you during the execution of your business. For example, they may offer you regular risk and opportunity reviews, support your performance controlling, help you with the selection of key partners.

References: Which other *e*Ventures has the VC supported and what were his lessons learned? He should be willing to introduce you to some of his earlier participations so that you can get a first-hand impression, how the VC executes his influence, to be able to check if that style of cooperation fits with your expectations.

As mentioned in the beginning, there are different money sources for the different phases. Let's have a closer look. In the initial phase, you need the seed capital, just to finance your launch activities, i.e. for a few months to maximally one year. The majority of that capital is usually to be provided by yourself (with all the financial support from your family you can get), and a smaller fraction (e.g. around one third) can be obtained from a VC company. Once your products and services have been introduced in the market, you need new money for your growth. As by then you have a clearer picture about the market dynamics, your cost structures and the profitability, you can combine the various money sources. Again, your own money, namely all the profits you are making, will be re-invested into the company. More money from the VC should be available by then – when you talk to your VC for the launch, check with him what his pre-requisites are for providing that additional money. Now you can also get some long-term loans from a bank if necessary. After a continuous growth, you can have your IPO and raise money at the stock exchange. This will allow you further investments into even larger growth – and into becoming one of the "established" companies. By then, the company should be able to generate enough money in itself to pay for all ongoing operations, continue with the investments, pay the banks and taxes, and satisfy the shareholders.

Long-term finance experience indicates, that the initial investment, the seed capital, is approximately ten per cent of the overall investment until the IPO. The ize of this initial investment is primarily driven by your private sources (and your risk appetite); so based on your currently available capital you can already extrapolate the expected size of your company-to-be.

Recommendation:

- Build your start-up company on own capital or on venture capital, respectively, but not on long-term loans.

12.5   CHECKLIST

The checklist below highlights the key aspects of the necessary financial considerations.

Table 12-39: Checklist for the Financial Considerations

Item	To check	Recommendation	Your view
Costs	*Are all cost aspects reflected in your business plan?*	To include: All cost items for the initial investment Operational costs External costs as well as internal costs	
		Are your estimates based on concretely available prices, proposals and assessments or are they guesswork? If you've made guesses you have to update your estimates once you have more concrete figures available.	
Benefits	*Are all benefit aspects reflected in your business plan?*	To include: Financial benefits such as additional sales, reduced costs (per sold item, for support, for supplies), reduced marketing / sales efforts	
		Non financial benefits like time to market, growth of market share, quality improvements	
		Reflection of the initial assumptions and strategic targets to adjust them to the changes in the market. Possibly recalculate the ROI based on the updated estimates.	
Sensitivity and risks	*What can happen to make your business plan obsolete?*	List the risks with their current probability of materialization.	
		Cover the financial impact, if risks materialize (how do the figures look then)?	
		Include the efforts for the risk mitigation in your cost estimates – possibly as optional costs depending on the further risk assessment.	
Return on Investment	*When do you start to be profitable?*	Your investment should be paid back after one or latest two years – if you allow longer times, you should know that it's not a business plan, but a gambling idea.	
Go or No-go?	*What are your reasons to start?*	Have a clear picture about the expected outcome, either as a financial return or as an achievement of strategic targets.	

For a softcopy of the website please visit my website.

12.6   DISCUSSION POINTS

Well, financials are a well-kept secret by the companies, but if you want to share some specific experience, e.g. on risk mitigation or some surprises you had during your launch, please share your views with your co-entrepreneurs on my website.

13

Getting ready

Organize a clear project plan with activities, deliverables, responsible staff and milestones.

Before you start the project, the objectives, deliverables and deadlines must be crystal clear. Step by step, define what your customers should be able to see on the web, on which part of the web (PC, mobile phone or TV), and what you want to get out of it. Initially, you may only want to provide information on a static website; while that doesn't qualify as an *e*Business in our terminology, it's still the necessary first step. I've included the appropriate tasks in my descriptions below. Next, you want to allow your customers to get individual offers from a dynamic website and then close the sale by traditional or slightly enhanced ways, e.g. mail, fax, telephone, *e*Mail. To support this, you need the appropriate customer care functions. Then, you should enable your customers to enter their orders in self service, obtain a confirmation and get information of the delivery status. And you probably want to get some payments.

The most important recommendation is to approach your Internet presence as a real project – don't believe, that you can create a professional impression just by a bunch of freelancers and a bit of time from you here or there. Instead, a clear description of the project targets is necessary together with the assignment of the right staff for achieving those targets. Legal approval may be necessary, e.g. if you want to launch in some countries an ISP, and it may be necessary that you have to obtain the licences to start your business. Additionally, the necessary funding for the project and for the subsequent operation and maintenance as reflected in the financial plans needs to be prepared as described in the previous chapter. You may think it not necessary to spend the money on external support and professional consulting – but the contrary is true: it will be cheaper for you to use an external consultant for dedicated activities where you don't have sufficient skills than to try several options by yourself. With external help your overall cost of learning will be actually less and delays in the implementation are less probable.

The next important advice is to start with a clear subset of objectives. Your initial offerings should contain those products most easily explainable via the web and those customer targets with the easiest Internet accessibility and the best risk profiles. This requires only a fraction of the overall investment and thus reduces your risks. Once this initial launch has been successful, you should be ready for a quick boost to a larger eVenture: establish early a relationship to someone with a big wallet like a venture capitalist and include options in your contracts with system vendors to quickly deploy additional features.

In your project team you should have members with the following backgrounds, either from within your company or assigned from outside, e.g. from professional consultancies or as freelancers with well-defined work packages:

- Programmers for your website with HTML or Java background;
- IT specialists to set up the interfaces and networks;
- the providers of the contents like your marketing and sales people;
- graphic designers for a good layout of the website;
- specialists from the software and hardware providers for the necessary customization and configuration;
- representative customers for designing and testing the interactions.

In this chapter, I've outlined some project plans. Please don't expect, though, to get complete project plans – each situation is too different. What I want to achieve is to provide you with a starting point for the refinements of the plan according to your specific situation. The plans are structured in a way to allow you to do the important and critical things early enough for your launch, but to save your investments for the less critical items up to the latest possible point in time. So the plans are rather meant to tell you what NOT to do in the various stages.

13.1   PROJECT PLANS FOR THE BUSINESS SCENARIOS

The plans relate back to similar business scenarios as discussed earlier. The business scenarios are:

Launch of Internet based sales: The company intends to sell some physical goods (e.g. books, traditional mail-order articles, innovative mail-order articles like flowers or grocery) or provide brokerage services (e.g. for real estate, insurances, investments). They want to start with a small investment, but prepare for quick growth. We assume that the business vision is documented and the business partners – in particular the suppliers – have agreed to engage with the company. The initial project phase has to prepare for launching the sales.

Growth of sales activities: After a while, this company has grown and the investments for customer care and logistics can be made according to the business growth. The second phase addresses the additionally necessary functions. In this phase, also an outlook is provided what options can be framed after becoming an international player.

ASP services provided via the Internet: In this scenario, the company has been successfully in business for quite a while. They've decided to use Internet as an additional sales and distribution channel. The project has to implement the environment additionally necessary for the new channel.

Launch of ISP activities: A company wants to start as an Internet Service Provider. They need to establish an appropriate infrastructure and start business with some key accounts. The project has to deal with the set up of this infrastructure. In later phases, after the initial business plans are achieved, the next steps to offer full retail business can be taken.

As a pragmatic approach, I've framed all project plans in four phases:

1. Pre-launch
2. The actual launch
3. The initial growth
4. The full blown *e*Business operation.

Those phases are discussed below; in the project plan outline I combine some of those phases as appropriate.

During Pre-launch, the strategic considerations are made, i.e. the market research is performed, the target markets and propositions are defined, the financial and organizational business plan is outlined and the partners are identified. In that phase, you should look for input and help from several sources: ask the local chamber of commerce, your tax accountant, venture capitalists, your banker. Also during that phase, some initial "static" presence can be published on the web, but except for some *e*Mail contacts no additional integration with ordering, delivery or payment happens. The Pre-launch activities should be pretty much completed once you have prepared all the documentation (checklists) suggested by the book. In this chapter, the creation of the web presence is highlighted.

The objective of the Launch phase is to hire the appropriate staff, perform the initial marketing campaigns and implement the most important IT infrastructure for the launch. By the end of that phase, the first offerings can be made via the Internet, orders can be entered, and some customer care interaction with the customers is possible.

During the Growth phase, the components you decided not to implement initially in order to save some investments need to be covered according to the speed of growth; of course this will be different in each case, but in the example you find some useful general indications.

Finally, you can look for optimizations and a fine-tuning of your focal areas: depending on your adjustments of the business proposition you can deploy additional IT.

As this section is focused on the IT perspective, we won't discuss the hiring and marketing activities further, but please don't interpret that these areas are less important – the contrary is true: technology is just the enabler for the new business activities. Before we go into the details of the implementation of the web presence for the various scenarios, one piece of advice up front:

Recommendations:

- First of all, check on the Internet how the current offering is – use global (e.g. Yahoo.com, Lycos.com) and regional search engines (e.g. from the global providers, but with their regional implementation such as Yahoo.co.uk or Lycos.de) to find providers with similar offerings you want to launch.

- This research will take some time, but you get a first-hand impression of the activities of your future competitors. Use their services by some test orders, so you will realize their strengths and you also should be able to identify areas you can outperform them. Additionally, check the websites of research agencies (see Chapter 14 for addresses). There, and from your local chamber of commerce you can get the most recent forecasts for the various market segments.

13.1.1   Launch of Internet-based sales

The assignment of activities to the project phases is roughly depicted in Figure 13-51 below; the areas relevant up to the launch are highlighted.

During the Pre-launch phase, a static website is to be published with basic information regarding the company and the offering; possibly also a dynamic website allowing some searches or the access of databases can then be prepared.

For the Actual launch, the customer care functions, in particular order entry, need to be implemented with the necessary integration of the back office. Initially, you should do the order entry and customer care in a small call centre. Later you should offer self service via the Internet, after you have tested the self service with a small pilot used initially by your customer care representatives and then by a small number of test customers.

Static website

For the static website, I assume that you initially outsource the hosting to a third party, e.g. your ISP. The activities listed below are based on that assumption. If you decide differently, please adjust the activities accordingly.

Selection of partners for website: You'll need at least two companies for your website publishing:

- Your ISP/web-host. Dozens to hundreds of companies exist in every country where you can host your website. Use the criteria explained in Chapter 11 for your decision. To list them once again: Domain name, Security sophistication, eMail, Statistics, Support times, Service levels, Flexibility as well as Value added services, Payment features, Interfaces, Marketing support – as well as cost.

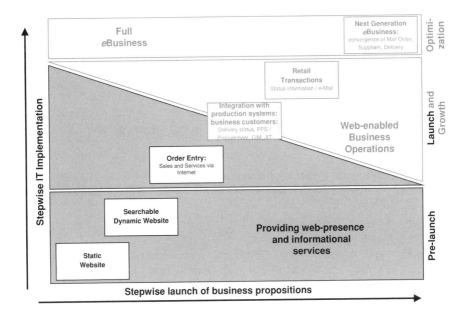

Figure 13-51: Project activities for launch of Internet-based sales

The large global ISPs are listed in Section 14.2 as a first point of contact. Smaller local providers may be a better choice in the long run depending on your exact business requirements, but initially the large providers are a "safe bet".

- A professional design company to design and enter your information. Actually, you may be able to set up HTML-pages yourself, but you should avoid any homegrown impressions, as you want to be perceived as a professional provider. In the same way as you don't want to have your sales brochures handmade and photocopied, you should engage professionals for your website implementation. At a later stage, you may then perform the updates yourself. The criteria for the selection of your website designer should include: samples of earlier designed websites (go for what you believe fits to your company culture), flexibility and service commitment (e.g. working at the time when you need them, guaranteed deadlines), cost. Avoid being carried away with glossy pictures – your offerings have to be nicely packaged, but don't bore your customers with useless figures. A good design partner can best be found by checking the local publications on Internet topics or by asking other *e*Businesses about their experience with their design company.

Get your domain registered: Choose a name for your company which can be well remembered by the customers and get it registered early. Don't use a sub-domain, but a real domain like www.mycompany.com (instead of www.nameprovider.com/mycompany). The companies doing the US/international registration (i.e. the .com domains) are listed in Section 14.2; for a registration in a particular country check the local information source or ask your ISP.

Definition of contents: The contents of the website needs to be written up. This should include:

- Up-to-date information relevant for your customers, e.g. recent news regarding their community, recent news about changes in your offerings.
- Links to other providers that may be interesting for your customer community.
- Product and service offerings, i.e. the various propositions for your targetted customer groups with their unique differentiators from the competitors' offerings. You also can announce future offerings as soon as you are committed to launch them.
- Job opportunities, i.e. the roles and responsibilities where vacancies exist, the skill profiles you require and the reasons why you believe, a new hire would feel well in your organization. You also should quote such job opportunities in the various search engines with up-to-date links to your own website.
- Your team and company profile in order to build the trust of your customer. That is, the experience of your developers, the service mentality of your sales and customer care staff, your mission statement, the location of your premises, your size (staff or financial background), key people in the company and their organizational responsibilities, your alliances.
- Contact possibilities, at least a telephone number and an *e*Mail-address or better separate addresses for service or product requests from consumers or from professional prospects, for job applications or information requests from investors.

Design: The key design has to be decided. This should cover:

- The graphics and colours to be used fitting to your other company materials.
- Navigation aids such as a site-map and search functions for key words.
- Consistent format layout for all frames allowing a quick orientation on the screen. Important information and buttons, for example, should be at a place where the viewer doesn't need to scroll up or down to find it again. Like the shopping cart should always be visible or a quick access to the site-map.
- Reduced pictures and graphics without meaning which eat up a lot of disk space and data transmission times – focus on meaningful graphics or photos, e.g. sample products or demo application, revenue breakdown, or pictures of your board members.

Implementation of website: Once you have defined the contents, you can enter it – or actually your design partner should do that.

- Editing the text: entry of the information with the tools provided by your web-host.
- Scanning of Pictures: entry of the selected graphical information, e.g. photos.
- Set-up of eMail connection and processes to answer incoming eMails.
- Configuration of links with your partners, e.g. advertising partners, search engines.
- Review of the website.
- Release of the website.
- In addition to the one-time set-up of the website by your design agency, you should make someone within your company responsible to regularly update the text, e.g. offerings, prices, job opportunities.

Awareness and advertising: In addition to the "electronic" marketing activities listed below you should pursue several parallel approaches like advertising in newspapers, magazines or possibly even radio and TV in order to maximise the market awareness. Both traditional and electronic marketing activities will be an ongoing task; this is to be started early and will require massive budgets. Whenever the hit rates on your website are below your expectations, you should engage a professional marketing agency. Here's my initial advice for the start of electronic marketing activities.
Search Engines: Register with several search engines to allow all prospects looking for your services to actually find you. Many websites can only be found, if the customers already know the webiste – you should avoid that mistake and allow everybody looking for your type of offerings to get to your website. The commonalities of all search engines are that they automatically check websites for index words. The differences now are how

the index words are defined (e.g. by authors of the search engine providers), which parts of the web are checked (e.g. only a specific country or all websites). Moreover, the various search engines use different algorithms for the identification of key words and the rankings of the findings, i.e. the sequence in which the search results are shown.

- Search Engines with regional usability: As you probably plan a regional offering in the beginning, e.g. for one country or a continent, you should check, if the search engine candidates provide a regional check for those countries and if the regional providers also show up in the overall search.

- Register with the Search Engines (e.g. through your ISPor by one of the registration companies – see the screenshot below of www.searchenginewatch.com and Section 14.2 for list of companies).

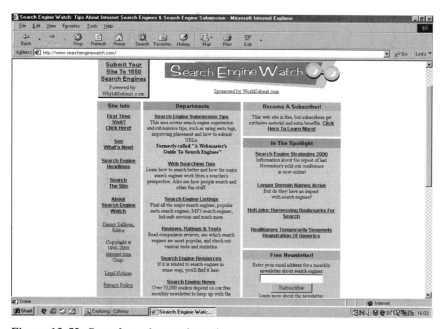

Figure 13-52: Search engine registration

- Hit the index words: the search engines usually check the Internet address for occurrences of the index word, they look in particular at the beginning of the text on the website and at headlines, some also in the source code of the HTML file. Additional criteria for the search engines include how often the relevant index words show up on your website, how long the overall text is, and sometimes even how many links lead to your website. Therefore, you should describe your offering on your homepage in one concise sentence in the beginning plus provide a broader description with various alternative wordings.

- Multiple websites: In order to get a reasonable rank in each of the relevant search engines, you should open a variety of websites that all refer to your master website. On each of the multiple websites, you should tune the website design in the best way for a specific search engine. This may require some trial and error regarding the words and their sequence until you've achieved the appropriate position in the search engine, but the effort will pay off.
- What not to do: It violates the Internet rules and some laws, to attract surfers by using key words that are protected by others' copyrights or trademarks, e.g. the brand names from the competitors or names of individuals not related to your offering like politicians or show stars.

Links from other websites: Another way to attract attention are links you get established from other websites. it may be permanently established links you have with another content provider. The sequence in which the search results are shown.

- Free links: you can talk to other content providers to establish a link from their website to yours. Such links increase the credibility of your offering, because your link partner sheds some of the trust he has earned with the consumers onto you. Often, your link partner will appreciate, if you provide a returning link from your website to his. So you can achieve a synergy in your awareness raising activities – as I'm doing with McGraw-Hill regarding my book: the websites www.success-at-e-business.com and www.mcgraw-hill.co.uk/books/morath refer to each other.
- Paid links: you can get links from some companies against the payment of some fees. That's like a printed ad in a newspaper. As long as that company can show you how it increases the number of prospects visiting your website, it may be a good investment.
- Banner ads: such advertising is good if you can monitor those web surfers that were attracted by a specific banner. Then you can pay your marketing partner placing the ad based on the rate of web hits generated by him.

Mailings: Mailings are a standard tool for marketing and awareness creation. With the Internet you can do it much cheaper than with the traditional methods.

- *e*Mail/SMS: Inform the customers and prospects regularly about your recent developments highlighting special offers. Given that these are unexpected messages, you should be very crisp in order not to bore the recipients. You can use all the *e*Mail addresses the customer has voluntarily given to you. Therefore, you should ask for the surfers' *e*Mail addresses at each request for information they submit to you on the web, and also when someone dials your call centre. Additionally, you should ask for their mobile phone number in order to send them SMS-Messages. In both cases, some customers may not like obtaining such information, so be ready to stop such unsolicited mailings.

- Mailing lists: Encourage your customers and prospects to subscribe to your mailing lists. Those subscribers have probably a higher affinity to your company than those without a subscription. Therefore you can inform them in more detail about your activities. Your ISP should provide you with mailing list functionalities or you can check with a search engine or bot provider.

Dynamic website

For the dynamic website, I assume that you keep your homepage with the same hosting partner, but that you link the website with some of your internal IT systems to provide information stored in your company's databases via the web. The nature of such information is very dynamic and thus would require too much effort to reflect it in updates of the text information on your static website. Examples of such information may be product availabilities, delivery status, mail-order catalogues, newspaper articles, product configuration samples.

The activities listed below are based on that assumption. If you decide differently, please adjust the activities accordingly.

Business design of contents: The offerings you want to show with a direct interface to some of your operational systems, need to be detailed. The design should cover:

- Which business objects can be presented to the public directly, i.e. without clean-up effort (e.g. you can show released price plans, but you must not share your future pricing scenarios).
- Who is allowed to access which data, e.g. customer having access to his personal customer master file.
- Which legal requirements have to be considered.

Database access: Once the business objects have been identified, the data files in the IT systems need to be found where those objects are stored. Then, those objects need to be provided in a way that enables them to be transmitted via the Internet.

- Analysis of existing data structures (data models, file descriptions, actual implementation) to identify the fields to be transmitted.
- Definition of data architecture: I recommend to keep the data which can be accessed by the public in a separate database, which is kept redundant to your operational databases. Thus, you can prevent hacker entries disturbing your production runs most effectively. For this intermediary database, the data model and database description has to be defined.

- Definition of data extraction frequencies and development of data extraction routines from the operational databases into the intermediary database.
- Implementation of Internet enabled database viewer on the intermediary database.
- Implementation of Search Engine for advanced and user friendly searches in your database.

Security design and implementation: Features for various levels of security need to be designed and implemented:

- *e*Mail encryption, Virus-Checking and Firewalls.
- Identification, authentification of customers entitled to view the databases; encryption of identification and authentification data.
- Access control for database access from the Internet to intermediary databases.
- Access control and encryption for data file downloads.

Review and test: None of the changes and enhancements may go without review and test. For every update, perform an internal review, then check it using different Internet browsers (in particular Netscape and Microsoft Explorer). Before you roll the Catalogue and Order Entry out to your customers, you should have it tested by your Customer Care Representatives. If they need any training for it (e.g. for looking up a product ID required for the input), don't have it used by your customers. Rather redesign it for ease-of-use. Similarly, if they get annoyed because they have to wait several seconds on the response from the system, redesign and tune it until it's really ready for the market. Finally, for important areas have some customers test your site as well – you may get interesting feedback on what to improve.

Takeover in production and maintenance: The operational concepts need to be defined as to which activities to run regularly, responsibilities including support in case of problems and service level commitments.

Order Entry

With the activities above completed, the Internet world can see who you are and can get informed about your offerings. If someone likes them he would need to pick up a phone or send you an *e*Mail asking for your product or service. But that's not the way to lower the decision hurdle for your customer! Instead, you have to make it as easy as possible for your customer to just say YES to your offering. Avoid to puzzle the customer with long questionnaires or application forms, just build bridges for him to do the final mouse click confirming the purchase at your virtual cashier or to press the buy-button at his Internet-extended remote control while watching your TV spot.

Design and implementation of order entry: The approach, processes and data necessary to capture an order have to be defined. The approach should be in a way that an order will be entered just once and no re-entry in the various steps of execution takes place:

- Decide who can enter the order: As a long-term target, your customers should be able to enter the orders directly via the Internet (PC, mobile phone or TV). As intermediary steps it may be applicable that the customers express their desires via phone, eMail or paper mail (like the classical mail-order) and your customer care representatives enter it in the systems. This may lead to slow downs in the process and to mistakes – consider what happens if a customer forgot in his mail to tell you the quantity of an item he wants, then you need to call him back and close the gap.

- Identify the data necessary to execute an order: First of all, you need to get the itemized information of what the client is ordering. With the same importance, you need the customer ID such as address or customer number and contact information (telephone numbers, eMail address) plus the data you need for payment or credit checking, if applicable. To facilitate the entry of those data, you should refer to data entered before from the same customer. This can be done by an alias name in combination with a password (both to be defined by the customer); or you can place a cookie on the customer's PC – on this cooky you can store the data for customer identification in order to recognize him again at the next interaction.

- Design, development and implementation of the screens to capture the customer information and the order information. If the entry is handled internally, then normal GUI front ends for your customer care system can be configured, if you want to use the web, Internet forms have to be set up for the appropriate channel (PC, mobile phone, TV). In either case the interface with the order entry and your back end application need to be developed, too.

Review and test: As discussed before. Additionally, you should perform an end-to-end test, i.e. check if the orders really go through from the Internet to your processing systems. This test is now pretty crucial. You need to perform the test with some carefully selected group customers in a kind of "blind" test, i.e. don't tell them it's a test – send them the same mailings about your Internet launch that you intend to send to all your customers once everything is properly tested. Make the same type of offers to them that you intend to make to all customers later. And observe, if they behave according to your expectations. If not, ask them by eMail, by telephone or face-to-face what went wrong. With this aproach, you don't spoil your reputation and you get early insights that allow you to tune your website and/or your offering.

Takeover in production and maintenance: The operational concepts need to be defined as:

- Which activities to run regularly and at which times of the day/week/ month
- Responsibilities including support in case of problems
- Service level commitments.

Recommendations:

- Test your offering and your website with a small subset of products and services and with a clear group of target customers, e.g. a group of existing customers in a specific region.

- Create awareness for your offering by search engine entries, links and traditional marketing means.

- Focus your IT activities on your ISP interaction and a solid catalogue with order entry.

13.1.2   Growth of sales activities

After the launch of your *e*Business, you will quickly see how your offerings are accepted by the market. This will indicate where you need to set the next priorities. The sequence shown in Figure 13-53 below therefore is just indicative – it may well be that you implement the additional consumer features before the business customer features or that you skip one of those activities completely, because they don't support your business model.

In any case, the key point will be the integration. Your front end with the order entry needs to be integrated with the back end, i.e. ERP systems, and with the supply chain which in itself needs to be supported by quick procurement approaches. Once you have integrated your delivery capabilities in a way that you can get a status information of the progress of an order, you can then exchange this status information with your customers. For business customers, this can include an integration into their business processes (e.g. for Just-in-Time logistics).

For consumers, *e*Mail information at certain stages should be the appropriate approach. Additionally, you can then consider to adopt a one-to-one marketing approach and offer customized websites; also your system must become very quick in response to the customer data entries in order to allow them to navigate through a personalized website session. At this stage, statistical analysis, customer segmentation and automatic decision support become advisable.

Finally, you should strive for operational excellence: e.g. customer calls to the call centre mustn't be aborted or service commitments have to be targeted, such as 80 per cent of orders to be delivered within 24 hours.

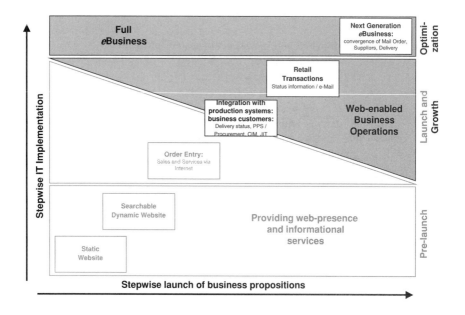

Figure 13-53: Project activities for growth of Internet-based sales

Some work on your back end systems

Once you've completed the activities of the launch project, the orders pop up somewhere in your premises – and someone needs to run around and deliver the ordered items. Initially, delievery can happen because you were courageous enough to buy some goods up front and store them somewhere in a little storehouse. So you are lucky, that for the first deliveries, you can send a courier to the storehouse, package the goods and mail them to your happy customers.

Soon, there will be more orders and you realize at one of your early morning walks through the storehouse, that you'll quickly run out of stock. So you make some urgent calls to your suppliers and beg that they send you some additional goods – they are ready to cut back on their normal delivery procedures and send you an urgent delivery provided that you pay the express fees. Well, if that's what it takes to keep your customers happy, you accept the attack on your margins. But you want to do better!

That's the latest time when you should stop doing your morning walks to the storehouse but implement an Enterprise Resource Planning (ERP) system instead. Actually, in theory a better time would be to start the implementation parallel to the launch as discussed in the last section. But that depends on your ability to handle many activities in parallel and I've recommended you stay focused at any time, anyway. Plus, the cost you spend on express delivery is only eating some of your margin, while an unnecessary investment in an ERP system might have been throwing money out of the window. So, now let's go for it.

As an interim step, you will probably use a spreadsheet reflecting the key aspects discussed in Section 10.2. For each item you are selling, you record the number ordered by your customers, for each item from your suppliers, you record the number ordered by you – and when you can expect delivery depending on standard shipment or express. Now you can give your customers an indication when they can expect the delivery. Also, you need to monitor your financial performance: the prices for purchased and sold items need to be recorded, too. And you have to deal with different pricings depending on the way of shipment, you offer special prices at certain seasons or for certain customers and your customers sometimes get express delivery, too. So your spreadsheet starts looking more and more awkward!

Thanks to your patience while reading this book, right before the confusion in your spreadsheet starts to drive everybody crazy, you have your real ERP system ready. That's good for getting a sound impression of the various piles you are handling, in particular your inventory and your money together with your expectations (i.e. budgets) and trends. Additionally you need to monitor the processes, how speedy they are (what's the minimum time from order to delivery, what's the average, what's the maximum), in order to be able to tune them and because you may want to keep your customers informed. Again, in the beginning this can be done manually, but once you have thousands of orders to monitor, you'll need the support of a workflow system as we discussed in the IT section.

Now, suppose you grow even faster and even larger, and it's not sufficient any longer to just see your updated figures every day and to re-order supplies based on best prices with some phone calls? Well, then you need an automated procurement system. In such a system you can configure such aspects like the minimum levels of inventory, ordering policies (e.g. what packaging sizes from which supplier), the required reviews of automatically prepared orders, the release of automatic payment for the supplies. Refer to Section 14.9 for vendors of the appropriate solutions.

But didn't I say that we would shoot for integration in this phase? You are so right – we only have to lay the groundwork first to integrate the customer facing systems with it. So let's briefly summarize the tasks you're up to:

Design of ERP and preliminary implementation: No matter if you use a spreadsheet or a dedicated ERP system, you need to configure the following areas:

- Inventory planning
- Chart of accounts for the financial figures (budget and actuals)
- Accounts payable and receivable
- Suppliers in order to have the payment information handy
- Staff in order to generate pay cheques.

Design of procurement approach and implementation: Once you decide to implement a procurement system, you need to set up your procedures and configure the software accordingly. You have to:

- Assign competency levels to your individual staff members, i.e. up to which amounts and from which suppliers they can order
- Enter the agreements with your suppliers, e.g. product descriptions, prices and ordering quantities
- Set up the payment instructions.

Design of workflow approach and implementation: You need to monitor your customer oriented processes and their efficiency either by using watches, calendars and checklists or with a workflow software. Therefore you have to define:

- Key customer oriented processes
- Expected duration of the processes
- Exception handling once certain limitations of the processes are passed (e.g. in case you commit to a three-day delivery: once more than three days have passed since the order entry, the customer will get a pro-active information indicating that you are pushing to get his delivery soon)
- either description of manual processes or configuration of workflow software.

Design of status tracking database and implementation: For the feedback to the customers you need to integrate your back end systems with the customer facing areas. The tasks below assume, that your various components are covered by separate systems; you may well create a solution where some of the components are handled within one system (e.g. order tracking being part of workflow software, or order tracking being part of customer care front end). Then the interface will be covered within that particular system. In general, the following interfaces need to be implemented:

- Interface between inventory keeping (ERP) and order management system. This interface will be bidirectional. The inventory has to report to the order entry system the number of items on stock. Once an order is made the order entry system has to report the number of ordered items back to the inventory system and the inventory number has to be decreased accordingly.
- Interface to procurement system either from order management (if the procurement system handles the inventory thresholds once reorders are necessary) or from inventory. This interface triggers the re-orders of goods.

- Interface from procurement system to inventory system with the average ordering time for each item to be reported.
- Interface from procurement system to status tracking/order management system with the date of expected receipt from supplier reported.
- Interface between workflow system and status tracking. This interface has to be bidirectional, too. From workflow system to status tracking, the information regarding average delivery times is to be reported. From status tracking to workflow system the actual date for each particular order is to be reported.

Review and test: As discussed before; the integration of the different components is highly complex and many "misunderstandings" between the various systems are possible. So, again, testing is a key task!

Takeover in production and maintenance: As for the earlier discussed systems, the operational concepts need to be defined. As you keep adding staff, you should take your new employees through a training on the extended processes. For the operations of the various components, you also need to monitor the dependencies. It won't longer suffice to have just one or two technical support persons available for fixing of problems; instead you need representatives from all key functions.

Integration with production systems of business customers

Once you have integrated your delivery capabilities in a way, that you can get a status information of the progress of an order, you can then exchange this status information with your customers. So you can provide similar information to your customers as you receive from your suppliers. For business customers, this can include the integration into their business processes.

The best known examples for supply chain integration are in the automotive industry. Already in times before the Internet was available, they had created standards for the electronic transmission of orders, delivery status information and payments – all via electronic data interchange (EDI). Also the logistical concepts "just-in-time" have been invented by them in order to minimize the inventory keeping. The particular complexity in the automotive industry is, that items from plenty of suppliers (and sub-suppliers) are needed to fabricate one car. An end-to-end integration of the supply chain, the transportation between the suppliers and the car production site, the monitoring of delivery status via satellite communication, and the flexible readjustment in case of problems has made car fabrication an IT venture.

For your probably less complex sales activities, more basic types of integration and information should be sufficient. Information from you to your customers can be: Do you have the item ordered by your customer in stock? When will it be shipped to him? If it's not in stock, how long does it take you to get it from your suppliers? Can the supplies be expected on time or did delays happen? Are partial or complete shipments ready? What's the account and payment status? What new items are on sale or special promotions?

Manually or automatically generated requests from your customers which you need to respond to (ideally also automatically) include: Pricing information, availability of certain items, expected time for delivery, orders, account information – i.e. exactly the same information you are about to send to the customers. The difference is, that in the first case you submit the information to the customers when you believe it's appropriate. In the second case, your customer triggers the submission of the information by his request.

The tasks necessary for this integration are:

Definition of interfaces to customers: The data to be sent to the customers and the approach and the timing of the submission have to be defined:

- Identification of systems from which data have to be submitted, e.g. order status tracking.
- Analysis at which steps of the processes updates of the relevant data are recorded.
- Decision for each step of the processes and for each data element, if the data transmission can be initiated by the customer (pull information) or by you (push information).
- Definition when the pull and push information is used for each item and for each customer, e.g. by information exchange profiles.
- Definition of data transfer structures, e.g. file descriptions, for each of the different process steps and data submission events.

Review and test: As discussed before; the tasks listed above seem to be straightforward, but as you want to interface with your customers you should test this connection with some key customers first, before you roll it out to all business customers.

Takeover in production and maintenance: The operational concepts need to be defined, again, and this time you need to include the customer in that definition because the regular processes have to be synchronized between both companies.

Retail transactions – status information

For your consumer customers, you need to cover similar aspects as for the business customers. If you want to see how the information is shared with the consumer, make some orders at amazon.com and wait for the *e*Mails confirming your order, announcing the shipment or apologizing for delays. In addition to the push messages at key events of the order and delivery progress, you may also envision to allow your customer to pull additional information, e.g. if he has lost specific *e*Mails about the order progress, he can request specific information

(like expected day of delivery) or he can inquire the invoicing and payment status.
The tasks necessary for this integration are:

Definition and development of interfaces to consumers: The data to be sent to the customers and the approach and the timing of the submission have to be defined:

- Identification of systems from which data have to be submitted, e.g. order status tracking.
- Analysis at which steps of the processes updates of the relevant data are recorded.
- Decision for each step of the processes and for each data element, if the data transmission can be initiated by the consumer (pull information) or by you (push information).
- Definition when the pull and push information is used for each item and for each customer, e.g. by information exchange profiles.
- Definition of information contents and configuration, e.g. *e*Mail wording and lay out, paper mail wording and lay out, for each of the different process steps and data submission events.
- If you allow also pull information: Definition of web frames or forms to request particular information and interfacing with your databases providing such information.

Review, test and production takeover: As discussed before; as many customers will receive the information and observe their quality, you have to test very thoroughly. You should perform this test end-to-end; i.e. doing real Internet sessions with simulated or better with real customers and performing real cycles from order to physical delivery.

Outlook: next generation eBusiness

With all the business going on, the monitoring of customer transactions and financial performance and the formal and informal feedback you receive from your customers, you can step up to a more effective approach. You will strive for operational excellence, efficient processes and a high financial performance. In addition to ongoing internal process improvements, you can grow your business activities organically by adding staff and products, by tuned cooperation with your partners or by mergers and acquisitions.

Quick organical growth is best possible, when your customers like specific products from you much more than others. So you can specialize and extend your offering in that area. For example, if your sales in HiFi and TV sets outperform your other areas you can specialize as entertainment provider and add to your offering products like discs, videos, games and maybe even concert tickets. Alternatively, you can specialize as electronics provider, always keep up with the latest inventions like digital satellite broadcasting, multi-norm equipments, video films on laser discs, and add to your offering high end modules for HiFi freaks as well as tuning extensions for the sets like gold cables and connectors.

With the possibilities of the Internet, you can use your contact zones in order to embrace with your customers more and more intensively. Going back to the specializations as mentioned in the paragraph above, you should organize your contact zones around the topics interesting for your communities, e.g. let your customers chat about why they like a hardware brand, which strategies are most successful to win the latest games or discuss how they liked the last Back Street Boy concert, respectively. Or, they can exchange technical tricks on how to get even more brilliance off the monitor and how they link the analog and digital HiFi equipment with their PCs.

Tuned cooperation with partners is advisable, when the activities between you and your customers stretch over many companies. Optimize the supply chain, e.g. reduce the numbers of suppliers or sub-suppliers, or you may insource some aspects of your delivery or your telecom related activities. This is a long and cumbersome process, but the automotive industry has shown the way. Volkswagen in Europe went so far as to push their suppliers for how they deal with the sub-suppliers, what service levels are to be agreed between the suppliers and sub-suppliers – and of course what cost optimizations and price cuttings have to be implemented.

The most drastic tuning and "insourcing" is if you acquire one of your partners or if you merge fully or partially with him. Two basic settings for mergers and acquisition can be thought of: complementary combinations in order to cover additional aspects of the value chain and thus offer broader services to the customers or overlap situations where you can cut back on costs because both companies were handling similar business processes. For the latter, many examples exist in the traditional mail-order business. Only a few providers stay as independent competitors after the first booming years have passed. The evolution in virtual Internet malls has still to be awaited; possibly the proximity of electronic sales and electronic payments may lead to interesting constellations of mail-order companies and financial organizations. Consider a mail-order company running also a bank or a bank buying a mail-order company.

Project activities for this stage of your business need to be defined once you have achieved that stage; they will include a new iteration of your strategy considerations and very intense discussions with your partners. Once you agree on tuned business approaches, your processes and systems need to be adjusted. Sometimes a solution of one of your partners (or acquired companies) may be better than your original system, so you need to adopt and extend that. For all the changes, the new cycle of design, development, configuration, test, training and roll-out has to be gone through. Additionally, you need to extend your data bases in order to keep the ability to perform the various analysis covering the trends of buying behaviour, order histories and payment transactions. And your organization has to go through the adjustments too.

Recommendations:

- Focus on processes supporting quick interactions with your customers.

- Upgrade your environment once there are performance bottlenecks.

13.1.3   ASP services provided via the Internet

The *e*Venture activities for ASP services are similar to the sales scenario above. Some key differences exist, though, like the fact that the ASP services are targeted at business customers, in particular SMEs and that the service provider usually has some ongoing business not related to the Internet. Therefore, I describe the tasks again, but now within their different context. I assume for the descriptions, that the back end system actually providing the value proposition (e.g. accounting services) does exist already, so just another way of accessing and using the services is to be provided via the web.

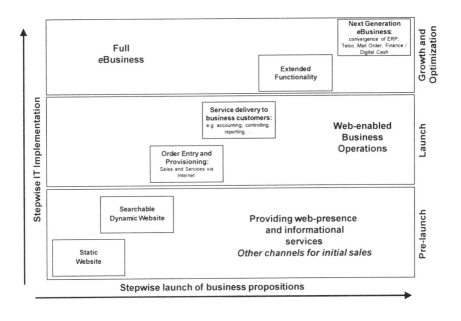

Figure 13-54: Project activities for creating an Internet channel for ASP

During the pre-launch of Internet enabled services, while the traditional business of the company continues, a static website is to be published with basic information regarding the company and the offering; possibly also a dynamic website allowing some searches or the access to databases can be prepared.

For the actual launch of the Internet services, the customer care functions, in particular order entry and provisioning, need to be implemented with the necessary integration of the back office. As the configuration of the ASP services is probably relatively complex, the order entry and provisioning will be handled by a technical customer care group that also is in charge of hotline support.

Also, the "delivery" of the services to the customers needs to be organized. For a better understanding I describe the tasks based on the example of a company offering ERP services. Let's assume a service like accounting as it's now offered by SAP/mysap.com and JDEdwards with JDe.sourcing. The delivery of such ASP services has to include data transmissions from the customer to the provider and the other way round. The customer has to enter the transaction data (e.g. his bookkeeping entries) and send them to the service provider, then the service provider does the agreed calculations (e.g. update the accounts and generate the balance sheets) and submit the reports back to the customer.

In order to achieve a quick implementation, the initial Internet enabled offering will cover the core functionalities. In a next step now those functionalities can be expanded. As an ERP provider you could now offer sophisticated controlling in addition to accounting, or staff and payroll services.

Eventually, the offering can be further extended; with strengthened partnerships (e.g. with a finance institution) the IT service provider can include related business activities (e.g. secure payment transactions).

Static website

For the static website, I assume that you initially outsource the hosting to a third party; soon this will change, though, so you should agree on a quick termination and easy move to your own environment. The activities listed below are based on that assumption. If you decide differently, please adjust the activities accordingly.

Selection of partners for website: You'll need at least two companies for your website publishing:

- Your ISP/web-host. Dozens to hundreds of companies exist in every country where you can host your website. Use the following criteria for your selection: points of presence in all places where you want to offer your services to allow your customers dialling in at low cost, possibility for a brief domain name, commitment for sufficiently high bandwidth to support quick data exchange with your customers, service quality (e.g. support for your website implementation, entry to search engines and links), cost. The large global ISPs are listed in Section 14.2 as a first point of contact. Smaller local providers may be a better choice in the long run depending on your exact business requirements, but initially the large providers are a "safe bet". In either case, you should check that your ISP doesn't end up as your competitor, rather look for synergies where the ISP supports your ASP plans.

- A professional website design company to design and enter your information as attractive as your sales brochures and annual reports are. The criteria for the selection should include: samples of earlier designed websites (go for what you believe fits to your company culture), flexibility and service commitment (e.g. working hours as you need them, guaranteed deadlines), cost. A good design partner can best be found by checking the local publications on Internet topics or by asking other eBusinesses about their experience with their design company.

Get your domain registered: Choose a name for your company which can be well remembered by the customers and get it registered early. Don't use a sub-domain, but a real domain like www.mycompany.com (instead of www.nameprovider.com/mycompany). The companies doing the US/international registration (i.e. the .com domains) are listed in Section 14.2; for a registration in a particular country check the local information source or ask your ISP. Also, the search engine providers need to be informed early. Some of them take more than three months to reflect new entries.

Definition of contents: The contents of the website need to be defined by those responsible for marketing and sales. Those contents should include:

- Company profile, i.e. your mission statement, the location of your premises, your size (staff or financial background), key people in the company and their organizational responsibilities, your alliances.
- Product and service offerings, i.e. the various propositions for your targetted customer groups with their unique differentiators from the competitors' offerings. You also can announce future offerings as soon as you are committed to launch them.
- Job opportunities, i.e. the roles and responsibilities where vacancies exist, the skill profiles you require and the reasons why you believe a new employee would like to join your organization. You also should quote such job opportunities in the various search engines with up-to-date links to your own website.
- Contact possibilities, at least an eMail-address – better separate addresses for service or product requests, for job applications and for investors.

Design: The key design has to be decided. This should cover:

- The graphics and colours to be used fitting to your other company materials.
- Navigation aids such as a site-map and search functions for key words.
- Consistent format layout for all frames allowing a quick orientation on the screen. Important information and buttons, for example, should be at

a place where the viewer doesn't need to scroll up or down to find it again. The shopping cart should always be visible as well as a quick access to the site-map.

- Reduced pictures and graphics without meaning which eat up a lot of disk space and data transmission times – focus on meaningful graphics or photos, e.g. sample products or demo application, revenue breakdown, or pictures of your board members.

Implementation of website: Once you have defined the contents, you can enter it – or actually your design partner should do that.

- Editing the text: entry of the information with the tools used by your design partner.
- Scanning of Pictures: entry of the selected graphical information, e.g. photos.
- Set-up of eMail connection and processes to answer incoming eMails.
- Configuration of links with your partners, e.g. advertising partners, search engines.
- Review of the website.
- Release of the website.
- In addition to the one-time set-up of the website by your design agency, you should make someone within your company responsible to regularly update the text, e.g. offerings, prices, job opportunities.

Awareness and advertising: See Section 13.1.1.1; this task is as described there.

Dynamic website

The nature of the information on your dynamic website changes very frequently and thus would require too much effort to reflect it in updates of the text information on your static website. Examples of such frequently changing information may be current stock price quotes, researched newspaper articles, expected arrival time of planes or trains, current bids during auctions, or the results (e.g. account balances) from the application you run in your premises crunching the data of your customers.

Moreover, this website will be the portal to your interactive service offerings. Therefore I assume, that you build up your own hardware environment. At that time, it will also be appropriate to insource the static website. The activities listed below are based on that assumption. Please adjust the activities accordingly, if you have a different setting.

Selection and configuration of software and hardware: You need to implement your web hosting software and hardware (including firewall):

- Identify the required functionality for your software implementation, based on the checklists and recommendations from Chapter 11.
- Request proposals from the vendors and review your requirements based on the proposals.
- Select a software vendor and obtain his hardware recommendations.
- Do a test installation of the software.
- Define the needed availability of the solution, e.g. >90 per cent if you handle a few dozen customer interactions per day or >99 per cent if you handle several hundred interactions per day.
- Install the hardware.
- Implement the web hosting software.

Business design of contents: The offerings you want to show with a direct interface to some of your operational systems, need to be detailed. The design should cover

- Which business objects can be presented to the public directly, i.e. without clean-up effort (e.g. you can show released price plans, but you must not share your future pricing scenarios).
- Who is allowed to access which data, e.g. customer having access to his personal customer master file.
- Which legal requirements have to be considered.

Database and software application access: Once the business objects have been identified, the data files in the IT systems need to specified out where and how those objects are stored. Then these objects need to be provided in a way that enables them to be transmitted via the Internet.

- Analysis of existing data structures (data models, file descriptions, actual implementation) to identify the fields to be transmitted.
- Definition of data architecture: I recommend to keep the data which can be accessed by the public in a separate database, which is kept redundant to your operational databases. Thus, you can prevent hacker entries disturbing your production runs most effectively. For this intermediary database, the data model and database description has to be defined.
- Definition of data extraction frequencies and development of data extraction routines from the operational databases into the intermediary database.
- Implementation of Internet enabled database viewer on the intermediary database.
- Implementation of Search Engine for advanced and user friendly searches in your database.
- Agreement on Service Levels with Internet Access Provider in order to make sure, that the entries from the customers and the responses back are transmitted in time. It may be appropriate to define distinct service

quality levels, e.g. for "normal" transmission and for "express" transmission.

- Implementation of Service Level Management tools.

Security design and implementation: Features for various levels of security need to be designed and implemented:

- *e*Mail encryption and Virus-Checking.
- Identification, authentification of customers entitled to view the databases; encryption of identification and authentification data.
- Access control for database access from the Internet to intermediary databases, Firewalls.
- Access control and encryption for data file downloads.
- Encryption and authentification for data submitted by the customers.

Review and test: None of the changes and enhancements may go without review and test. For every update, perform an internal review, then check it using different Internet browsers (in particular Netscape and Microsoft Explorer). Finally, for important areas have some customers test your site as well – you may get interesting feedback on what to improve.

Takeover in production and maintenance: The operational concepts need to be defined and the tools to support the operations need to be configured appropriately – this has to include automatic restarts, backup and recovery processes, fallback solutions in case of problems (like alternate routing in case of network problems). Also, the support responsibilities (like 24 hour-service) need to be defined.

Order Entry and Provisioning

With the activities above completed, you only publish information about your company and your services, but no interaction is possible yet. If someone wants to use your services he would need to pick up a phone or send you an *e*Mail asking for an offer. But that's not the way to do *e*Business. Instead, you have to make it as easy as possible for your customer to just say YES to your offering. Avoid puzzling the customer with long questionnaires or application forms, just ask for the key information necessary to initiate the customer relationship and to configure the services. If your offering is too complex, you should adopt a call centre approach, where your customer care representatives walk the prospect through the configuration of your services. In this case, you should have a button on your website to allow the customer to get immediately connected with a customer care representative.

Design and implementation of order entry and provisioning: The approach, processes and data necessary to capture an order have to be defined. The approach should be in a way that an order will be entered just once and no re-entry in the various steps of execution takes place:

- Decide who can enter the order: As a long-term target, your customers should be enabled to enter the orders directly via the Internet. As intermediary steps it may be applicable that the customers express their desires via phone, eMail or paper mail (like the classical mail-order) and your customer care representatives enter it in the systems.
- Identify the data necessary to configure the services. If we refer to our ERP provider, he needs to package his offering in a way to avoid asking questions like "how many accounts do you need in your general ledger". Instead he should offer the appropriate pre-configured packages for the various groups of users, e.g. accounting solution, payroll service, accounts receivables management, cash management, with different target groups like small retail shop, small craftsmen company, medium sized software house. With the same importance, you need the customer identification and characteristics such as address or customer number and contact information (telephone numbers, eMail address) plus size of the company (number of employees, annual turnover, number of suppliers and customers).
- Design, development and implementation of the screens to capture the customer information and the order information. If the entry is handled internally, then normal GUI front ends for your customer care system can be configured, if you want to allow self service on the web, Internet forms have to be set up. In either case the interface with the order entry and your back end application needs to be developed, too. Those interfaces may need some additional bidirectional interaction to start the services. In our ERP provider example, this would mean, that for each new customer, automatically a new user needs to be opened in the ERP processing system like a new general ledger loaded from the appropriate template. Then, the opening balance needs to be generated based on the figures generated by the former accountant which can be entered by either the customer or the ERP provider staff.

Review and test: As discussed before. Additionally, you should perform an end-to-end test, i.e. check if the orders really go through from the Internet to your processing systems.

Takeover in production and maintenance: The operational concepts need to be defined as:

- Which activities to run regularly and at which times of the day / week / month
- Which responsibilities exist including support in case of problems
- Service level commitments.

Service delivery to business customers

So far, your back end systems are ready to process the customers' transactions, but those transactions need to get to your back end system first of all, and the results of the calculations then need to be reported back to your customers. Therefore, you need to integrate your customers' processes with your back end processes.

Your customers have to submit their data to you – as you can experience when doing homebanking transactions: you tell your bank's IT system what payment transfer to execute or what stocks to purchase or buy. If your customers have only a few daily transactions, they can enter them through Internet forms and you get them immediately on your back end system. Alternatively, you can provide them with a data entry tool which they can run on their PC in their premises and then they send you a file with a bulk of transactions, e.g. the performed sales of the day and the received invoices. The same applies for the reports you generate: you either can publish them on an encrypted Internet frame (visible only for the respective customer) or you can provide a file to be downloaded to the customer's PC and printed there. The tasks necessary for this integration are:

Definition and development of interfaces with customers: The data to be received from and sent to the customers and the approach and the timing of the submission have to be defined:

- Identification of transaction types to be obtained from the customers, e.g. budget figures, accounting entries, invoices, salary agreements.
- Identification of the data to be sent to customers, e.g. general ledger report.
- Definition of data transfer types and structures, e.g. forms or files, format or file descriptions, for each of the different transactions.
- If you decide for an entry via Internet forms, you need to develop them accordingly.
- If you decide for file transfer, the appropriate data entry programmes need to be developed and sent to the customer. This software distribution can be organized via Internet, e.g. new versions of the software can be downloaded to the customer's PC, whenever a new version is available. As a more advanced approach, you could use the same programmes which you have developed for the form entry, but allow that the customers keep a copy locally on their PC, for the bulk entry and submit the whole file then. Thus, your customers save Internet connection time (and money) and you save the effort (and money) to maintain two separate versions of code.

Review and test: As discussed before; the integration with your customers (like the downloading of your transaction entry programmes) require a thorough test; in particular you should ask some customers to do a pilot test before you roll it out to all business customers.

Takeover in production and maintenance: The operational concepts need to be defined, again, but this time you need to include the customer in that definition because the regular processes have to be synchronized between both companies.

Extended functionality

The tasks above were for the core set of transactions – and you probably find out, that you need quite a lot of forms to do all the data entry necessary to perform the services in your back end system. You also need to balance enhancements in your back end system with the need to upgrade all your Internet customers to the additional features (or to maintain separate versions of the back end software). But you will make enhancements, anyway, and offer additional services. For those services, you can go through the same tasks as described above plus one addition, namely the support for the customers with the "old" services while some "new" approaches are already implemented. Various options exist:

- Ideally, the "new" services don't interfere with the "old" services – then you can just keep the transaction entry and the reporting back to your customers as you developed it before.
- Next best, all your customers use Internet forms (or download automatically the new software whenever there's a new release) and the new data which can now be entered by the customers are not necessary for the old customers – they can just leave the fields blank or your software automatically inserts some default values. In this case, you only give a brief message to your customers or you explain that on the data entry form.
- It is pretty bad if the semantics of certain old data fields change. Your customers will get upset, data entry errors will occur and you will be busy fixing operating problems. So you should avoid that whenever possible. If you can't avoid such changes, you should provide some automatic "translation" from the old semantics to the new semantics for quite some time to allow a smooth migration, but that requires some more software overhead.

Outlook: next generation eBusiness

So far, you have a pretty advanced service approach and you can even extend it by adding new services regularly. However, your competitors will try to catch up, so you have to step up, too, to a more effective business. You will strive for operational excellence, efficient processes and a high financial performance. In addition to ongoing internal process improvements, you can grow your business activities organically by adding staff and services, by extensions of your value propositions by tuning your cooperation with your partners or by mergers and acquisitions.

The implementation tasks for the organic growth have been discussed before; in parallel you need to grow your staff – both by numbers and by experience.

Extensions of the value propositions are advisable, when the activities between you and your customers stretch over many companies. The ERP provider might add tax advice as a forward integration on top of the traditional accounting services, or he might add the payment handling and fund management as a backward integration. In the first example, a closer cooperation with tax advisers would be appropriate, in the second case with banks and investment companies.

The most drastic tuning of the cooperation with partners is an "insourcing" of their services by acquiring one of your partners. Two basic settings for mergers and acquisitions can be thought of: complementary combinations in order to cover additional aspects of the value chain and thus offer broader services to the customers or overlap situations where you can cut back on costs because both companies were handling similar business processes.

Project activities for this stage of your business need to be defined once you have achieved that stage; they will include a new iteration of your strategy considerations and very intense discussions with your partners. Once you agree on tuned business approaches, your processes and systems need to be adjusted. Sometimes a solution of one of your partners (or acquired companies) may be better than your original system, so you need to adopt and extend that. For all the changes, the new cycle of design, development, configuration, test and roll-out has to be gone through. Additionally, you need to migrate your customers' data in your operational systems in order to maintain your trend analysis functions. And your organization has to go through the adjustments, too.

Recommendation:

- Start with a clear set of initial services for a concise customer group, e.g. for small or medium enterprises who currently tend to reject your offerings because they would require a too large up front investment.

13.1.4   Launch of ISP activities

The eVenture activities for ISP activities are similar to the ASP services scenario above. Significant differences exist, though. Some examples:

- ISPs approach the mass market and have very large numbers of consumers as their users;
- the ISP services are the foundation upon which value added services can be carried;
- the ISP services are often offered for very little charges or free of charge to the consumers, so revenues need to be generated either from the content providers or from advertisers.

As the ISP approaches are still new for most of us, let me share some of the research results before we discuss the tasks in more detail.

Possible sources of revenues

The traditional sources of revenues for ISPs are charges for telephone connection times and subscription fees. Both those types of revenues are dying out. ISPs with subscription fees and with call by call charges are continuously cutting back the fees and the challenge of free ISPs continues pushing for further decreases of the fees. The attempt to recover from that revenue decrease by bundling the ISP subscription with the telephone connection in order to get at least the revenues for the switched connection[23], isn't successful any more. Also the telephone revenues for the connection from the consumers' PC to the point of presence of the ISP are eroding due to the competition in the deregulated markets.

So, new sources of revenue must be identified based on new value propositions. Even a new terminology is necessary: If your customers don't pay for your services, can you call them customers any more? And if your allies or partners have to pay you for your survival, shouldn't you treat them as the real customers? Anyway, in this book, we have been using the term customer (or consumer) for those people surfing the Internet demanding your services and partner (or ally) for the companies offering the contents via the ISP backbone. New types of revenues can be obtained by the ISP, e.g. from:

Advertising partners: fees for marketing activities like advertisement banners seen by the consumers, commissions for customer responses to marketing campaigns run by the ISP, per centage of sales price for ordered products.

Telco partners: participation in telephone charge for connection time, interconnect charges for transit of web traffic.

Content providers: fraction of micropayments for chargeable contents, e.g. for software payable by digital cash, or for chargeable dictionary inquiry.

Subscribers of value added services: fee for membership in community.

Such communities are the foundation of your revenues. Therefore, you should carefully create the environment where they want to stay and where they are happy to obtain the information from your advertising partners. Some examples: If one of your partners is

An airline or a travel agency, you can market their offerings to members of Frequent Traveller Community. To create this community, you can publish

---

[23] A comment for the US readers: In Europe, local telephone calls (e.g. to the point of presence of an ISP) are usually to be paid and the cost depends on the duration of the connection time. This is different from the US approach with free local calls (or a small fee independent of the duration of the call). Therefore, different business models have to be adopted in the US and in Europe.

special transportation information, e.g. flight delays, hotel availabilities during peak times like trade fairs, plus the travellers can chat amongst each other about best airlines, best hotels, or entertainment in cities abroad.

A gift shop or flower shop, you can highlight their offerings to subscribers of a calendar service, e.g. for birthday reminders. Plus the members could chat about gift ideas.

A bank or investment company, you can offer automated advise, e.g. implement buy/sell triggers for stocks to members of an Investment community. Plus the members could chat and share their experience in a forum about tips and tricks (e.g. taxation, special insights, stock recommendations).

An insurance or a book store, you can offer book reading advise and insurance comparisons to a community of parents. And the community could organize child care amongst the members, or chat about education and safety issues.

A virtual shop, you can do "best buy" marketing to a Browsing/auctioning community. Plus the members could establish their private communities ("talk to your friends while they are online, too"). These friendships could then be assessed for common transactional/buying behaviours.

Above are examples of creating communities driven by the offerings of your partners. Many community offerings, though, are established driven by the demand of a specific community. A region where such communities have at the same time led to the foundation of free ISPs (currently more than two hundred) is the UK. You find communities/ISPs for members of specific churches, for specific professions, for specific interests, for certain political and society targets. These types of communities usually are not pursuing business purposes (with only some thousand members/subscribers they would be pretty small, anyway), but they have their primary purpose in representing and furthering the interests of their members. So the community-specific ISPs are bundling the demand of their members and provide a marketing and sales channel for the offerings in case a provider can convince their opinion makers. Once you've convinced the opinion makers, the communities can link from their portal to your offering – and for some of those links you may be even willing to pay some commissions.

Task summary of ISP activities

Figure 13-55 below indicates the key areas for the project and their approximate sequence. The launch of an ISP requires teams of several dozen to hundred staff, so it's out of the scope of this book dealing with the specific considerations of SMEs. I still want to give you the background of the complexities of the ISP offerings to allow you more profound discussions with the ISP you're dealing with.

The launch phase has three objectives: implement the technology, create the contents in cooperation with the partners, recruit a large number of subscribers. If the ISP starts as a small provider (a tier three or tier four provider as it's called), he can peer with other tier three or four providers, i.e. he can exchange data free of charge. He has to negotiate with the tier one and two providers for the data exchange that he still needs due to the gaps in global access and due to performance bottlenecks in his peering network. At the same time, he needs to prepare the contents. For the initial contents the creation of the relationships with the content partners is equally important as the technical implementation of his network. The content is displayed in the portal, which has to be created in a way attracting the consumers.

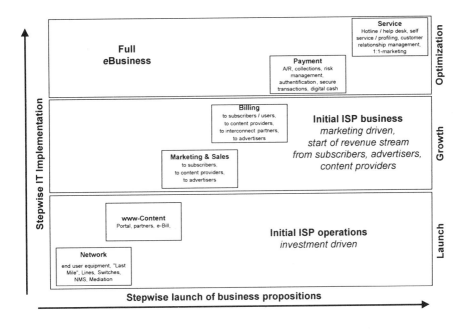

Figure 13-55: Project activities for ISP launch

In the portal, a search function is usually provided, some frequently requested information is packaged such as news and weather and community specific updates, and links to the partners are included. If the ISP charges for the use of the services or is a telco provider as well, the bill can be presented online. The consumers can view the contents provided by the ISP in cooperation with his partners. They will find any combination of static websites, dynamic websites, order entry for the ISP's sales partners, ASP offerings, forums and chat rooms.

In the second phase, while continuing the fast growth of subscribers the focus will be to materialize the designed revenues. Therefore, all the customer value management systems, one-to-one marketing systems and sophisticated billing systems have to be implemented and configured. This is a phase in itself, because it can easily take nine to eighteen months until the complex systems are up and running.

For the optimization, the payment transactions between the ISP's subscribers/ consumers, and his partners can be handled by him in conjunction with his settlement partners like credit card acquirers or banks. Moreover, he needs to add service components like consumer and partner support, and he has to optimize his marketing automation by tuning the underlying customer behaviour models.

13.2   IMPLEMENTATION EXPERIENCE – WHAT NOT TO DO

In this section, I want to share some project experiences with you. The underlying recommendation is to regularly step back and check if the original assumptions are still right, if the market and competition has changed and if your value proposition is still strong.

13.2.1   Don't build on improvisation

You will need to improvise more often than not, but you should avoid it whenever possible, otherwise you will fail like a little retailer in Austria. He thought his web presence was for free. He subscribed to a web host, where he placed his website for € 10 a month, purchased Microsoft Frontpage and started editing his frames. After five weekends were over, his presence in the Internet read still "Soon you will find here the attractive website of xyz.retail.com". So he hired a local student and asked him to come up with his website. This worked well, and when the student returned to university everything was up and running. Every weekend the retailer went through the eMails of the week to check if he could close additional business. Unfortunately, over time the eMails sounded more and more upset that no immediate responses were given. And the contents of the website was outdated, because the retailer sold the goods from another supplier now, so the packaging and pricing was different. After six months, the dealer was frustrated about the new technology and closed his website. A better way would have been to design the activities from the beginning to the end, to prepare for responses to received eMails, and to anticipate updates of the website.

13.2.2   Don't outsource your core capabilities

An ISP provider considered to outsource all operational activities. After the 300+ requirement paper was compiled, they found out that if all these services were run by an outside company, this would be a huge competitor. Actually this competitor would be able to offer the services cheaper, because he wouldn't need to carry the overhead of the company having initially the idea. So they restrategized and decided to build a team of IT specialists and to build up all the infrastructure internally. They had lost three months in their time to market and it required a much bigger investment than with the initial approach, but now they had a much better approach than educating and nurturing future competition.

13.2.3   Don't hesitate to communicate

A smart entrepreneur in France did all the necessary things as discussed in this book, he hired excellent staff and established a solid IT infrastructure. Unfortunately, he didn't ask his team for feedback during the creation of the business plan, so he had to realize after six months that his sales figures were at only one third of his market research results. What was different about his customers' needs than anticipated? When he started to share his assumptions with the observations of his call centre and sales force staff, he found a rich set of experience and was able to double his sales figures in only two months, so he was almost back on track regarding his business plan.

13.2.4   Don't disregard experience from others

It's easy to make mistakes and you should forgive yourself and others if it's the first time such a mistake is made. But if you could have known better, shame on the person who disregarded experience from others. And the market is even harder than only putting shame on such a person; many entrepreneurs fell bankrupt due to only a little mistake. Like the American HiFi equipment retailer, who had a quick and successful launch of his eVenture, made good revenues, had nice and cooperative partners and for a long time had the right instincts regarding the number of supplies to order. His banker and his friend recommended him to implement a little ERP system to be able to forecast sales, but he believed this would be throwing money out of the window. He grew larger and hired a guy to help him monitor the inventories and trigger the supplies. After the next Christmas sales were over, the poor fellow realized that they had ordered way too much and that they had compiled unsellable equipment that had eaten up one year's revenue. The bank closed the shop and now the entrepreneur is back in his earlier profession of a disc jockey.

13.2.5   Don't take success for granted

Doing business on the web is still experimental. Whole industries are currently collecting their experience. You cannot expect that everything can be designed properly, therefore you need to have clear steps with check marks allowing you to adjust the contents and speed of the subsequent step.

Surprises will come all along. Your ISP may go out of business and you quickly need to move your website. A competitor may copy or even extend your value proposition and you need to counteract quickly. And your customers may show a different buying behaviour than you thought. So, keep all your senses activated and stay flexible!

13.2.6   Don't try to do everything at once

No matter how big your appetite for risk is, your investments shouldn't be more than the assets you own, or your family and friends would be ready to lose in the worst-case, or a venture capitalist would be willing to invest in your eVenture. In fact, when you are serious about your business idea you will take all your own money, plus your family's money, plus all the venture capital funding you can get. But you shouldn't use it up in the first project phase! Cover in your investment plan for the growth phase as well!

Don't build your enterprise on long-term bank loans – you would need to pay them back no matter how stretched your business situation may be at certain times. With your bank you need to have a credit line for short-term overdrafts, e.g. for three-month expected revenues in order to maintain liquidity during cyclical revenue decreases, but no long-term loan.

Again my recommendation: plan your project with clear milestones in order to adjust the next steps according to the most recent development.

13.2.7   Don't repeat the mistakes of others

A recent survey at more than 500 start-ups showed the following reasons for a failure:

- Seventeen per cent ran out of money – if you have prepared your business plan properly, have done your ROI calculation, have enough own money or venture capital available and only little debts plus a good financial monitoring approach you should be able to avoid that risk.
- Gaps in the plan and concept led to a mis-positioning at 13 per cent – we've discussed the business concept, the electronic interaction, your organization and IT in depth in this book. If you have done the indicated "homework" properly and have it cross-checked by an investor you should be on the safe side.
- Lack of qualification or over-optimistic self-assessment led to another 12 per cent of failures. So, be honest to yourself to make sure that you are not day-dreaming but preparing a challenging and hard time of getting your company launched.

Therefore, be extremely thorough in your preparation – pull out the checklists another time and assess, if you have considered all relevant points.

13.3   CHECKLIST

The following checklist is now the summary of all the chapters of the book, in a way it's also a cover sheet for the other checklists. A softcopy of this checklist (as also of the others) can be obtained on my website www.success-at-e-business.com. With the compilation of the checklists you have your project initiation documentation prepared.

Table 13-40: Checklist for your project execution

Item	To check	Recommendation	Your view
Strategy	*Are the strategic targets defined and documented?*	The strategic considerations are described in Section I of the book; here's a summary: • Definition of Target customers with a breakdown of which customer segments to approach at the various stages of the project • Definition of Products to be offered with a breakdown of which products to be sold via Internet at the various stages of the project	
Clear decision	*Does the business plan indicate an ROI supporting the project?* *If not, what other reasons are in favour of the project?*	Have a clear sponsorship for the project from the investors or the board of your company. Prepare a list of success criteria to check at the various project milestones; e.g. • Costs incurred up to the milestone • Updated benefit expectation • Reflection of the initial assumptions and strategic targets to adjust them to the changes in the market. Possibly recalculate the ROI based on the updated estimates. • List of risks, current probability of materialization, impact of risks, mitigation strategies	
Resource availability	*Do you have the funding (and liquidity) to finance the project at the various stages?* *Is this the case even if the benefits come "a bit" later than planned?* *Do you have the internal staff or the external support identified and available to execute the project?*	I personally wouldn't start an *e*Venture based on a loan, the interest needs to be paid and you need to pay back the loan, this is a legacy for your future activities. Instead you should use own or external venture capital. With that approach, you can expect more patience from the capital side in case of later paybacks. Regarding the staffing, you have to have a project manager with the appropriate experience. Additionally the project team should be comprised of at least half internal staff in order to prepare for the know-how transfer into your organization.	
Project organization	*Is the project plan ready?*	The project plan should include • The tasks (with deliverables and milestones) • The staff with the team responsibilities and cooperations between team members and the environment, e.g. contact persons in the partner organizations	

GOOD LUCK!

14

Useful websites and other information

The providers and vendors mentioned in this book are listed below and their websites and some background information are provided. I've categorized their offerings, therefore those companies show up in various places that provided various tools or offerings.

The listings are structured by type of service in the sequence you will probably want to get in touch with them; each of the listings is sorted alphabetically. As far as pricing information is given, this was valid at the time of editing; no liability for correct figures at the time of reading can be accepted.

14.1 RESEARCH AGENCIES/INFORMATION SOURCES

From the research agencies, you can obtain current statistical information in order to estimate your market size. Additionally, some of the research agencies provide market surveys and solution vendors.

Research agency	Coverage	Website
Fletcher Research Ltd	Market Research	www.fletch.co.uk
Forrester Research	Market Research	www.forrester.com
GartnerGroup	Information Technology Research	www.gartner.com
GfK	Market Research, Focus: Germany	www.gfk.de
IDC	Market Research	www.idc.com
INSEAD	Business School	www.insead.fr
Jupiter Communications	Market Research, Focus: Europe	www.jup.com
Meta Group	Information Technology Research	www.metagroup.com
Patricia Seybold Group	Internet Research and Consulting	www.customers.com
Tower group	Information Technology Research	www.towergroup.com

The local chambers of commerce should be contacted for regional statistical information, and the local press checked for special editions on electronic business.

Newspaper / Magazine	Website
Computer weekly	www.computerweekly.co.uk
Computerzeitung	www.computer-zeitung.de
Financial Times	www.ft.com
Informationweek	www.informationweek.com
InternetNews.com	www.internetnews.com
Internet world	www.internetworld.com
PC world (publishes ranking of ISPs)	www.pcworld.com
Tomorrow	www.tomorrow.de
Wall Street Journal (offer Internet directory each third Thursday in month)	www.wsj.com
w&v	www.efv.de + www.w&v.de

14.2   WEB HOSTING ENVIRONMENT

14.2.1   Domain registration

The first thing to do for your web presence is registrating your domain, i.e. your name. You can do it directly, e.g. with the companies listed below, or through your ISP.

Website	Comments
www.networksolutions. com	Ex-monopolist for the US domains .com, .org, .net Registration costs $ 70 for two years, an extension $ 35 per year.
www.register.com	New player for international domains; currently same pricing scheme as Network Solutions
+ Separate companies for each country	e.g. Germany: www.denic.de, www.strato.de, www.puretec.de

14.2.2   ISPs

The ISP is your "point of contact" with the Internet. If you are smaller, he can provide you with the full services of helping your set up your website, hosting it and providing the necessary technical infrastructure. If you are larger, he will handle the data interchange between your webserver and the Internet users.

ISPs	Website
AT&T WorldNet	www.att.net, www.att.com

Atlas of Cyberspaces (by University College London)	www.geog.ucl.ac.uk/casa/martin/atlas/isp_maps.html
AOL	www.aol.com
Cable & Wireless	www.cw.net, www.cw-usa.net, www.cwplc.com
CompuServe	www.compuserve.com
Ebone	www.ebone.com
GTE Internet	www.gte.net
IBM	www.ibm.net (now served by www.att.net in most countries)
InternetWatch Foundation (UK)	www.internetwatch.org.uk
KPNQwest	jv.eu.net
Mannesmann Arcor	www.arcor.net
MCI worldcom	www.mci.net
Nacamar	www.nacamar.net
Qwest	www.qwest.net
Sprint	www.sprint.net
Uunet	www.uunet.com
Xlink	www.xlink.com
Yahoo	www.yahoo.com

Also, you should check the offering of the former public PTTs; they often have also a very broad ISP offering. Usually, there are up-to-date evaluations for each country, what the characteristics of each ISP are. Those evaluations can be found on the web, in computer and business magazines, through chambers of commerce and from business angel institutions.

14.2.3   Search Engines and agents

Search Engines (SEs) are the primary tool on the web of raising the awareness about your offering. You should register with many search engines and a broad set of key words to make yourself widely known.

	Website	Indexed pages*/comments
Altavista	www.altavista.com	SE: 150 Mio. Websites
artificial-life.com	www.artificial-life.com	Provide Avatars for easier navigation in the web
Botspot.com	www.botspot.com	Survey of search agents/bots
Dsr1.com	www.dsr1.com	Registration service for various search engines (cost: $ 100 annually)
Excite	www.excite.com	SE: 250 Mio. websites; expected focus on online shopping
Fast	www.alltheweb.com	SE: 200 Mio. websites
HotBot	www.hotbot.com	
Infoseek	www.infoseek.com	

Search Engines (continued)

	Website	Indexed pages*/comments
Intkomi	www.intkomi.com	SE: 110 Mio. websites
Lycos	www.lycos.com	SE: Expected focus on community sites
Northern Light	www.northernlight.com	SE: 161 Mio. websites
Search Engine Watch	www.searchenginewatch.com	Ranking and comparison of search engines, e.g. regarding market reach for specific segments; possibility to register to the search engines
WebPosition Gold	www.webposition.com	Software for automatical re-registration to search engines (cost: $ 149)
World Submit	www.worldsubmit.com	Registration service
Yahoo	www.yahoo.com	SE: Offers added services, e.g. auctions, web hosting for private websites. 1 Mio. websites listed.

* Of overall more than 800 Mio. websites. Source: Search Engine Watch

14.3 WEBSITE DESIGN AGENCIES

The design is usually handled by local agencies – therefore, you should check in the search engines what companies are identified in your region. One multi-regional provider is razorfish (www.razorfish.com).

14.4 VENDORS OF INTERNET FRONT OFFICE SOFTWARE

14.4.1 Shopping/Catalogue

The online catalogue is the major vehicle of presenting your offering on the web. If you select a vendor with a good functional scope and performance, most of the requirements for your launch should be covered at little cost.

Provider	Core offering	Website	Comments/size*
The ISPs	Small online shops (catalogue and order entry)	See ISP section	
Blaze Software	Web personalization and self service	www.blazesoft.com	Formerly: Neuron Data
Cat@log	Online shop	www.catalogint.com	Award winning application; easy integration with broad set of databases; good analysis of customer behaviour (click stream)

* Financial figures and staff sizes in this chapter are based on publications of the companies unless otherwise indicated.

Shopping/Catalogue software (continued)

Provider	Core offering	Website	Comments/size
Clarify	Front end for telecom customer care and sales	www.clarify. com	Revenues 1998: $130 Mio. (growth >75% annually, again to be expected in 1999)
IBM	Hardware, *e*Business packages (including hardware and software), consulting	www.ibm.com	Revenues 1998: $35,419 Mio. Licence fee for start-up package Net Commerce: > € 5,000
ICat	Order entry and tracking	www.icat.com	Good integration concept with back end systems
Intershop	Catalogue and Order Entry	www.intershop. com	Currently > 20,000 websites supported (largest number of installations for catalogue and order entry) Licence fee: > € 5,000
Interworld		www.interworld .com	
Lotus	Domino.Merchant: online shop for medium to large providers	www.lotus.com	Integrated with Lotus Domino
Microsoft	Frontpage	www.microsoft. com	HTML editor for publishing websites
NetObjects	Fusion	www.netobjects .com	
OpenShop	Ordertainment	www.openshop. com	Java based flexible shop support including auctions, interactive comunication, entertainment
Smart Order	Order Entry for Sales representatives with interface to delivery	www. smartorder.com	

14.4.2   Call Centre software

If you run your own call centre, the interactions of the customer care representatives need to be supported by the call centre software.

Provider	Core offering	Website	Comments/size
Clarify	Customer Relationship Management focused on telecom providers	www.clarify.com	Revenues 1998: $130 Mio. (growth >75% p.a., again to be expected in 1999)
Genesys	Computer Telephony Integration	www.genesyslab. com	Revenues 1999: $139 Mio. (growth > 70% annually)
Siebel	Customer Relationship Management	www.siebel.com	Revenues 1998: $391 Mio. (growth >80% p.a., again to be expected in 1999), > 2,000 professional staff
Vantive	Customer Relationship Management	www.vantive.com	Revenues 1998: $163 Mio. (growth >20% p.a.), >600 staff

14.4.3   Delivery servicing/workflow/ERP

If your supply chain is complex or difficult to manage, you have to monitor each item ordered by a customer to present up-to-date status information.

Provider	Core offering	Website	Comments/size
Baan	ERP	www2.baan.com	Revenues 1998: $ 791 Mio
FileNet	Document Imaging, Workflow	www.filenet.com	Revenues 1998: $ 310 Mio
Integratio	Implementation of eProcurement	www.integratio.de	
JDEdwards	ERP	www.jdedwards.com	Revenues 1998: $ 932 Mio
Lucent	Network services	www.lucent.com	Revenues 1998:$30,147 Mio
Peoplesoft	ERP	www.peoplesoft.com	Revenues 1998: $ 1,314 Mio.
SAP	ERP	www.sap.com	Revenues 1998: € 4,300 Mio., > 19,000 employees

14.4.4   Automatic eMail response systems

When your customers use eMail frequently for interactions with you, an automatic response system can cut back your efforts significantly.

Provider	Website
Aptex: SelectResponse	www.aptex.com
Millenium: Echomail	www.millenium.com, www.echomail.com
Message Media: Response Now	www.messagemedia.com, www.responsenow.com

14.5   LOGISTICS SERVICES

To deliver physical items to your customers and for related services, you'll need a logistics partner. In addition to international providers as listed below, the traditional PTTs of many countries have interesting service offerings, too.

Provider	Core offering	Website	Comments/size
DHL	Delivery of letters and parcels	www.dhl. com	Specialized in customs regulations around the globe
FedEx	Delivery of letters and documents	www.fedex. com	Specialized in America–Europe transportation
UPS	Delivery of letters and parcels	www.ups. com	
Sellbytel	Outsourced call centre	www. sellbytel. com	Startup operating throughout Europe, has won international awards like "Service Globe 99". (Use as benchmark for the offering of your local provider.)

14.6   PAYMENT AND RISK MANAGEMENT PROVIDERS

Your ISP should support your payment approaches. In case he doesn't provide you with the appropriate services, you can configure the payment solution yourself. As a minimum, you will need a credit card company acquiring your transactions and the SET software to encrypt the transmission of the financial transactions. Additionally, you can implement cybercash solutions.

In case you allow your customers to draw credits, you need software support for the management of the financial risks.

14.6.1   Credit card companies

Provider	Website
American Express	www.americanexpress.com
GZS	www.gzs.de
MasterCard International	www.mastercard.com
Visa Card International	www.visa.com

14.6.2   SET

Provider	Website
Brokat	www.brokat.com
Compaq	www.compaq.com
Data Design	www.datadesign.com
IBM	www.ibm.com
Trintech	www.trintech.com
Verifone	www.verifone.com
Xlink	www.xlink.com

14.6.3   Cybercash

Provider	Website
Adobe	www.adobe.com
Afor	www.afor.com
Bull	www.bull.com
Cybercash	www.cybercash.com
Inatec	www.inatec.com

14.6.4   Risk management

Provider	Core offering	Website	Comments/size
American Management Systems	System Integration for telecom and eBusiness providers	www.amsinc.com	Revenues 1998: $ 1,008 mio, > 8,000 staff
Dunn & Bradstreet	Credit Bureau	www.dnb.com	
Experian	Consumer rating	www.experian.com	
Moody's	Rating agency	www.moodys.com	
Standard & Poors	Rating agency	www.standardandpoors.com	

14.7   BUSINESS-TO-CONSUMER SOFTWARE VENDORS

For individually addressing large numberrs of customers, personalization tools are necessary.

Provider	Core offering	Website	Comments/size
Broad-vision	One-to-one relationship management	www.broadvision.com	13% market share*
Fair, Isaac	Decision Support for Marketing and Risk Management	www.fairisaac.com	Revenues 1998: $ 245 Mio
Janus	Simulation of market dynames	Anathanson@ flashnet.it	
Netscape	Portals (and browsers)	www.netscape.com	5.7% market share
Open Market	Customer transaction applications: authentication, ordering, payment, tracking	www.openmarket.com	7% market share
Oracle	Software development tools: Java, Portals, Database management, Service Bureau	www.oracle.com	5.6% market share
Vignette	Story Server: web personalization tool	www.vignette.com	Revenues Q3/1999: $ 24 Mio

* Market shares in this section are quoted from IDC 1999 unless otherwise indicated.

14.8   VENDORS OF DATA WAREHOUSE AND ANALYSIS TOOLS

For monitoring the behaviour of large numbers of customers, a data warehouse is necessary, if the current IT environment is so much inhomogeneous that no integrated view of the customer situation would be possible.

Provider	Core offering	Website	Comments/size
AMS	System Integration and Consulting for large enterprises	www.amsinc. com	Revenues 1998: $1,008 Mio, >8,000 employees.
ATG	Dynamo/click stream analysis	www.atg.com	
Broad-vision	One-to-one personalized web access	www. broadvision. com	Revenues 1998: $51 Mio, >400 employees
Business Objects	OLAP tools	www. business objects. com	
Cognos	OLAP tools	www.cognos. com	
IBM	Hardware, eBusiness packages (including hardware and software), consulting, Data Mining ("Intelligent Miner")	www.ibm. com	Revenues 1998: $35,419 Mio
Micro Strategy	ROLAP: DSS Products Server	www. microstrategy .com	
NCR	Hardware (cash registers, teller machines, data bases), software (DWH, data mining) and system integration	www.ncr.com	Revenues 1998: $6,505 Mio
Oracle	Database systems, programming languages (Java), Data Mining ("Thinking Machines/ Darwin"), MOLAP ("Express"), eBusiness portals and CRM	www.oracle. com	Revenues 1999: $8,800 Mio, >41,000 employees
Platinum Technology	Data extraction and analysis tools, e.g. Prodea	www. platinum.com	
SAP	CRM, campaign management, workflow, R/3, mysap	www.sap.com	Revenues 1998: $4,300 mio., > 19,000 employees
SAS Institute	DWH, MOLAP, EIS, Analysis and financial consolidation (e.g. "Enterprise Miner"), balanced scorecard	www.sas.com	Revenues 1998: $873 Mio
Seagate	MOLAP ("Holos")	www.seagate software.com	Revenues 1999: $142 Mio, 1,100 employees
SPSS	Data Mining ("Clementine") and DWH	www.spss. com	Revenues 1998: $121 Mio

14.9   BUSINESS-TO-BUSINESS APPLICATION VENDORS

14.9.1   Electronic procurement

Key component of the supply chain management is the procurement software.

Provider	Core offering	Website	Comments/size
AMS	Procurement desktop	www.amsinc. com	1998 revenues: $1,008 Mio, > 9,000 staff
Ariba	Electronic procurement	www.ariba.com	1999 revenues: (estimate) $40 Mio 14% market share
Commerce One	Purchasing and procurement	www.commerce one. com	5.6% market share
Harbinger	Internet gateway, WebEDI/procurement	www.harbinger. com	5.6% market share
Intelisys	Internet procurement	www. iecsolutions. com	6.1% market share
Infobank	Electronic procurement	www. intradeonline. com	European focus
Oracle	Enterprise Applications, CRM, Internet servers, Procurement	www.oracle. com	5.6% market share
Netscape	Portals	www.netscape. com	15% market share
Sterling Commerce	System connections: file transfer, forms, mailbox, XML	www.sterlingco mmerce. com	6.7% market share

14.9.2   Billing

For ISPs, ASPs and telco providers, that handle very large numbers of customer transactions, high performant billing solutions need to be implemented.

Provider	Core offering	Website	Product/Comments
American Management Systems	System Integration for telecom and Internet providers	www.amsinc. com	Tapestry: platform for high performance rating and billing, integration of third party software Prices > € 1 Mio.
Architel	Telecom service activation and interconnect software	www.architel. com	ASAP: with interfaces to the major telephony switch providers
ATG	Click stream monitoring	www.atg.com	Dynamo: 2 million users worldwide

Billing solution (continued)

Provider	Core offering	Website	Product/Comments
Comptel	Telecom service activation and Call Data Record collection	www.comptel.com	MDS/AMD
IMS Belle Systems	Internet billing and integration with network access servers, web servers and *e*Mail servers	www.belle.dk	IMS Internet Management System (ccoperation with Cisco) Price range € 100,000–150,000
Intec Systems	Interconnect billing systems	www.intec systems.co.uk	
Kenan	Telecom Billing systems	www.kenan.com	Arbor Subsidiary of Lucent Usage based costing; expects more than 100,000 subscribers
Portal	Internet customer management and billing software	www.portal.com	Infranet Price range € 500,000–800,000
Solect	Internet billing	www.solect.com	IAF Horizon Price range € 500,000–750,000
XaCCT technologies	Internet account activation and billing	www.xacct.com	

14.9.3   Supply Chain Management

In addition the electronic procurement software, sophisticated SCM approaches require proper planning and well-established interactions between the suppliers and their customer.

Provider	Product	Website	Comments
Baan	Supply Chain Solutions	www.baan.com	
i2 Technologies	Intelligent *e*-Business	www.i2.com	
J.D.Edwards	Supply Chain Advantage JD*e*.sourcing	www.jdedwards.com	Based on cooperation with IBM and Synquest
Logility	Value Chain Advantage	www.logility.com	
Manugistics	*e*-Chain	www.manu.com	
Matrix One	*e*Matrix	www.matrix-one.com	
Oracle	Oracle Applications	www.oracle.com	
Paragon Management Systems	Supply Chain Planner	www.paragonms.com	
Parametric Technology	Windchill 2.1	www.ptc.com	

Supply Chain Management (continued)

Provider	Product	Website	Comments
Peoplesoft	Peoplesoft	www.peoplesoft.com	
SAP	Advanced Planner, mysap.com	www.sap.com, www.mysap.com	Includes an electronic marketplace for cooperation between all registered users.

14.10 OTHER PROVIDERS

Provider	Core offering	Website
Cisco	Internet routers	www.cisco.com
Lucent	Communication systems hardware and software	www.lucent.com
Netscape/ ASP	Internet browser (Netscape Navigator), and other shareware	www.netscape. com
Sun	Technology solutions, in particular high performing servers	www.sun.com
Weblogic	Middleware to enable web interactions for larger companies	www.beasys.com

GLOSSARY

Account	All Internet accesses are handled through the user's account. The account is held with the IAP or ISP.
ActiveX	Microsoft's collection of techniques, protocols and APIs to standardize the interactions between objects within webpages. Integrated in Microsoft's OLE (Object Linkage and Embedding) philosophy.
Agent	Software application in charge of performing specific services, e.g. identifying specific updates on websites, launching particular jobs at specific times, searching specified information.
Algorithm	Specific sequence of activities describing the solution for a certain constellation.
Applet	Application code downloaded from the Internet and executed on the user's PC; often written in Java.
ARPANet	Advanced Research Project Agency Network: Developed by the US Department of Defense in order to allow quick and cheap exchange of research information between scientists dealing with defense issues. Architected in a decentralized way to allow continued operation in parts of the network even after a possible destruction of other parts of the network.
ASP	Application service provider: Company that runs software applications on their IT environment and makes it available to external users. The data interchange between the ASP and its users can be handled via Internet.
Attachment	File attached to an eMail. An attachment may contain text, spreadsheets, audio data (e.g. music), pictures, animated graphics, video. Attachments should be encrypted in order to avoid viruses.
ATM	Asynchronous Transfer Mode: Data Transmission which can happen either in one direction, or in the other direction or in both directions at the same time.

Avatar	Representation of a human being in a Virtual Reality environment. Can serve as a guide in a shopping mall. Example: see Einstein alife from www.artificial-life.com
Backbone	Network connection for high speed exchange of Internet services; in particular between ISPs.
Bandwidth	The throughput capability of data connections; measured, e.g. in Megabit per second. ISDN connections, for example, have 64 kBit/second.
Banner	Advertising block from third parties inserted on the website of a provider. The viewer can get to the website of the advertiser by clicking on the banner. The display of banners can be suppressed by special software.
Bookmark	The preferred Websites of a user can be defined in some browsers. So the user can simply select the bookmark and doesn't need to type the whole URL. Also called Favorites.
Browser	Shows the information stored in the Internet (which is encoded in HTML or XML) on the screen of the user and allows the printout. Two primary products exist currently: Netscape Navigator and Microsoft Internet Explorer.
Cache/Proxy server	Server for intermediary storage of websites. The Cache is placed close to the location of the users and replicates frequently requested websites from physically remote providers in order to reduce the times and cost necessary for data exchange with the remote provider.
Certification	For payment transactions, Trust Centres issue certifications to consumers. With the certification, the consumers can obtain eCash from their bank. The Trust Centre together with the bank guarantee to exchange the digital cash against real money. This digital cash can be transferred electronically, e.g. to a service provider to pay for his services. The service provider then can cash it in.
CGI	Common Gateway Interface: Possibility for a Web-client (e.g. the consumer's PC) to launch Programmes on the Web-server (e.g. the Information Provider).
Chat	A realtime conversation between two or more visitors of a website using a chat room. The text typed by any of the chatting visitors shows up at the screen of all participants in the chat. The conversation is usually deleted when the conversation is finished.

Cookie	Files downloaded from the web to the PC of a user. The cookies can contain the name of the user, profile information, e.g. buying preferences, and can be read back by the information provider. Well designed websites should inform the users about the fact that a cookie is placed on his PC and what the content is. Cookies shouldn't contain sensitive data, e.g. credit card numbers, as they could be read by a hacker who intercepts the Internet session.
CSR	Customer Service Representative (also: customer care representative)
Cybercash, cybercoin	Trademark of Cybercash; see eCash
Decoding	See Encoding
Decryption	See Encryption
DHTML	Dynamic HTML: Extension to HTML allowing dynamic loading of websites – good, if you have pictures on your screen: the customer can read the text while the pictures still build up, i.e. getting sharper and sharper. He doesn't need to wait until the site is completely loaded, before he can surf onto the next information.
Dial-up connection	The communication between the computers (e.g. your PCs and the servers of your web host) is built up at each occasion when you need to transmit data. See also: leased line.

The telephone costs will be charged by unit (e.g. by second or minute) according to the tarrif for such connections, e.g. local tarrif, long distance tarrif.

This approach is advisable, if you have only occassional data transmissions, e.g. to check a few incoming mails or to update infrequently your website contents. |
Digital cash	See Certification and eCash
Domain	The Internet domain is a semantic label for the URL of a website, e.g. mcgraw-hill.co.uk. The domain name contains the top-level domain (e.g. .com for North American companies or .de for German providers). The domain names are assigned by specific institutions in each country.
Domain name server	The Internet routers and servers only use the IP-addresses. When a domain is requested by a user, the domain name server translates the domain name into the IP address. The domain name servers are usually run by the institution maintaining the domain names.

Download	Getting files from the Internet and loading them on their own computer. Such files can contain text, pictures, audio, video, software or business data. Those data don't need to be encoded in HTML, but can use the format of any application.
DSL	Digital Subscriber Lines: Technology used primarily in the US for Internet connection. In contrast to ISDN, no dial-up is necessary, because with DSL a permanent connection is switched to the ISP.
Dual Band	Mobile phones that can be used in two different GSM environments.
Dual Mode	Mobile phones that can also be used as cordless phone using the fixed wire connection in the houshold.
eBusiness	Overall business approach exploiting electronic interaction in all areas. Types of services and products reflect the possibilities provided by interactive marketing and selling, interactive production and supply chain management, interactive ("just in time") delivery, and integration with suppliers and partners.
eCash	Electronic Cash, also trademark of Digicash. The customer loads electronic cash from his bank onto his computer or onto his smartcard. The electronic cash is certified by a Trust Centre and is only valid if it's presented together with the certificate. At each transmission of the electronic cash, the validity of it needs to be verified by the Trust Centre. The owner of the electronic cash can obtain real money in exchange for the digital cash (provided it'' properly validated). See also Certification.
ECML	Electronic Commerce Modeling Language: Format standardizing the primary features necessary for electronic commerce, e.g. order, payment. Developed jointly by AOL, American Express, Cybercash, IBM, Mastercard, Microsoft, Setco, Sun, Transactor Networks, Trintech, Visa.
eCommerce	Use of an electronic channel for one particular aspect of the overall business, such as sales via the Internet, electronic procurement or electronic payment.
EDI	Electronic Data Interchange: Standards agreed before the Internet activities were established in a business context. EDI was performed via the normal telephony network or package switched data transmission, respectively. Electronic procurement approaches were implemented via EDI in the 1970s (e.g. in the automotive industry). Now, some of the EDI standards are upgraded to a usage on the Internet.

*e*Mail	Electronic mail: Brief messages can be exchanged between the mail partners. Most of the ISPs allow also to attach data files. Strengths of *e*Mail are the delivery is much quicker than traditional mail, virtually no costs and mailing lists that allow a distribution of messages and data to a large group of addressees.
Encoding	Transforming binary files (e.g. spreadsheets, video) into text based files. Two often used approaches are Uuencode and MIME. Used for *e*Mail attachments. Not all encoding protocols are transparent, i.e. not all allow to easily decode the encoded files; some also have problems with special country specific characters.
Encryption	In order to protect transmitted data against interception and illegal copying, the data are encrypted. The recipient needs to decrypt the data with the same key in order to make them readable again.
	Encryption algorithms are the more secure the longer the encryption key is. Currently 64 bit keys are standard, because the US government was blocking the exportation of the encryption software with longer keys (e.g. 128 bit keys). This policy has changed in January 2000, so it can be expected, that the key length for the standard encryption routines will increase soon.
*e*Venture	Project initiative to launch a new *e*Business (as a start-up or as the transformation of an existing business) or *e*Commerce activity. Requires the mindset of a pioneer, ongoing balancing of risks and opportunities and the quick implementation of a forceful organization with lean business processes and a dedicated IT support.
Extranet	Making an Intranet accessible for selected external partners, e.g. suppliers or customers, for exchanging data and applications. The users of an extranet are a well-defined group and access is protected by identification routines.
Favorites	See Bookmark
Firewall	A security device put in between an inhouse IT environment and the Internet. Usually run on a specific server in order to encrypt confidential data which are transmitted via the Internet and to prevent illegitimate access from outsiders to the inhouse IT environment.
Forum	A discussion between various visitors of a website. The contribution of each visitor is stored in a database and can be retrieved and presented to subsequent the visitors.

Frame	Method developed by Netscape to split the window visible by a browser into multiple separate areas.
FTP	File Transfer Protocol: Set of rules of how data files can be transmitted between two or more computers. Needed for uploading your website definition to your host, for transmitting data e.g. from a dynamic catalogue, order entry and similar databases
GPRS	General Packet Radio Service: Standard for mobile data transmissions with up to 115 kBit/sec.
GSM	Groupe Special Mobile/Global System for Mobile Communication:
	The European standard for communication for mobile telephony and data transmission. GSM 900 is implemented in approximately 100 countries, GSM 1800 in twenty countries, GSM 1900 in particular in the US.
GUI	Graphical User Interface: displayed on the screen of a computer using colour icons, radio buttons, pull down menus (to name some key elements) and allowing multimedia features. Initially developed by Apple for the Macintosh computers, now widely used. In contrast to that, the earlier 3270-screens just were able to display 24 lines of 80 characters each in black and white.
Homepage	The starting page of the website; usually all underlying pages should refer back to the homepage.
HSCSD	High Speed Circuit Switching: Standard for accelerated data transmission with up to 57.6 kBit/sec. in GSM networks.
HTTP	Hypertext Transfer Protocol: Document transmission rules between computers. Each system linked to the Internet must be able to handle HTTP; for end user devices this is included in the browser software.
HTML	Hypertext Markup Language: Description syntax for Web pages; most of the websites are stored in HTML format. Non-graphical HTML-documents can be created by text-editors (e.g. Microsoft Word); graphical HTML documents require a more sophisticated editor. The display functions are included in the browser software for end users.
Home page	The cover page of a website. This is the entry to your whole Internet presentation of a provider. Homepages often contain the site map, i.e. a table of contents, and search functions to directly access the desired information.

Hypertext	Is an overlay structure to traditional text documents. In hypertext documents, references ("hyperlinks") are included to specific parts of the text itself or to external items. Within hypertext documents, you can use those hyperlinks to jump directly to the location of the referenced text.
IAP	Internet Access Provider: A small provider without own network. They operate usually only in a small region.
ICANN	Internet Corporation for Assigned Names and Numbers
Identrus	International Banking consortium dealing with security approaches.
Interconnet	Agreement between fix wire telco providers to mutually use their lines and to reimburse each other appropriately.
Intermediary	Is in touch with buyers and with sellers and matches the demands and the supplies. Traditional examples include real estate brokers, investment brokers or travel agencies. Internet examples include online auctioneers.
	In a broader sense: everybody in the supply chain.
Internet	Network of millions of servers around the globe that are connected by using the same standards for data interchange. Internet servers are run by private persons, companies, public services and ISPs.
Intranet	Network of servers within one enterprise, where only the staff has access to provided data and information. The same standards for data interchange are used as in the Internet. Intranets are shielded against outside intruders by firewalls and additional password protection.
IPO	Initial Public Offering: The dream of many Internet pioneers – getting the company traded at a stock exchange. With the money raised by the IPO, additional investments can be made – and the founders can get rich.
IPP	Internet Presence Provider: Companies doing the concept, design and development of web presences for electronic commerce and electronic business companies.
IP-Number	Unique physical address of each computer connected to the web (e.g. 162.70.95.131).
ISP	Internet Service Provider; Tier 1 = large organizations organizing the global data interchange, Tier 2 (and below) = providing access to the retail market. The ISPs can also host the websites of the content providers, in particular private persons and small businesses that don't want to afford an own server for the website. The ISP services can be accessed at the PoPs.

ISDN	Integrated Services Digital Network: Allowing telephony using digital transmission of the signal (instead of analog transmission). Data transmission is possible via Internet with a better quality than via analog lines. The standard bandwidth is 64 kBit/sec, but higher bandwidth is possible depending on local implementations.
Java	Programming language for applications on the web developed by Sun to reflect the latest research in software engineering such as object orientation. Java is independent from differences in hardware and software platform, as Java is executable in itself.
	The structure of the language is similar to C++. For Internet applications, Java is used to build small applications (see applet), which can be run on the consumer's PC. Java is usually interpreted at the time of execution by the browser.
Leased line connection	The communication between the computers (e.g. your inhouse web server and your Internet provider) is kept up permanenty. See also: dial-up connection.
	The telephone costs will be charged on a "rental" basis, e.g. monthly, depending on the bandwidth you have subscribed to.
	This approach is advisable, if you have frequent data transmissions (i.e. more than 1 GByte per month), in particular, if you run your own web server.
Link	Connection between two websites. One presentation can refer to another presentation to allow the user quick jumps between the websites just by a mouse click.
Mall	Website combining several online shops and added services in a user friendly GUI.
Micro-payments	See: eCash
Millicent	Trademark of DEC; see eCash
MIME	Multipurpose Internet Mail Extensions; see Encoding.
MMM	Mobile Media Mode: Beginning of the Internet address of a service provider when called from a mobile (WAP) phone – like www for PC based Internet.
Modem	Modulator/DEModulator: Used to translate the digital signals for data transmission (e.g. Internet) to analog signals used in traditional voice telephony connections.
MOLAP	Multidimensional OLAP: Prepares internally data for often used inquiries in a way to allow very performant responses to complex analytical analysis.

Name server	The server that translates the URL (e.g. //http:www.success-at-e-business.com) into the physical location of the website. This translation can be handled by global name servers (e.g. with the company where the site is registered), by national name servers, or by a server in your own company.
NAP	Network access point
NSP	Network Service Provider = Provider of the physical telephony network (cable, switches, satellites.)
OLAP	Online analytical processing: Tool to define ad hoc queries in large databases. Often used to identify customer segments and profiles, e.g. for customer relationship management.
Peering	Agreement to mutually exchange the data transmission at no cost between the large ISPs.
Plug-in	Software which can be downloaded from the Internet on an as needed basis. It's configured to be immediately executable on the user's PC without additional set up.
PoP	Point of presence: Physical locations where the services of an ISP can be accessed. In regions with good Internet coverage, the PoPs should be scattered in a way allowing the consumers to dial in with a local call.
Portal	The presentation you see when you connect to your IAP or ISP. In the portal, the provider has bundled all his offerings and those of this partners. Benefit for the visitor is to do "one stop shopping", because many providers of services needed by the target group of the portal are bundled. Benefit for the portal provider is to increase the traffic by channelling many value added services and to generate additional revenues like sponsoring or advertising fees for customer specific links and banners.
POS	Point of sales
Proxy-Server	Storage of frequently viewed websites close to the location of the viewers. This is useful in the case when the content provider is very distant from the viewer in order to save data transmission time and cost.
Roaming	Agreement between mobile telco providers to mutually use their infrastructure and to reimburse each other appropriately. International roaming is common, because so far nobody has built up truly cross-border mobile infrastructures. National roaming is only applicable in countries with little mobile infrastructure.
ROLAP	Relational ROLAP: Predefined inquiries running regularly against the database.

Router	Select the best physical connection to the server where the website is located. Frequently used websites can be stored redundantly on the routers in order to minimize the cost of data transmissions between the router and the physical website location.
Server	The hardware where the websites are stored. Those servers can be accessed from remote places via the Routers in order to view the contents of the website. Also the maintenance of the website can be done remotely. The software for the administration of the websites is also part of the server.
	Term to define the logical entity that provides certain services.
SET	Secure electronic transaction
Set-top box	Device to connect a standard household TV with the Internet by using the fix wire telephone lines.
SGML	Standard Generalized Markup Language: The international standard (ISO 8879) for the definition, identification and use of the structure and contents of documents. The standard used in the Internet, HTML, is one specific implementation of SGML.
Site	See Website
SSL	Secure Socket Layer: Approach for data encryption using a private key and a public key for secure HTTP data transmissions. Is supported by all web browsers and the industry standard for data encryption.
Smart Phone	Mobile Phones combining telephone capabilities with palmtop computer functions.
SMS	Short Message Service: Brief text provided on the display of the mobile handset.
SOHO	Single office/home office
Surfing	Viewing the Internet contents via a browser by moving from website to website in order to get entertained or research information.
TCP/IP	Transmission Control Protocol/Internet Protocol: Standard for data transmission used between all Internet Routers and Servers.
TriBand	Mobile phones that can be used in three different GSM environments.
UMTS	Universal Mobile Telecommunication System: New global standard for mobile telephony; will be rolled out in 2002. With UMTS, data transmission up to 2 Megabit/sec. Will be possible.

Unified messaging	Approach to make messages accessible via different devices (e.g. *e*Mail, SMS, voice mail), no matter how the message was originally sent. This includes that the provider needs to perform conversions, e.g. from text to speech.
Upload	Copying data files from the user's PC to the Internet. Opposite of download.
URL	Unified Resource Locator: Globally unique address within the Internet of a website.
Virtual Reality	Representation of reality on computer. Covering at least visual aspects (usually three-dimensional) and acoustical aspects. For video games and robot applications, sensor gloves are often utilized to replace the steering of a device (e.g. a camera), which was earlier done by commands, function buttons or cursor steering.
WAP	Wireless access protocol: A "dialect" of HTTP for the data transmission to the mobile Phones. Can be used in GSM, GPRS and UMTS networks. Initial gateway-servers to translate HTML into WML have been developed by Software AG, Mannesmann, Nokia and Linkedwith based on an XML data format. Infowave is working on a Microsoft Exchange based gateway.
Website	Totality of the presentation of a company, private person or public service. The website is usually accessed through the homepage. Specific subdivisions of the website can be accessed, if the internal structure of the website is known, or if a link from another website refers to the respective subdivision.
WML	Wireless Markup Language: A "dialect" of HTML to describe websites for the display on mobile Phones. Some ISPs offer to "translate" HTML into WML to allow the access by mobile phones.
WWW	World Wide Web: Was developed by the European CERN in order to allow easy access to a user friendly display of information stored in distributed locations. Uses HTML to define the presentation. This presentation can include multimedia components, i.e. text, images, audio and video.

XML   Extended Markup Language: Extension of SGML in order to add more tags describing the contents of the document. With XML, Internet frames can be formatted as a data entry form for the customer in a way that the data can be directly further processed by the IT of the content provider. Also, searches for specific contents can be simplified for the customer provided that the XML tags have been set accordingly as an additional index.

FURTHER READING

Dieter Ahlert	Mega-Trends in Marketing und Einzelhandel (Mega trends in Marketing and Retail), IfHM, University Muenster (Germany) 1999
Michael Bloomberg	Bloomberg, John Wiley & Sons, New York (NY) 1997
Peter Buxmann	XML – Extensible Markup Language, Johann-Wolfgang-Goethe University, Frankfurt (Germany) 1998
W. Chan Kim and Renee Mauborgne	Creating New Market Space, Harvard Business Review, Boston (MA), Reprint 99105
Daryl R. Conner	Managing at the Speed of Change, Villard Books, New York (NY) 1992
Michael A. Cusumano & Richard W. Selby	Microsoft's Secrets, HarperCollinsPublishers, London, 1996
Larry Downes, Chunka Mui, Nicholas Negroponte	Unleashing the Killer App. Digital Strategies for Market Dominance. Harvard Business School Press, 1998
Howard Gardner	Leading Minds: An Anatomy of Leadership, Basic Books, 1996
Edgar K. Geffroy	200 Ways to Better Selling (to be published 2000)
Jerrold M. Grochow	Information Overload! Creating Value With New Information Systems Technology, Yourdon Press, Upper Saddle River (NJ) 1997 www.prenhall.com
Milton S. Hess	A task based approach to Risk Mitigation, American Management Systems (AMS) Best Practice Topic Papers, Fairfax (VA), 1996

Tony & Jeremy Hope	Transforming the Bottom Line, Managing Performance with the Real Numbers, Nicholas Brealey Publishing, London (UK) 1996
William H. Inmon	Building the Data Warehouse, John Wiley & Sons, 1996
Bruce Judson	Hyperw@rs: 11 Strategies for Survival and Profit in the Era of Online Business, Scribner, New York, 1999
Reginald Foster, Gerhard Plenert	Teaching Dinosaurs to Fly: Transforming Your Company into a Next Generation Enterprise (to be published 2000)
Spencer Johnson, Kenneth H. Blanchard	The One Minute Manager, Berkley Publication Group, 1993
Dr Ravi Kalakota	e-Business: Roadmap for Success, Addison-Wesley, Reading/MA, 1999
Robert Kaplan/David Norton	Balanced Scorecard. Translation Strategy into Action, Harvard Business School Press, Boston 1996
Otto Kalthoff, Ikujiro Nonaka, Pedro Nueno	The light and the shadow – How Breakthrough Innovation is Shaping European Business, Capstone, Oxford (UK) 1997 www.bookshop.co.uk/capstone/
Marshall McLuhan	The Global Village: Transformations in World Life and Media in the 21st Century, Communication and Society (New York, N.Y.) 1992
Thomas J. Neff & James M. Citrin	Lessons from the Top Doubleday, New York, 1999
Ikujiro Nonaka, Hirotaka Takeuchi	The Knowledge-Creating Company: How Japanese Companies Create the Dynamics of Innovation, Oxford University Print, 1995
Michael E. Porter	On Competition, Harvard Business Review, Boston/MA, 1979 – 1998
S. M. Roberts	Global regulation and trans-state organization, In: Geographies of Global Change, Oxford (UK) 1995

Eike W. Schamp   Globalization of Production Nets and Locational
                          Systems,
                          In: Geographische   Zeitschrift,   Stuttgart
                          (Germany), 1996, Heft 3+4

Patricia B. Seybold   Customers.com: How to create a profitable
                          business strategy for the Internet and beyond,
                          Times   Business,   New   York,   1998,
                          www.atrandom.com

D. H. Stamatis   Documenting and Auditing for ISO 9000 and QS-
                          9000; Tools for Ensuring Certification or
                          Registration,
                          Irwin Professional Publishing, 1996

James Teboul   Managing Quality Dynamics,
                          Prentice Hall, 1991

Frederick E. Webster   Market-Driven Management – Using the New
                          Marketing Concept to Create a Customer-
                          Oriented Company,
                          John Wiley & Sons, New York (NY) 1994

INDEX

The following generic words are not in the index as they are the core substance of the book and thus are dealt with throughout it:

Best practices
Business
Change
Commerce
Customer
Information, Information Technology, IT
Launch
Market, Marketing
Offering
Order
Organization
Product
Sales
Service
Software
System

Combinations of those words or their context, though, like customer relationship or customer interaction, are included in the index.